MEDIEVAL STUDIES at MINNESOTA 3
The Medieval Mediterranean
Cross-Cultural Contacts

MEDIEVAL STUDIES at MINNESOTA 3

The Medieval Mediterranean
Cross-Cultural Contacts

Edited by Marilyn J. Chiat and Kathryn L. Reyerson

NORTH STAR PRESS OF ST. CLOUD, INC.
St. Cloud, Minnesota

CARL D. SHEPPARD

ISBN 0-87839-049-0: Paper
ISBN 0-87839-050-0: Cloth

Library of Congress Cataloging-in-Publication Data

The Medieval Mediterranean : cross-cultural contacts /
    edited by Marilyn Chiat and Kathryn Reyerson.
       p.   cm. — (Medieval studies at Minnesota ; 3)
      ISBN 0-87839-050-2 : $22.95 ISBN 0-87839-049-9
      (pbk.) : $16.95
     1. Mediterranean Region—Civilization. 2. Mediter-
ranean Region—Religion.   I. Chiat, Marilyn Joyce
    Segal.   II. Reyerson, Kathryn.
III. Series.
DE60.M4 1988   88-28150
909′ .09′822—dc 19   CIP

Published by:
    North Star Press of St. Cloud, Inc.
    P.O. Box 451
    St. Cloud, Minnesota 56302
Printed in the United States of America by Sentinel
Printing Company, Inc., Sauk Rapids, Minnesota. All
rights reserved.

A Tribute to Carl D. Sheppard

The theme of this book, and of the conference that preceded it, cross-cultural contacts in the medieval Mediterranean, was selected to honor Carl D. Sheppard's many contributions to medieval studies. Carl D. Sheppard, professor and chair for twenty-three years of the Department of Art History at the University of Minnesota and former professor of art history at the University of Michigan and the University of California, Los Angeles, has continually challenged his students and colleagues to recognize that art is not created in a vacuum, but is the creation of an individual, or individuals, living in a specific time and place. Although never denying that a formal study of an art object can yield a great deal of data, Professor Sheppard maintains that much more can be known if only we place that object within its larger historical context. Because of his interest in the historical context—the complex society in which an artist lived and worked—it is appropriate that a conference and volume honoring Carl D. Sheppard's scholarship should honor as well his interest in stretching the boundaries of the study of art.

As one whom he challenged to investigate an area largely ignored in American art historical scholarship, the ancient synagogue, I feel particularly qualified to speak about the enormous influence Carl D. Sheppard has had on his students and the field of medieval art history. By stretching boundaries, he encouraged me, and others like me, to explore new areas of research; to ask questions not usually asked by art historians; to take risks; to publish the results of research; and to be prepared for scholarly disputes. Through his own impeccable scholarship, he has demonstrated how important it is to be imaginative but thorough in research, to prepare documentation, and to support arguments. Carl D. Sheppard has lived up to this philosophy of scholarship; his students can only hope to do the same.

Professor Sheppard has been aware that to realize his philosophy of the study of art, it is necessary to cross disciplinary boundaries. Art history yields certain types of data, but not enough to provide all the information necessary to evaluate completely the place of an object in history. Carl D. Sheppard's recent venture into the field of archaeology reflects this commitment. Not content to study objects and/or buildings still standing or unearthed by others, he undertook in 1983 to mount his own excavation in Andravida, Elis, Greece. Professor Sheppard, along with colleagues in other disciplines, excavated and studied the Frankish cathedral of Haghia Sophia, an excellent example of cross-cultural influence clearly demonstrating that cultural characteristics, including aesthetics, can cross geographic boundaries.

The papers included in this volume honor Carl D. Sheppard's scholarly philosophy; they illustrate how scholars from various disciplines can enhance our understanding of the cross-cultural contacts that contributed so much to the vitality and vibrancy of life in the medieval Mediterranean world.

Marilyn J. Chiat
January 20, 1988

Carl D. Sheppard Publication Fund

Benefactors

Dr. Fouad G. Azzam and Nancy C. Azzam
Dr. Christine Sheppard
Nancy Allen Sheppard and S. Peter Poullada
Katharine Sheppard and Lewis Sage

Sponsors

Dr. Theodore C. Boyden
Sage and John Cowles
James T. Demetrion
Gertrude B. Ffolliott
Dr. Sheila ffolliott
Dr. Ruth Mellinkoff
Charles Parkhurst
Mr. and Mrs. Peter Willis

Donors

Dr. Robert H. Beck and Corrie W. Beck
Dr. Margaret I. Bouton
Dorelen Bunting
Catherine Fels
Richard Hubbard Howland
Donald W. Judkins and Elizabeth W. Judkins
Prof. Joseph J. Kwiat and Janice M. Kwiat
Muriel Monette
Mr. and Mrs. Peter L. Morawetz
Henry Nuelsen and Margaret Nuelsen
Miss Eleanor A. Pernell
Herbert G. Scherer
David W. Scott
Prof. Robert Trotter and Claire Trotter
Henry and Ruth Trubner
Matt and Ann Walton
Erma Wheeler
Richard S. Zeisler

Contents

List of Illustrations

PLATES

MAPS

The Pilgrim as Tourist: Travels to the Holy Land as Reflected in the Published Accounts of German Pilgrims between 1450 and 1550

Introduction

Three faiths—Jewish, Christian, and Muslim—became the dominant religions of western civilization in the course of the Middle Ages. Within each, there is and was great cultural and ethnic diversity. The complex relationships today among Jews, Christians, and Muslims in the Mediterranean, the tensions and attempts at resolution of conflicts among these groups, have their roots in the Middle Ages. Although much has been written and continues to be written about the hostilities dividing Jews, Christians, and Muslims, little scholarship to date explores the more positive forms of interaction that mark the long history of coexistence of these groups in the Mediterranean world. This volume, through its varied contributions, explores other forms of interaction than that of hostility. The occasion for this examination of cross-cultural contacts was the third biennial conference on Medieval Studies at the University of Minnesota, held in May 1987 in honor of Emeritus Professor Carl D. Sheppard.

For people to understand and evaluate events transpiring around the Mediterranean world today, they must know the history and culture of the region and the many shared traits and values that arose from significant borrowings among diverse religious groups. A keynote address by Oleg Grabar, Aga Khan Professor of Islamic Art at Harvard University, on the Dome of the Rock in Jerusalem, inaugurates this investigation of cross-cultural contacts. This volume contains further contributions that we have assembled in sections on medieval religion, art and architecture, history, learning and technology, and literature.

Few previous works have taken as ambitious a look at cross-cultural contacts as does this collection of conference papers. Contacts between East and West—within Christianity—have been treated in works by Deno Geanakoplos.[1] Bernard Lewis has provided the Islamic perspective in his book, *The Muslim Discovery of Europe*.[2] Bernard Bachrach has explored the fate of the Jews in the Christian kingdoms of the West.[3] But no previous collection assembles studies of such varied lines of interaction—pagan Roman, Western Christian, Byzantine, Jewish, Coptic, Russian, and Islamic—spanning the domains of art history, architecture, religion, linguistics, technology, hagiography, literature, and history.[4] With the exception of prostitution of Muslim women by Christians in Valencia—a topic with negative overtones concretely treated by Mark Meyerson from a study of juridical documents—the contacts that these studies reveal were neutral, if not positive, in impact. That so many productive interactions could take place is witness to the possibilities for cooperation and harmony, even among vastly differing societies.

Three great religions, Islam, Christianity, and Judaism, took form in the same area of the Eastern Mediterranean.[5] All three share the concept of the unity of God; Muslims refer to the adherents of the two earlier faiths as "Peoples of the Book," acknowledging their respect for Abraham, the Prophets, and their scriptures. The early Jews, Christians, and Muslims came from the same area and lived similar lives. By the fourth and fifth centuries, a transitional era between the end of the ancient world and the beginning of the Middle Ages, Jews were widely scattered around the Mediterranean world and beyond. Christianity had become closely identified with the political power of the Roman Empire, and subsequently with that of its successors, the Barbarian Kingdoms of the West and the Byzantine Empire in the East. In the seventh century, the armies of the Islamic states began advancing along the southern shores of the Mediterranean and a period of dramatic confrontation began between religions and cultures. These armies reached the Strait of Gibraltar in 699, entered Spain in 711, and had conquered the Visigothic kingdom and crossed the Pyrénées by 720. Through the remainder of the Middle Ages, Islamic states covered half of the perimeter of the Mediterranean and Christian states the other half, with Jewish communities scattered throughout both.

Continual interaction followed, although its nature often has been misunderstood, perhaps exacerbating some of the region's tensions today. Historians writing in the Middle Ages stressed military history and kept theological disagreement in the foreground.[6] To a degree, scholars take the same tack today.[7] The picture medieval contemporaries and modern historians often present is one of unremitting ideological incompatibility and active hostility. The hostility they depict was real, but it was not the entire story. Although each religion saw the other as a monolithic force, intragroup divisions often exceeded intergroup enmity, as is the case today. Furthermore, totally separate groups, such as Zoroastrians and Cathars, continued to exist.[8]

Peaceful coexistence was possible. For a time, Christians and Jews lived in relative harmony in Byzantine Palestine: A study of their places of worship indicates a mutual borrowing of architectural forms and decoration.[9] When the Christian states grew intolerant, the Islamic world continued to provide a field for fruitful interchange. Christians and Jews lived quietly and in freedom under Muslim rule in Spain, North Africa, and the Near East.[10]

Islamic theologians studied Greek philosophical texts and Western scholars first learned of these texts by contact with Arab scholars in Córdobá and other Islamic centers in Spain.[11] Arabic love poetry influenced the songs of the twelfth-century troubadours in France.[12] During the Abbasid Empire (754-1250: the Muslim state stretching from North Africa to the Euphrates River), Jews established trading communities throughout the Muslim world.[13] They also were found in all the major trading centers of the Christian world. Studies of financial documents tracing the development of international commerce and banking show the influence and interchange in commercial techniques.[14] These facts are known from scattered, discrete past studies. This volume provides a more concentrated emphasis on the issue of cross-cultural interchange, revealing the great range of assimilation and interaction, direct and indirect, deliberate and unconscious, at the level of high culture and at the more practical level of techniques.

Oliver Nicholson in his study of late antique eschatological work points to an example of profound borrowing at a basic level of belief during the conversion experience of the western half of the Roman Empire in the fourth through sixth centuries. Three religious traditions, pagan, Jewish, and Christian, came together in Christian eschatology to produce a fusion of the Golden Age/End of the World myth from the Eclogues and the Book

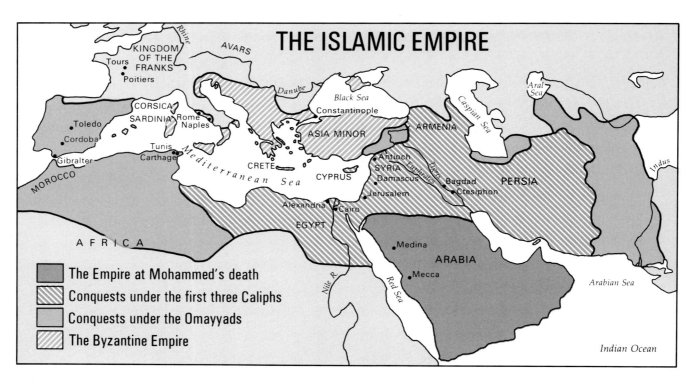

THE ISLAMIC EMPIRE

■ The Empire at Mohammed's death
▨ Conquests under the first three Caliphs
▨ Conquests under the Omayyads
▨ The Byzantine Empire

of Daniel. The imperial court scholar Lactantius linked the pagan Golden Age with the age before Jupiter when Saturn reigned. Borrowing from Vergil to describe this era of bliss, he implied that the Christian righteous would enjoy similar conditions for one thousand years after the Second Coming of Christ.

A further example of cross-cultural religious influence is isolated by Father Ivan Havener. He identifies borrowings from Greek writings in the construction of the Latin hagiographic tradition of Pope Gregory the Great. Ironically, the epithet "Great" came from a Greek anecdote that gained currency in the Latin West but not in the Byzantine East.

Conscious and unconscious borrowing undoubtedly were at work in the interchange of architectural elements among cultures in the Mediterranean world. Catherine Asher traces a Roman tradition of baths on Spanish soil into the Umayyad period:

Structures retaining basic Roman principles of cold, warm, and hot areas adopted ornament and internal design from the eastern Umayyad realm. Eastern Umayyad architecture and decoration were also the model, according to Jonathan Bloom, for the Great Mosque of Córdobá. Opposed to this thesis is the interesting scenario of Marvin Mills, suggesting that the mosque of Córdobá was originally a Roman grain warehouse transformed by western Umayyads to meet their religious needs. The scarcity of evidence surrounding the building of the mosque makes radically differing scenarios of construction possible, enhancing the excitement of scholarship. It is for the reader to decide which seems more satisfactory.

A further investigation of architecture in techniques of planning is offered by Eugene Kleinbauer. After a valuable historical survey of architectural planning across ancient Greek, Roman, and Byzantine culture, he then examines the techniques illus-

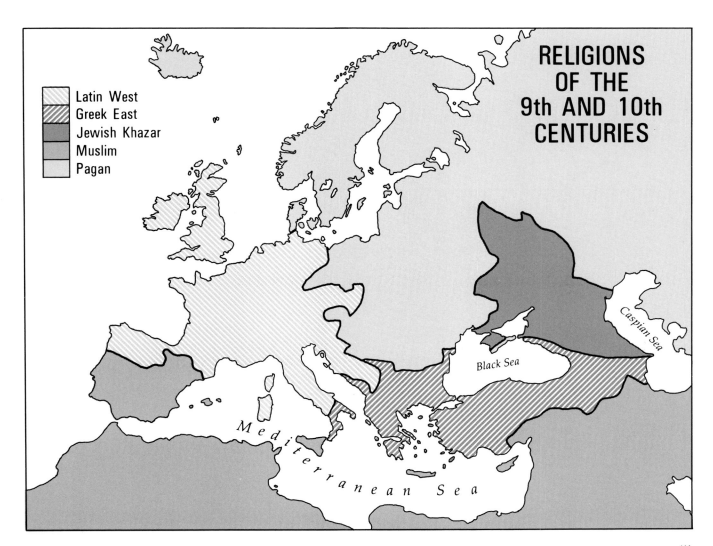

RELIGIONS OF THE 9th AND 10th CENTURIES

Latin West
Greek East
Jewish Khazar
Muslim
Pagan

Caspian Sea

Black Sea

Mediterranean Sea

trated in the renowned St. Gall plan for a ninth-century Carolingian monastery. In the process, he highlights the truly innovative features of scale drawing of forty monastic buildings that the plan contains.

Sybil Mintz presents further evidence of artistic interchange in a study of the carpet pages of the Farhi Bible, produced in fourteenth-century Spain during the heyday of Spanish Hebrew codex output. The Bible combined motifs of Christian and Hebrew inspiration with Islamic configurations of layout and design. Ann Walton traces the influence on Christian iconography of the pictorial literary image of the Three Hebrew Children in the Fiery Furnace from the Book of Daniel. The furnace scene, first appearing in catacomb frescoes, enjoyed considerable resonance in Byzantine and Western Christian art through the late Middle Ages.

On the level of high culture and technical interchange, the Mediterranean world and its extensions offer interesting examples. Familiarity of Jews with Arabic works of philosophy, medicine, literature, music, engineering, and statecraft is clearly demonstrated by the Genizah booklists of Egypt analyzed by Moshe Sokolow. On a linguistic level, Leslie MacCoull demonstrates interesting Arabic/Coptic interchanges occurring in the technical terminology of the textile industry and of alchemy. A far-flung but significant example of actual technology transfer is reconstructed by Thomas Noonan. Greek artisans in Kiev introduced the Rus' to Byzantine glass-making techniques, which Rus' artisans then adopted and adapted as the basis for a successful indigenous glass industry.

Beyond the realms of art, religion, and technology, complex interaction of a social nature inevitably

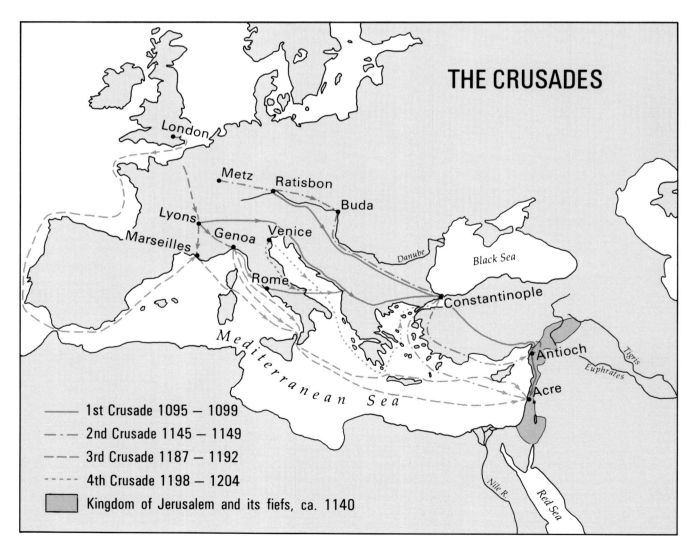

THE CRUSADES

— 1st Crusade 1095 – 1099
—·— 2nd Crusade 1145 – 1149
– – – 3rd Crusade 1187 – 1192
---- 4th Crusade 1198 – 1204
Kingdom of Jerusalem and its fiefs, ca. 1140

occurred. Jews and Christians were the beneficiaries of protected status under Islamic rule as Peoples of the Book, often leading to a delicate balance of privileges and restrictions. In the Islamic kingdom of Granada and in Morocco, Clara Estow shows, the legal position of the Jews was clearly articulated as one of inequality, as prescribed by the Koran, but not one of outright persecution. Punishment was reserved for specific offending individuals. Nevertheless, the potential for abuse of a subjugated religious group by the ruling faithful remained strong in situations of coexistence. In Christian Valencia, Mark Meyerson finds that Muslim women, marginalized or rejected from their own societies, were enslaved by Valencian royal authorities to staff official brothels.

The proximity of differing religious groups in Spain and North Africa led both to accommodation and to exploitation. More distant perceptions of the "infidel" or the "other" have been preserved in Western Christian literature. Stephanie Van D'Elden has discovered that in medieval German epic and romance, the image of the infidel ran the gamut from worthy enemy to abominable heathen, according to the needs of the plot and the whims of the author. Inconsistencies of approach to the religious alien, rather than influence from Crusade experiences or from instincts of proselytization, were the rule. The Mediterranean world, peopled by diverse infidels, proved an exotic framework for a good tale. Pursuit of and fascination with the exotic also were characteristics of Christian pilgrim travel literature of the late Middle Ages and early Modern Era. Gerhard Weiss explores the rich accounts of German pilgrims to the Holy Land in the Islamic Near East. The trials and exultation

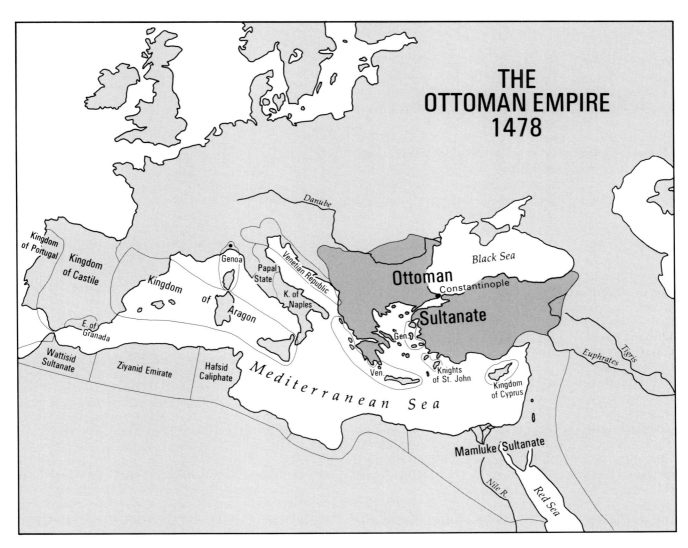

of the journey exposed these travelers to foreign cultures and broadened for these few directly, and for their readers vicariously, the previously narrow horizons of medieval Europeans.

These selected case studies show the breadth and depth of cross-cultural interaction in the medieval Mediterranean world occurring simultaneously with the military hostility of Islamic expansion, the Crusades, and the final conquest of Constantinople by the Turks in 1453.[15] Although day-to-day contacts of individuals of differing religious persuasion may not always have been harmonious, the positive balance sheet is far from blank. The great cultures of the Mediterranean had much to teach each other. More often than not, left to their own devices without the intervention of ruling officialdom, these cultures engaged in cross-fertilization that did much to enhance western civilization.

Special thanks for support of the conference giving rise to the papers of this volume are due the Medieval Studies Committee of the University of Minnesota, the Minnesota Humanities Commission, the College of Liberal Arts, the Departments of History, Religious Studies and Ancient Near Eastern and Jewish Studies, the Department of Professional Development, Continuing Education and Extension, the Dworsky Center for Jewish Studies, the Episcopal-Lutheran Center, the Hillel Foundation, the American-Arab Anti-Discrimination Committee, Church Women United of Minnesota, the Center for Jewish-Christian Learning of the College of St. Thomas, the Islamic Center of Minnesota, the Jewish Community Relations Council/Anti-Defamation League of Minnesota and the Dakotas, the Minnesota Council for the Committee for Peace and Justice in the Middle East, the Minnesota Rabbinical Association, the National Conference of Christians and Jews, Inc. of the Minnesota and Dakotas Region, the Program for Cultural Cooperation Between Spain's Ministry of Culture and United States' Universities, and the United Theological Seminary. Professors Marilyn Chiat and Sheila McNally were the co-chairs of the conference. Dr. Ann Walton raised funds from individuals, listed in the beginning of this volume, to create a publication fund in honor of Emeritus Professor Carl D. Sheppard. Without Dr. Walton's assistance, this volume would not have appeared. This volume and volume two of the series Medieval Studies at Minnesota have been published with the generous financial support of the Carl D. Sheppard Publication Fund.

Kathryn L. Reyerson
Marilyn J. Chiat
March 9, 1988

Notes

1 Deno Geanakoplos has published numerous studies on Byzantine/Western relations. See *Byzantine East and Latin West: Two Worlds of Christendom in the Middle Ages and Renaissance; Studies in Ecclesiastical and Cultural History* (New York: Barnes and Noble, 1966); *Emperor Michael Palaeologus and the West, 1258-1282. A Study in Byzantine-Latin Relations* (Hamden, Conn.: Archon Books, 1973); *Interaction of the "Sibling" Byzantine and Western Cultures in the Middle Ages and Italian Renaissance (330-1600)* (New Haven: Yale University Press, 1976); *Medieval Western Civilization and the Byzantine and Islamic Worlds. Interaction of Three Cultures* (Lexington, Mass.: D.C. Heath, 1979).

2 Bernard Lewis, *The Muslim Discovery of Europe* (New York: W.W. Norton, 1982).

3 Bernard S. Bachrach, *Early Medieval Jewish Policy in Western Europe* (Minneapolis: University of Minnesota Press, 1977). A very stimulating book that examines cross-cultural contacts in the world arena is Philip D. Curtin, *Cross-Cultural Trade in World History* (Cambridge: Cambridge University Press, 1984).

4 One exception to this statement is the collective volume, edited by Joseph Gutmann, *The Image and the Word: Confrontations in Judaism, Christianity and Islam* (Missoula, Mont.: Scholars Press, 1977).

5 For general background on the three religious traditions one can consult Michael Grant, *The Jews in the Roman World* (New York: Scribner's, 1973); Peter R.L. Brown, *The World of Late Antiquity* (New York: Harcourt, 1971); Jacob Neusner, *First Century Judaism in Crisis* (Nashville: Abingdon Press, 1975); Bernard Lewis, *The Arabs in History*, 3rd ed. (New York: Harper & Row, n.d.).

6 The best example of such focus for Islamic and Western historians alike is, of course, the era of the Crusades. See Francesco Gabrieli, *Arab Historians of the Crusades* (Berkeley and Los Angeles: University of California Press, 1969); and Edward Peters, ed., *The First Crusade. The Chronicles of Fulcher of Chartres and Other Source Materials* (Philadelphia: University of Pennsylvania Press, 1971).

7 Again, the Crusades remain the most prominent context in which interaction, particularly between Christians and Muslims, is treated in the Middle Ages. See for background on the Crusades, Hans Eberhard Mayer, *The Crusades*, trans. John Gillingham (Oxford: Oxford University Press, 1972).

8 On the Cathars, see Malcolm D. Lambert, *Medieval Heresy: Popular Movements form Bogomil to Hus* (London: Edward Arnold, 1977). For background on the Zoroastrians, see Mary Boyce, *A History of Zoroastrianism*, 2 vols. (Leiden: Brill, 1975-82), and *Zoroastrians. Their Religious Beliefs and Practices* (London, Boston: Routledge & Kegan Paul, 1979).

9   Marilyn J. Chiat, "Synagogues and Churches in Byzantine Beit She'an," *Journal of Jewish Art* 7 (1980): 6-24.

10 Lewis, *The Muslim Discovery of Europe*, pp. 74-75.

11 Bernard Lewis, *The Jews of Islam* (Princeton, N.J.: Princeton University Press, 1984) and Eliyah Ashtor, *The Jews of Moslem Spain*, trans. from Hebrew by Aaron Klein and Jenne Machlowitz Klein (Philadelphia: Jewish Publication Society of America, 1973).

12 The issue of Arabic influence has spawned an enormous literature. Representative discussions include Peter Dronke, *Medieval Latin and the Rise of European Love-Lyric* (Oxford: Clarendon Press, 1966), pp. 50ff.; and Herbert Moller, "The Social Causation of the Courtly Love Complex," *Comparative Studies in Society and History* 1 (1959): 137-63.

13 Louis Finkelstein, ed., *The Jews: Their History*, 4th ed. (New York: Schocken Books, 1970), p. 192.

14 John Pryor has explored cross-cultural origins for the *commenda* partnership in "The Origins of the Commenda Contract," *Speculum* 52 (1977): 5-37.

15 For background, see Bernard Lewis, *Islam: from the Prophet Muhammed to the Capture of Constantinople* (New York, 1974).

The Meaning of the Dome of the Rock

Oleg Grabar

Together with the Alhambra and the Taj Mahal, the Dome of the Rock in Jerusalem is without a doubt the best known monument of Islamic architecture (Fig. 1). Thousands of tourists visit the Dome every year, it appears on posters and stamps, and the strikingly simple profile of a gilt cupola on a high drum rising from an octagon covered with glittering tiles has been copied in recent years on nearly all possible materials—from textiles to prints—as the Dome of the Rock also has become a symbol of Palestinian nostalgias and aspirations as well as of

fundamentalist—and not so fundamentalist—Islamic ambitions and piety. This mixture of national, ethnic, and religious associations around a monument or a place on earth is, of course, not unusual and, in our days of ideological conflicts, it is intensified whenever sacred places or national monuments are *in partibus infidelium*. Curiously, this situation occurs with the Alhambra and with the Taj Mahal as well as with the Dome of the Rock, so that three of the most famous monuments of Islamic architecture are not in territories under the im-

Fig. 1. Jerusalem, Dome of the Rock.

mediate control of Muslims. Accidents of history perhaps, but, as I shall try to show in the case of the Dome of the Rock, the complexity of contemporary meanings associated with it, whatever modern reasons led to the complexity, is more than matched by those of the past.

This is not, of course, true in a simple and literal sense, the sense of the tourist guides, who provide for it a traditional explanation fully established by early Mamluk times, let us say by about 1300. The Dome of the Rock, according to this tradition, was built over the rock whence the Prophet ascended into heaven on his night journey, the *isra*, from Medina to Jerusalem, alluded to in the first verse of the 17th *surāh* of the Koran. The event itself, barely intimated in the Koran and the subject of some exegetical debate in early Islamic times, was embellished over the centuries by folk as well as mystical piety. Eventually it became fully accredited by the orthodox *sunnah*, or tradition, and incorporated with a great wealth of details in the account of the Prophet's Ascension, or Mi'raj. Various components of the event found their place in a number of specific spots around the Dome of the Rock, where Buraq, the prophet's steed, knelt and waited, where it was tied, where the Prophet prayed, and so on. In addition, although less frequently mentioned, at least by tourist guides, a series of eschatological themes were woven around the Dome of the Rock, the most dramatically powerful one being that the Ka'abah in Mekkah will join the Rock in Jerusalem at the end of time. Finally, in ways that still seek their full investigation, the sacred history of Jerusalem from Adam to Jesus, and obviously with particular emphasis on Abraham, also finds its way to the Dome of the Rock and its surrounding areas in the *fada'il*, which, since the twelfth (and perhaps already eleventh) century, served as guidebooks and as spiritual helpers to the Faithful.[1]

A specific Muslim meaning (the Ascension of the Prophet); an old and peculiarly Jerusalemite association with the Resurrection, the Judgment, and the end of time; and an intimate relationship to the monotheistic prophetic succession as seen through the Muslim faith—these three themes combined to create around the Dome of the Rock, on the platform of the Haram, to its north and to its west, that extraordinary Mamluk Jerusalem which Suleyman the Magnificent, the new Solomon, enclosed in a stunningly powerful curtain wall. This monument has very recently been made available to the learned and general public thanks to the tremendous work carried out by the British School of Archaeology in Jerusalem.[2]

Mamluk Jerusalem is well provided with monuments, inscriptions, texts, descriptions, *waqfiyahs*, and now even the fascinating archive discovered in the Aqsa Museum and slowly being published by Prof. Donald Little and his colleagues.[3] Matters are much more complicated when we go back to the three and a half centuries of Islamic Jerusalem before the Crusades. How many of the associations demonstrable for the later Middle Ages can be carried back to the early centuries? Is it justified to do so? Although less systematic than in Mamluk times, information is plentiful. There are inscriptions:[4] an important group of geographical texts, one of which, Nasir-i Khusro's, is an account that almost can be followed on the terrain;[5] archaeological studies like Robert Hamilton's masterful unraveling of the Aqsa mosque's complicated history; or the largely unpublished and, at first glance, less carefully controlled Israeli excavations to the south and southwest of the Haram;[6] and then there is the Dome of the Rock itself.[7]

It is a remarkably well-documented building, with an inscription dated in 691-2 during the reign of 'Abd al-Malik. Except for minor details, the basic shape of the building has not been altered: a high cylindrical dome, gilt initially, over the mysterious Rock; two octagonal ambulatories; and four identical entrances preceded by a porch on slender columns. The building was lavishly decorated with marble plaques and with mosaics that sheathed it almost entirely, both inside and outside. The interior mosaics have been reasonably well preserved, but only minute fragments remain of the original external decoration. The history of repairs and modifications, such as they were, in the building are unusually well recorded, for the most part through inscriptions, and, leaving aside a number of technical problems that are bound to remain unsolved for lack of adequate documentation, it is only around the mosaics of the drum that feasible additional investigations are needed to determine the extent and date of restorations. Once again it is Suleyman the Magnificent who sponsored the last major overhaul of the building and who provided it with its beautiful exterior tile decoration, which, in a sixteenth-century technique, re-created the colorful brilliance of earlier mosaics. Some twenty years ago a major reconstruction of the Dome of the Rock was completed that was superbly documented during the work itself. To my knowledge, however, this documentation has not been made available.

I have summarized the history of the building, probably well known to most scholars and visitors to Jerusalem, to make two points. First, whatever changes occurred, it is relatively easy to imagine and visualize the building apparently completed in 691-2. Second, the building contains an unusual number of inscriptions from its early period. There is the 240-meters-long inscription with Koranic fragments from 691-2. In an unusual but, as we shall see, highly significant gesture, the 'Abbasid caliph al-Ma'mun replaced 'Abd al-Malik's name with his own, without, however, changing the date. Several 'Abbasid caliphs and members of their families, especially women, recorded their repairs in nearly inaccessible parts of the building, and major Fatimid work was recorded in more formal and more visible inscriptions. What this means is that the Dome of the Rock was from the very beginning what may be called a "talking" building, or perhaps better a "recording" building that incorporated its history within its own fabric, but not necessarily in a form or in places visible to all. Its history was, so to speak, given to the building.

I shall return shortly to some further lessons to be drawn from this practice of providing inaccessible information, but it is important to note that it appears from the very beginning, as the long Umayyad inscription is only decipherable from below when properly lit by sunlight, which means that it can never be easily read in its entirety.

Over a quarter century ago I proposed an interpretation of the Dome of the Rock that has been accepted, at least in its broad implications, by most non-Muslim scholars, ignored by some, rejected by one or two, but, to my knowledge, refuted by none.[8] Since I will propose some major modification to it, I am taking the liberty of summarizing it briefly. On the basis of the inscription that contains the whole Christology of the Koran; of the presence of Byzantine and Sasanian royal insignia in the mosaics facing the rock; of its location on the abandoned and desecrated Herodian space of the Second Jewish Temple, by then replete with popular associations with nearly every major personage of Biblical history; and of a number of other arguments that need not be repeated here, I interpreted the Dome of the Rock as a monument celebrating the victorious presence of Islam in the Christian city of Jerusalem by resacralizing with the new and final revelation a space made holy by Judaism.

Like everybody else I attributed the building of the Dome of the Rock to 'Abd al-Malik and saw it—together with the reform in coinage, the change of the administrative language from Greek to Arabic, the forceful if not at times brutal activities of al-Hajjaj in the Arabian peninsula, the truce with Byzantium, and the successful stemming of disorders

in Iraq—as another sign, a specifically visual one, of the middle Umayyad conscious assumption of discrete imperial rule, that is, the full awareness on the part of the Marwanids that theirs was a new empire continuing old Mediterranean and even Iranian ones but under the aegis of a new and final Revelation.[9]

I agreed with the prevailing formal explanation of the Dome of the Rock as a minor modification of a type of centrally planned martyria or churches illustrated by the Holy Sepulchre and the Church of the Ascension in Jerusalem, the cathedral of Bosra in southern Syria, San Vitale in Ravenna, eventually Charlemagne's palace church in Aachen.[10] The style and vocabulary of its mosaics seemed to me as correctly derived from the prevailing high styles of Late Antique and early Christian art, all probably executed by Christian mosaicists. Finally, I argued that this immanent and immediate message to the Christian world soon lost its point, but the monument that was the message became the visual and eventually semantic center of a religious and pietistic transformation. The Haram first became a mosque, as al-Walid constructed the Aqsa, then a unique mixture of mosque and shrine, with all sorts of associations leading up to, after the Crusades, the reasonably coherent, both visually and functionally, entity sketched out at the beginning of this paper.

Much in this explanation is still, in my view at least, entirely valid. But in two areas, curiously enough the areas where I fully agreed with everybody else's views of the Dome of the Rock, I do believe it to be based on erroneous or at least incomplete analyses of available data. These areas are: the involvement of 'Abd al-Malik in the building of the Dome of the Rock and the relationship of the Dome's forms to Mediterranean Christian or Late Antique art.

The date of the inscription, A.M. 72 (691-2 A.D.), is clear, and it has been demonstrated that the date was preceded by the phrase "built (*bana*) this cupola (*qubbat*) the servant of God 'Abd al-Malik (changed later into the *imam al-Ma'mun*), Commander of the Faithful" and followed with a eulogy: "may God accept (this work) from him and be satisfied with him; *amin*" and then a few damaged words. By a curious habit derived from the practice of painters and of manufacturers of objects, historians of art and by extension other historians, therefore, have tended to associate the building with events around 691-2 and to formulate through these events the psychological and ideological setting in which the Dome of the Rock was built, or rather created, for its completion may well have taken many years. In reality, however, as anyone involved with building anything, even in our times of computer controlled technology knows, it takes years to build and decorate a building of any magnitude. In the case of the Dome of the Rock, the following has to have taken place before 'Abd al-Malik's inscription could be put up: mosaics and marble had to have been set on the walls; tesserae and plaques of marble had to have been gathered from wherever they were manufactured and some designing of patterns should have taken place (a technical job for which actually a lot of information exists in the technique and composition of the mosaics themselves); building materials had to be assembled and put together, some of them taken from destroyed or abandoned ancient or Christian buildings, others cut or otherwise prepared.

So far I have mentioned only obvious building needs. In Jerusalem at this time, yet another requirement existed: the clearing of the space for the building. This clearing required the presence of the high platform on which the Dome stands, of a number of accesses (without the arcades that crown the stairs known today, most of which are dated to a later time), of the large esplanade in some sort of usable form, meaning in turn that the Double Gate, perhaps the Golden Gate, and possibly some access to the north all had to have been at least roughly cleared and flattened. I say "roughly" on purpose, for several later inscriptions indicate that work on the outer walls continued for several centuries and, as recent Israeli excavations have confirmed, the presence of a major (I suspect *the* major) early Islamic settlement south of the Haram, the southern and southwestern sections of the walls, precisely the ones that required most work, had to have been if not entirely rebuilt, at least made accessible and usable for movement. Recently it has even been suggested that the whole northern third of the Haram may well have been cut out of the natural rock under the Umayyads, and almost certainly before the Dome of the Rock was built.[11] I am not entirely convinced by the argument because, even though it solves a number of very important issues hitherto unresolved, it also creates new problems. How much really had to be done is difficult to say; the only visible documentation we possess, short of technically difficult and politically impossible excavations, consists in masonry analyses, a tediously difficult task with so many uncertainties that only general approximations can be expected from it. But, if we recall that Jerusalem was not a major center for what would nowa-

days be called a construction industry and that it was not a capital city bound to attract artisans seeking employment, the effort of creating a logical space for building the Dome of the Rock was enormous, requiring not only huge financial investments and sizable logistic support, but an organization in charge of the project. Even before much work had been done, someone had to have decided that it needed to be done. Even if one grants that our own progression from concept to brief, financing, design, blueprints, and execution is hardly a valid procedure for the seventh century, it is invalid only in the concreteness and specificity of the forms it takes, for the process itself is unavoidable, especially, as I shall show shortly, in a building with the peculiar visual characteristics of the Dome of the Rock. How long such a process would have taken is impossible to guess, but we are certainly talking about several years. And this is where the problem begins, for the ten years that preceded the alleged completion of the Dome of the Rock, in fact the twelve years that followed Mu'awiyah's death in 680 were years of almost unceasing internecine strife between various Arab factions, and it is not until the defeat of Ibn al-Zubayr by al-Hajjaj late in 692 that peace was restored within the half-urbanized factions of Iraqi cities. By then the Dome of the Rock already had been completed.

What this rather simplified sketch suggests is that the conceptual matrix in which the idea of the Dome of the Rock, its purpose, its location, and its shape were conceived is not from 'Abd al-Malik's time, but from Mu'awiyah's, an idea already proposed in a passing remark without substantiating evidence of the late Professor Goitein.[12] There is a world of difference between 'Abd al-Malik, fully conscious through his reforms of the "Islamic" character of the Umayyad empire, and Mu'awiyah, the brilliant and wily opportunist ready to acquire and consolidate power through any means. The further point, however, is that a demonstrable connection exists between Mu'awiyah and Jerusalem. According to a Syriac source "in 971 (i.e., 661 A.D.) many Arabs gathered in Jerusalem and made Mu'awiyah king; he went up to Golgotha, sat down there and prayed, then proceeded to Gethsemane, and then went down to the grave of St. Mary, where he prayed again."[13] An Arab Muslim source quoted by Tabari confirms a Syrian homage to Mu'awiyah in Jerusalem.[14] This is where he was offered the crown of king of the Arabs, says a third, this time Greek, source.[15] To my knowledge, no event or association of comparable importance connects 'Abd al-Malik to Jerusalem; such references as do exist are strictly within his caliphal prerogatives as ruler of an empire, for instance the militaries' recording the distances of various places to Jerusalem and a couple of other references to which I shall return. Mu'awiyah's relationship to Jerusalem is clearly that of a prince in the tradition of the pre-Islamic kings of the Arabian world. A verse from the *Mufaddaliyat*, identified and discussed by Professor Caskel, helps in providing a more specific explanation to the Syriac text: "I swear by Him, to whose holy places the Quraysh go on pilgrimage, and by that which is surrounded by the Hira mountains for sacrifice; by the month of the Banu Umayya and by the consecrated sacrificial animals, whose blood covers them."[16]

A parallelism is here indicated between a sanctuary of the Umayyads and one of Ibn al-Zubayr, the Qurayshite upholder of an old Mekkan tradition, who had recently destroyed the Ka'abah built with the Prophet's help and restored it to its earlier *jahiliyah* stage, the one, according to traditional lore and belief, which had been created by Abraham. In both cases the implication is downright pagan and tribal, not Islamic and imperial, reflecting a traditional Arabian perception of power struggles and power symbols, not a new one. It is in fact only within this Arabian context, still infected by paganism, that one can explain why a sanctuary would have been built around a natural rock whose only demonstrable (or at least preserved today) connotations *at that time* were with the Jewish Temple, if it is indeed *lapis pertusus* of a western pilgrim's text, or with Abraham's sacrifice through the ancient confusion between Mount Moriah and the land of Moriah.

Within this context, I propose to see the planning, foundation, and design of the Dome of the Rock as the expression of Mu'awiyah's rule, independent of a Hijaz to which, all texts say, he did not want to return. It was set around a rock with whatever Jewish associations this rock had because there also he was establishing an Abrahamic relationship and certainly with the memory of pagan lithocracy in pre-Islamic Arabia. It was also meant to be a message of power to the Christians, whose defeated rulers had their crowns hanging in the sanctuary, as similar trophies had been hanging in the Ka'abah, and it proclaimed the acquisition or appropriation by Mu'awiyah of *mulk*, that imperial power that had ruled the Christian world since Constantine, or possibly the kingship of the pre-Islamic rulers of the northern Arabian steppes and deserts. To Mu'awiyah, in short, what was meant to be created in Jerusalem was a dynastic or tribal shrine,

and Jerusalem alone made sense in the world conquered by the Arabs as the location of the shrine, because Jerusalem alone was endowed with the kinds of associations both with God and with kings that made an event there or a building reverberate throughout the world of Christians and of Jews as well as among the new Muslims. To try in a single monument to juggle messages to Arabs, Muslim or not, to the new leadership of a fledgling empire, to Christians and to Jews seems, to me at least, to fit beautifully with the striking and imaginative personality of the first Umayyad caliph.

One alternative to this scheme or scenario could be proposed. It is possible that the mosaic decoration and, more specifically, the inscription were chosen by 'Abd al-Malik and his pious entourage, and thus that, as the building was being built, parts of its program were being modified because of altered circumstances or additional meanings were given to it. The practice is not unknown in the history of mostly contemporary architecture and I know of one possible parallel in the Muslim world of the Middle Ages.[17] This hypothesis would explain Muqaddasi's celebrated text about the Dome of the Rock which mentions exclusively the caliph's intent to compete with Christian monuments.[18] It may also explain another more obscure statement in a late medieval text that 'Abd al-Malik incorporated the Dome of the Rock in the Aqsa mosque, which would mean then that it is 'Abd al-Malik who first sought to give it an Islamic meaning.[19] And al-Ma'mun's substitution of his name in the inscription can easily be explained as a last recognition of secular and imperial values in a building that by then had been transformed into a purely religious one. Solomonic lore, which has been proposed to explain certain motifs in the mosaic decoration,[20] would have influenced either Umayyad patron.

Before returning in conclusion to some additional remarks about the religious meaning of the Dome of the Rock, let me turn to the second part of my argument, the visual one. For, so far, the main justifications for my explanation of the building have been, first, that the process of designing a building of this magnitude in the peculiar conditions of the city of Jerusalem compels us to propose for the conception of the building an earlier date than the usually accepted one, and, second, that the contents of an inscription in Arabic, hardly yet the common language of the Christians and Jews to whom it was destined, but especially an inscription invisible to them and to nearly everyone else, makes this explanation most plausible.

The art historical argument about the Dome

of the Rock has centered almost exclusively on the question of the origins of its plan (Fig. 2), and scholars agree about the set of Mediterranean Christian monuments with which it is to be connected. It is difficult to disagree with series of plans that are indeed strikingly alike except on one point. Only the Dome of the Rock is perfectly symmetrical on any one of its axes and does not provide a particular preeminence of one side over the others; even the doorways are exactly alike. All the comparable Christian monuments are provided with a facade, if for no other purpose than to put a single entry into the building. Where the Dome of the Rock is even more different from any of its alleged models is in its elevation. Admittedly, most of the latter are known only as ruins, but in the Holy Sepulchre, Ravenna, or Aachen, the point of the building is always to compel entrance into it and, once in, to be overwhelmed by the central cupola. Things work out quite differently in the Dome of the Rock. Entry is difficult because of the narrowness of the doors and because not one of them has beckoning or in-

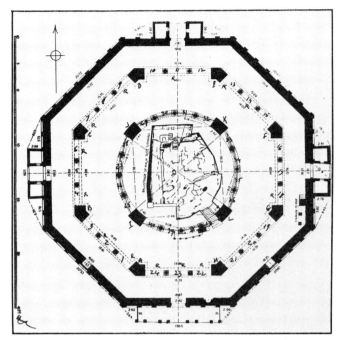

Fig. 2. Dome of the Rock, plan (after Creswell).

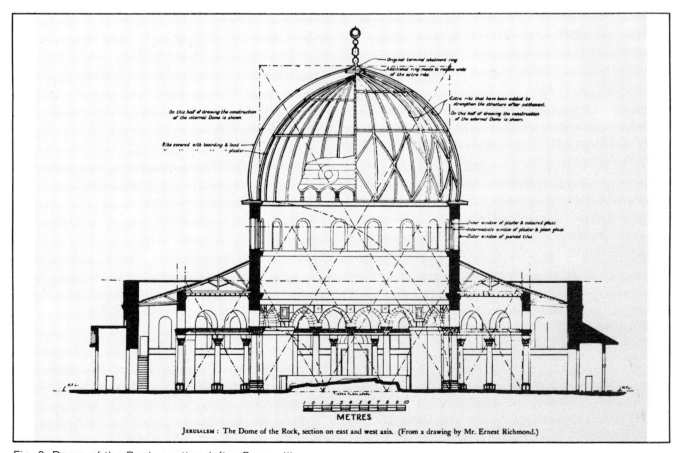

Fig. 3. Dome of the Rock, section (after Creswell).

viting signs (Fig. 3); the dome, twice as high as the ambulatory around it, has as its diameter the smallest circle that would encompass the rock and is therefore nearly invisible from the inside; in fact, slight alterations in the dimensions of intercolumniations always lead the eye across the whole building and over the rock rather than upward. These alterations are, however, minimal, and, on the whole, as many observers have noted, the Dome of the Rock is characterized by the precision of its geometric composition, both in plan and in elevation. As Ecochard and others have shown, the geometric principles involved are neither unique nor original. What is unique is that almost nothing breaks their harmony and proportions. The building is not only conceived in geometry, it *is* a geometric object.

In short, while the technical, phonetic, and, to a large extent, compositional structure of the building does indeed belong to the language of forms prevailing in the early Christian Mediterranean, the effect it produces is quite different from what is found in parallel buildings: separation between exterior and interior impacts; emphasis on the dome for the outside viewer, on a unified space with multiple supports from the inside; absolute equality of all sides. To these architectonic attributes must be added the mosaic decoration. Once again, the technique and most of the motifs belong to the Mediterranean tradition. The suggestion of an iconographic meaning for the crowns and possibly also for the trees in the spandrels and on the upper part of piers is legitimate to the extent that mosaics and paintings were used for visual messages in Christian and Classic art. The absence of living beings, certainly a willed decision, makes the means for the transmission unusual and raises some questions as to whether the messages were understood, but a number of formal components like relationship of motifs to each other, highlighting of some motifs over others, and so on, make an iconographic reading of the mosaics not only legitimate but likely. So far, however, only the crowns and jewels on the one hand and the large trees on the other have been given some attention.[21]

In two areas, however, the Dome of the Rock is entirely original. One is the nearly total sheathing of the building with colorful decoration, in this instance marble and mosaics. In ways that have never yet been fully analyzed and of which I shall provide only one example, this sheathing does much more than strengthen key architectonic parts; it actually modifies them, as in the intrados of arches, where the continuity of the surface design alters and softens the sharp edge of a stone arch and provides continuity to what is normally seen as contrast. The second originality of the decoration is that it also occurred on the outside. Exterior decoration is very rare in the prevailing Mediterranean *koiné* and, when it occurs there or in Iran, it tends to be limited to a specific message on the facade.

How can one explain these characteristics: differences between exterior and interior messages, perfect geometry, mosaics both inside and outside? (See Fig. 4.) Let me also add that no evidence exists before the Dome of the Rock for Muslim patronage of esthetically significant buildings. The earlier mosque in Jerusalem was described as "rude" by a western traveler and whatever can be reconstructed in Kufa and Basra does not compare in sophistication with the Dome of the Rock.

The explanation I am putting forward is that the Umayyad patrons were in fact affected or inspired by the one "monument" in their tradition, the Ka'abah in Mekkah (Fig. 5). It was a simple building with the function of a shrine-treasury inside and of a magnet for a ritual then in the process of formulation on the outside. Few were allowed inside, but all knew its contents. And it was covered with regularly renewed textiles that, according to al-Azraqi, were more frequently changed in pre-Islamic and early Islamic times than became the practice later on and especially whose colors varied considerably.[22] All of this means that the visual impression of the Ka'abah was that of a colorful textile fluttering under the impact of winds and covering a clearly delineated geometric shape.

It is perhaps reasonable to explain the outside mosaic decoration of the Dome of the Rock as seeking to give the colorful impression of textiles, but the building in Jerusalem hardly looks like its Mekkan counterpart. And yet, if we are mindful of the procedures of medieval architects outlined by Krautheimer many decades ago[23] and in line with my earlier suggestions about a historical context for the Dome of the Rock, a scenario for its construction can be proposed. Mu'awiyah in my hypothesis—but the process could apply to any comparable patron—decides to build in Jerusalem a shrine (understood here in a generic architectural and not religious sense as a unique monument for a singular purpose) to associate himself and perhaps his lineage with one of the holiest places in the Judeo-Christian and now newly Islamic world. He sees it primarily as a place competing in semantic value with Mekkah controlled by 'Ibn al-Zubayr, a representation of local pride; at least he does so with the eyes of a traditional Arab ruler. But with his eyes as the ruler of a fledgling world empire, he sees it also as a message to the People of the Book who form the majority of the population and, at least in the case of Christians, who had developed an elaborate and expensive art for their faith. Mu'awiyah turns to the building establishment of Syria and Palestine, perhaps even calls for artisans from more important centers like Constantinople, because he has extensive funds at his disposal and because, for at least one of his purposes, he has to use the language of the conquered world. Yet he also wanted to preserve something of the Mekkan world. Since no artisan was going to travel to Mekkah to look at the Ka'abah and since no appropriate architectural manuals or drawings were available, a brief was produced orally. The Ka'abah, someone would have said, is a geometrically clear building, it creates a colorful impression, it dominates its surroundings, it possesses treasures inside and serves as a visual magnet in the city and the surrounding valley. The Dome of the Rock then would have been the translation by Mediterranean artisans into *their* language of an orally transmitted description of the Mekkan sanctuary.

Two additional documents strengthen the possibility of this scenario. One is that several later writers did accuse the Umayyads of having tried to move the pilgrimage to Jerusalem. They understood the connection between the two buildings, but, because the Ka'abah had by then become exclusively the center of the hajj, they had to explain the connection in terms of the pilgrimage; the complex psychological and emotional components of generations with a foot still in *jahiliyah* times no longer made much sense to ninth-century Muslim writers. The other argument is that a reliance on geometric precision and geometric imagination is often the natural instinct of architects faced with a purpose with which they are not familiar. On a different level, neither the Dome of the Rock nor the Ka'abah were copied in later Islamic architecture, nor did they significantly affect the development of that architecture, some exceptions notwithstanding. By providing the Dome of the Rock with a unique and singular meaning at the time of its creation, its lack of impact may be explained as well, something which the traditional explanation was

Fig. 4. The Harem al Sharif, air view.

unable to do.

My argument tries to weave together two kinds of arguments: the analysis of a building as a perceived object and not, as is so often done in art historical research, as a bundle of influences; and, second, the elements of a process of building in which purpose, ambition, assets, surrounding events, people, ideas, and technological potential all intermingle. I have left out (or barely alluded to) a third component, which is the specificity of Jerusalem as a place and as a set of memories in the second half of the seventh century; the study of Jerusalem at that time could form a whole lecture in its own right.[24] What has emerged from this piecing together of a standing building and of processes issued from visual and written sources as well as from more general assumptions about the nature of building?

First of all, the uniqueness of the Dome of the Rock as a work of architecture can be explained by the unique circumstances of its creation. And the uniqueness of the circumstances explains in turn why, as traditional Islam was developing and codifying its piety and its sacred places, the Dome of the Rock, with a largely different agenda behind it, was difficult to fit into anything. It was a work of state, but of a type of state that was going to be radically changed by 'Abd al-Malik's reforms. It was also a work of art, but it was not a work of faith,

whereas the whole history of the Haram from the moment of the building of the Aqsa mosque by al-Walid becomes the history of Muslim religious and pious beliefs and practices overtaking an ancient sacred space and eventually the Dome of the Rock itself. This transformation was, I believe, finally achieved in a visually coherent form only under the Fatimids in the early eleventh century and the whole process is a fascinating one to which I hope to devote myself one of these years.

Second, even though the Umayyad period has been better studied than any other one in medieval Islamic history, insufficient attention has been given to what may be called its esthetic culture as different from its archaeology. Much too easily, we have all assumed that Arabia was forgotten once the visual riches of the conquered lands became available. What these riches provided was one or more new languages of forms, but they did not, at least not immediately, eradicate memories, visual impressions, and esthetic needs from the world of Arabian oases and probably tribes. Within these memories, the Ka'abah played a far greater role than has been imagined and a continuous one because of the Pilgrimage. On a more specific level, a very fascinating Mekkah-Jerusalem dialogue and competition seems to have existed, both in *hadith* literature and in eschatology.[25] Yet on another

Fig. 5. Mekkah, the Ka'abah, air view.

level, a pattern emerges of relationships between memory of things seen, ambitions for things to be seen, satisfying one's own sense of identity, and fascinating or seducing others. This pattern allows us to delve far more deeply than is usually the case into the web of motivations surrounding any work of art and, more specifically, this pattern has fascinating parallels with the architecture being developed today in the Arab world.

Finally, any interpretation of the Dome of the Rock raises issues that range from reconstructing the motives of patrons long gone to understanding how form and belief act with and react to each other. All these approaches help in explaining the Dome of the Rock, but none is the final truth about it, for like any work of art the Dome of the Rock will always remain something of a mystery. It is a fascinating and yet, to me, by now no longer a surprising fact that, at the other end of the grand tradition of Islamic architecture, the Taj Mahal, like the Dome of the Rock, is remarkably documented and yet equally elusive. Or perhaps the more one studies something the less one understands it. A depressing thought for an academic to expound, but a convenient way to end a paper or a lecture.

Notes

This paper was first given as the Antonius Lecture at St. Anthony's College, Oxford University, in 1985. A few modifications were made for delivery at Georgetown University and later at the Universities of Toronto and of Minnesota. For publication a basic complement of notes was added.

1 The earliest of these is Muhammad b. Ahmad al-Wasiti, *F. al-Bayt al-Muqaddas*, ed. Isaac Hasson (Jerusalem, 1979). The most celebrated is Muji al-Din, *al-Uns al-Jalil bitarikh al-Quds wa al-Khalil* (Cairo, 1283 fl.), partial trans. by Henri Sauvaire, *Histoire de Jérusalem* (Paris, 1876).

2 M. H. Burgoyne, *Mamluk Jerusalem* (London, 1986).

3 Among other places D. H. Little, "The Significance of the Haram Documents," *Der Islam* 52 (1980).

4 Max van Berchem, *Matériaux pour un Corpus Inscriptionum Arabicarum: Jérusalem Haram* (Cairo, 1925-27). Christel Kessler, "Abd al'Malik's Inscription," *Journal of the Royal Asiatic Society*, no. 3 (1970).

5 All these texts are conveniently summarized in G. Le Strange, *Palestine under the Moslems* (Boston, 1890), one of several such books.

6 Robert Hamilton, *The Structural History of the Aqsa Mosque* (Jerusalem, 1942); his results can be interpreted in other ways than he has proposed but the book is a model of its kind. Considerable information can also be obtained from the records kept at the so-called Rockefeller Museum in Jerusalem. For the Israeli excavations, see M. Ben-Dov, *In the Shadow of the Temple* (New York, 1985), a popular account.

7 Nothing has superseded the chapters in K. A. C. Creswell, *Early Muslim Architecture*, rev. ed. (Oxford, 1969).

8 O. Grabar, "The Umayyad Dome of the Rock," *Ars Orientalis* 3 (1959).

9 Much novel cultural history has been written recently on this period. As examples, see H. Kennedy, *The Prophet and the Age of the Caliphates* (London, 1986) and various works by Patricia Crone, like (with M. Cook) *Hayarism* (Cambridge, 1977).

10 All these examples are in Creswell. For a more imaginative but also more debatable view of the same monuments, see M. Ecochard, *Filiations de Monuments* (Paris, 1977).

11 F. E. Peters, "Who Built the Dome of the Rock," *Graeco-Arabica* 2 (1983).

12 In the article "Kuds" for the new edition of the *Encyclopedia of Islam*.

13 T. Nöldeke, "Zür Geschichte der Araber," *Zeit D. Morgenlandgesellschaft* 29 (1875).

14 Tabari, *Tarikh*, ed. M. de Goeje *et al.* (Leiden, 1890 and ff.), 2:4ff.

15 J. Wellhausen, *The Arab Kingdom* (reprint Beirut, 1963), pp. 100-107.

16 W. Caskel, *Der Felsendom und die Wallfahrt nach Jerusalem* (Cologne, 1963).

17 I mean the early fourteenth-century mausoleum of Oljaytu in Iran, whose study is yet to be made.

18 Muqaddasi's text is in Le Strange's book quoted in note 5, pp. 117-118.

19 Le Strange, pp. 144ff., among several places.

20 Priscilla Soucek, "The Temple of Solomon in Islamic Legend and Art," in Joseph Gutmann, ed., *The Temple of Solomon* (Missoula, 1976); Heribert Busse, "The Sanctity of Jerusalem in Islam," *Judaism* 17 (1968).

21 See articles by Grabar and Soucek.

22 Al-Azraqi, *Akhbar Makkah* (repr. ed. Beirut, n.d.), pp. 175ff.

23 R. Krautheimer, "The Iconography of Medieval Architecture," *Journal of the Warburg and Courtauld Institutes* 5 (1942).

24 See the suggestive recent books by F. E. Peter, *Jerusalem* (Princeton, 1985) and *Jerusalem and Mecca* (New York, 1986).

25 J. M. Kister, "A Study of an Early Tradition," *Le Muséon* 32 (1969).

Golden Age and the End of the World:
Myths of Mediterranean Life
from Lactantius to Joshua the Stylite

Oliver Nicholson

In the two hundred years between the beginning of the fourth century A.D. and the beginning of the sixth, Christianity took root as the established religion of the Mediterranean world. Some of the alterations are obvious: temples were abandoned and churches built, Christian emblems began to appear on everyday objects such as lamps, coins, and, gradually, military insignia. The change considered here is less obvious but may be more profound: the conversion of the Mediterranean world to Christianity affected the way that its inhabitants faced their future. Patterns of expectation deeply embedded in Mediterranean culture are involved: on the one hand, hope for the return of the Golden Age, which in the classical world had been articulated more often by poets than anyone else, and on the other, the convictions about the coming End of the World characteristic of Christian prophets.

Concern with the shape of the future obviously is particularly acute in times of trouble. Our study will proceed by contrasting the Christian authors who lived during two traumatic periods. These are, respectively, the early years of the fourth century, when Christians were troubled not only by a decade of civil war but also by the Great Persecution, and the early years of the sixth century, when a longstanding expectation that the world would come to an end five hundred years after the coming of Christ seemed about to be fulfilled in famine, disease, and foreign invasion. The authors well illustrate the change that had come over the pattern of expectations. Lactantius, a Christian Latin writer who ended his *Divine Institutes* with a vivid prophecy of the End, was well aware that not many of his contemporaries shared his convictions and elaborately included a Christianized version of the Golden Age in his predictions. Christian prophets around 500 seem, by contrast, more assured that they stand in the mainstream of contemporary expectation. In both crises, misfortune brought to the surface hopes and fears that had become deeply embedded

in the structure of Mediterranean life. At least so one assumes from the utterances that survive: Of those who faced their troubles in silence we have no record; we have to let their prophets speak for them.

501 A.D. was a calamitous year in the Eastern Mediterranean. From Antioch as far inland as the Persian frontier there was famine.[1] The whole harvest had been eaten by locusts.[2] The country people crowded into the cities, where many were forced to sleep in the open air.[3] A cold winter killed them in large numbers,[4] and survivors were driven to eating cabbage stalks picked up in the streets.[5] Plague followed famine.[6] As the year went on, matters improved very little. The corn harvest failed again;[7] the population faced 502 on a diet of dried grapes.[8] On August 22 of that year, the port of Acre (Ptolemais) was completely destroyed in an earthquake, and there was extensive damage at Tyre and Sidon.[9] At Nicomedia on the Sea of Marmara opposite Constantinople, a city in a notorious earthquake zone,[10] the people were tormented by demons.[11] On the same night, writes Joshua the Stylite, the chronicler who preserves for us this tale of woes, "a great fire appeared to us blazing in the northern quarter the whole night, and we thought that the whole earth was going to be destroyed that night by a deluge of fire; but the mercy of the Lord preserved us without harm."[12]

Worse, however, was to come. On the same day that Joshua saw fire in the north, the Shah of Persia mustered his army and marched against Roman territory.[13] He penetrated Armenia, and quickly captured the key fort of Theodosiopolis, modern Erzerum.[14] Then he turned south and in October laid siege to the black walls of the important city of Amida, modern Diyarbakir in Eastern Turkey. The most sophisticated artillery was used against the city; in the meantime, lighter troops killed and terrorized the people of the surrounding countryside.[15] This was the first serious Persian invasion for over half a century.[16] For one seer, a sibyl associated with the ancient temple city of Heliopolis, Ba'albek in the Lebanon, it seemed to be the beginning of the End of the World: "the Persians . . . will overturn with the sword the cities of the East together with the multitudes of the soldiers of the Roman Empire."[17] The sybil goes on to give details of further woes: "there will be much shedding of blood, so that the blood will reach the chest of horses as it is commingled with the sea."[18] At last, after much terror and suffering, the son of God will come with great power and glory and sit in judgment.[19]

This sybil, the *Oracle of Ba'albek*, was not the only prophet to express alarm. Another prophecy, made at roughly the same time but in the tradition of Daniel, displays similar desperation: "Only the Lord is the righteous judge and all is his work. All mankind shall open their mouths and shall cry and say, 'O Lord, Thou who art the Lord, lead us not into temptation but deliver us from evil.'"[20] This prophet too foresaw terrible natural disasters, the reign of the Antichrist, and the Last Judgment. He is echoed by another anonymous author of the time, whose work clearly included a chronicle of world history from Adam onwards, though only a summary survives, mostly in a Byzantine abstract known as the *Tübingen Theosophy*.[21] He too thought the world would come to an end five hundred years after the Incarnation of Christ.[22]

Such predictions of the End of the World were not hurried hallucinations brought on by panic. Famine and invasion fanned the flame, but eschatological expectation glowed constantly in the early Byzantine mind. None of the events that are foretold is ever an entirely new invention. During the reign of the Antichrist, for instance, two prophets, Enoch and Elijah, will arise and oppose him. The prediction is repeated from one prophecy to another;[23] the expectation does not alter because it is constantly present at the bottom of the mind. Sometimes one can see how an old prophecy is adapted to new circumstances. At one point the *Oracle of Ba'albek* inveighs against Constantinople: "Do not boast, city of Byzantium, thou shalt not hold imperial sway for thrice sixty of thy years."[24] The prophet of the early sixth century has altered an earlier utterance by adding the word "thrice"; an earlier version of the *Oracle* had threatened an end within only sixty years.[25] The prophets, such as the *Oracle of Ba'albek*, the Daniel-prophet, and the *Theosophy*, who spoke during the crises of the early sixth century were addressing dire present circumstances, but they were doing so in language that had become familiar to their hearers.

Their predictions also were based on a familiar theory of the history of the world. The *Tübingen Theosophy* repeated it. The world had been made in six days, and so, because one day in God's sight is equal to a thousand, would last for six thousand years in all. Christ came in the middle of the final thousand years, that is to say 5,500 years after the Creation, so the world would come to an end 500 years after his life on earth.[26] The End of the World was no sudden dream; rather it completed the natural trajectory of history. Christian chronographers had by exquisite calculations fitted the history of the world into the pattern of six thousand years; prophets who in the time of the breaking of nations described, in vivid if ambiguous language, how history was coming to an end would be retelling a familiar story, one which was reinforced by a coherent body of historical scholarship. The very familiarity of their predictions could help give to bewildered and suffering people some sense of where they stood.

Christian eschatology had not always been the familiar prophetic language of the Mediterranean world. Only two hundred years before Joshua the Stylite and the prophets of his time, people had been accustomed to interpret events according to a different pattern, based not on an overall theory of world history, but on the natural rhythms of life in the Mediterranean world. "All round the Mediterranean, a precarious living is won by painful labour," so we are told by a prehistorian who acknowledges her debt to Braudel. "When the population is low and labour is scarce, men work hard and acquire wealth, thus creating prosperity and generating a rise in population; but wealth brings corruption in its train, and since corruption leads to decay, the population eventually declines once more." There is never quite enough food to go around; each coastal enclave lives from year to year under the threat of famine; "the normal climatic and ecological pattern is one of local shortages."[27] It is not hard to see how such conditions could generate the myth that a Golden Age once had existed and the hope that one day its plenty, justice, and peace would return to the earth.

To look forward to the return of the Golden Age was as natural in the pre-Christian Mediterranean as to welcome the coming of spring. Poets wrote about both: "redeunt jam gramina campis, arboribusque comae."[28] But the Golden Age was not merely a literary motif; the theme had a place in the realities of public life. Diocletian, the last great pagan emperor, was remembered as "the father of the Golden Age."[29] In 298 one of his imperial colleagues was acclaimed by a panegyrist: "What mild autumns and springs are encouraging the trees which have been planted to grow! How the heat of the Sun is making the corn flattened by the rain stand up again! Everywhere walls are rising on old foundations which were so covered over that they could hardly be found! The fact is that the Golden Age which existed long ago when Saturn ruled, though not for a very long time, is now being re-born. . . ."[30] The panegyric-writers and poets spoke for many "Redeunt Saturnia regna";[31] in a hard world the Golden Age was a perennial dream of effortless prosperity:

> No plough shall hurt the glebe, nor pruning hook the vine;
> Nor wool shall in dissembled colours shine;
> But the luxurious father of the fold,
> With native purple and unborrowed gold,
> Beneath his pompous fleece shall proudly sweat.[32]

Hope that the Golden Age was returning might emerge when those things that the gods send, politics or the weather, might seem to justify it. The literary motif of the Golden Age expressed the familiar hopes of an entire culture. The myth was one of the permanent lines of tension that held in place the structure of ancient Mediterranean life.

Within two hundred years, as we have seen, it had been replaced by the Christian myth of the End of the World. How had this change been so complete? To ask this is to ask how it was that Christianity came to be the dominant religion of the Mediterranean world. But to ask in this way about the changing pattern of myths is to qualify in an important way the familiar question about conversion to Christianity. The Roman Empire did not become Christian simply because individuals, however numerous or however powerful, accepted Christ as their personal Lord and Saviour. Rather, conversion involved the transformation of an entire culture. Take geography: in the third century any-one could have told you that Delphi was the navel of the world; by the sixth it was equally obvious that the world had its omphalos at Jerusalem.[33] The same is true of the shift in myths. The conversion to Christianity of the Mediterranean world involved movements that went deeper than the changes of heart experienced by individuals.

One person who recognized the importance of Christian eschatological prophecy and the view of history that supported it was the great pagan scholar Porphyry, who wrote his massive *Against the Christians* in the generation before Constantine the Great.[34] In his work, Porphyry employed con-siderable learning to damage the *bona fides* of the Book of Daniel.[35] This was not done in the cause

of dispassionate scholarship. Images from Daniel sustained Christians afraid of persecution;[36] Daniel's visions of the beasts with horns, the Son of Man, and the Ancient of Days were the root from which grew the lush abundance of Christian eschatological prophecy.[37] The object of the attack was well-chosen; Christian controversialists rushed to the defense.[38] If Porphyry's arguments had persuaded people to ignore the Book of Daniel, little would have been left of the Christian myth of the End of the World.

The writings of one of Porphyry's Christian con-temporaries may help to explain why the sober warnings of the pagan scholar were not heeded and why Christian eschatology did in fact go on to take over the public mythology of the Mediterranean world. Lactantius had served as an official teacher of rhetoric under the emperor Diocletian, "the father of the Golden Age";[39] in his old age he was to be tutor to the son of Constantine the Great, the first Christian emperor.[40] His most considerable work, the *Divine Institutes*, ends with a long and dramatic account of the End of the World. The woes he describes follow one another in painful but traditional profusion until the Second Coming of Christ, who initiates the Last Judgment. As a consequence, the righteous will live on for a fur-ther one thousand years in a final millennium of bliss, before God brings the present world-process to a complete conclusion; those who worship idols will then be sent to perpetual fire while the righteous will serve him for all eternity.[41]

Lactantius' prophecy rests solidly on a theory of history which is similar to that in the *Tübingen Theosophy*: "Because all the works of God were finished in six days it is necessary that the world remain in this condition for six ages, that is for six thousand years."[42] The world was now in the sixth age: "Earthly prophets agree with those who speak from heaven in foretelling the fall and end of every-thing after a short time; it is as if they are de-scribing the last old age of the tired world as it falls apart."[43] The eschatological dénouement of the *Divine Institutes* is the final act of a drama whose pattern of construction is completely clear to Lac-tantius; his prophecy of the end of history is the natural consequence of his theory of the whole history of the world. Both prophecy and theory of history are distinctively Christian.

However, Lactantius was not living in a world that shared his convictions. The *Divine Institutes* account also, though in Christian terms, for the story of the Golden Age. God made man, about five and a half thousand years before the coming of Christ, to serve him and worship him in righteousness.[44] The qualities of equity and neighborliness that righteousness brings about persisted in the Mediterranean world until the second millennium before Christ, when an empire arose dominated by the family of a ruler called Saturn.[45] It was Saturn's son and successor, Jupiter, who first introduced strife and the worship of idols.[46] For the first time people were afraid: "who would not be afraid of this man surrounded by armed soldiers, encircled with the then unfamiliar flash of swords and steel."[47] For the first time food was not equitably shared; before, "the barns of just men stood generously open to all, for avarice had not yet come between men and the blessings given by God, in order to bring about thirst and famine." The time before Jupiter, when his father Saturn reigned, was, Lactantius averred, that which was recalled by poets as the Golden Age when "Rivers of milk flowed first, then rivers of nectar flowed after that."[48] It was righteousness, *justitia*, composed of *pietas*, the service of the Most High God, and *humanitas*, the quality that enables men to live in peace together, that had produced the conditions of the Golden Age.

These conditions would return in the final millennium of bliss that the righteous were to enjoy after the Second Coming of Christ. Lactantius used familiar lines from the *Fourth Eclogue* of Vergil to describe the peace and prosperity he and his fellow-Christians were to enjoy:

> No keel shall cut the waves for foreign ware
> For every soil shall every product bear.[49]

Contemporaries might feel that what was foretold was the Golden Age they were accustomed to hope for. But the lines of Vergil were only honey on the rim of the cup; the content of Lactantius' prophecy was Christian.[50] The Golden Age had been fitted in to the events Christians expected at the End of the World, and into the scheme of world history that sustained their expectation. Lactantius' Golden Age was to be enjoyed by only the righteous.

Lactantius' fusion of the myth of the Golden Age into his prophecy of the end is coherent, but how was it persuasive? One certainly could not give him credit for convincing the entire Mediterranean world to abandon its long-rooted hope in favor of the convictions of the Christians. But two features of his prophecy suggest reasons why such expectations spread.

First, for all the vivid language of his prophecy, Lactantius believed he was describing literally what was going to happen. Hope and fear contended in Christian attitudes about the end times, but such emotions were in the long run irrelevant. Lactantius

looked on his predictions as a matter of fact: "Res ipsa declarat,"[51] "it horrifies the mind to say it, but I will say it because it is what is going to happen."[52] What is more, it was going to happen soon: Expert Christian chronographers gave the world no more than two hundred years—that is, until about 500 A.D., "but we should worship and pray to the God of heaven . . . lest the abominable tyrant—the Antichrist—come more quickly than we think."[53]

There is a second reason why Lactantius' prophecy may have been particularly influential; it was uttered in peculiarly traumatic circumstances. Lactantius lived, as the old Chinese curse puts it, in interesting times; the *Divine Institutes* and the prophecy with which they close were written during the Great Persecution and the complicated civil wars from which Constantine the Great rose to supreme power. It was a time of confusion and heightened expectations. Emperors tried to bind each other through oaths sworn by the gods,[54] one welcomed the erection of a statue of Zeus the Friend of Men, which uttered ventriloqual oracles in support of his policies,[55] another had well-publicized visions of his divine companions.[56] In such circumstances some people in public life chose to interpret events in terms of Christian prophecy and of the pattern of history on which it depended. The emperor Constantine himself quoted Vergil's *Fourth Eclogue* in a sermon foretelling the coming of Christ.[57]

The conversion to Christianity of the Roman Empire was not achieved in a single generation, any more than it was achieved by the cumulative conversion of separate individuals.[58] But the first generation of the fourth century, the age of Lactantius and Constantine, had a particular importance in the protracted process. The great strength of the ancient gods had been that their worship was what came naturally. Under Constantine, the sacrifices they had received from time immemorial became illegal.[59] When, a generation after his death, the neo-pagan emperor Julian tried to reimpose the old worship, he did so as a partisan.[60] That is not to say that the old ways perished completely. The massive Roman temples still stood at Ba'albek when the sybil uttered her *Oracle* there in the early sixth century;[61] even in the age of Joshua the Stylite the people of Aphrodisias in Caria, faced with crisis and natural disaster, would turn once more to ancient divination.[62]

For the first time in the age of Constantine and Lactantius, however, evidence exists that the Christian pattern of prophecy was being taken seriously by those who lived in the worlds of courts and armies, those whose business was imperial politics.

The Christians had long made the remarkable claim that their God was not merely a supplement to existing divinities but was the only one who had power over public as well as private affairs; for the first time this claim was being put to the test. The imperial court was only one small world in the complicated mosaic of communities of the late Roman Mediterranean. Individual cities were to have their own crises that affected the worship they had been accustomed to offer to their own gods and the conversion of their local public life to the new pattern.[63] The introduction of Christian prophecy into the minds of those at the imperial court was one step in the transformation in public life that we call the conversion of the Mediterranean world to Christianity.

In about 500 A.D., at the same time as the events described by Joshua the Stylite and the prophets with whom we began, Zosimus, a pagan civil servant, considered the causes of the rise and fall of empires: "whereas Polybius tells how the Romans won their empire in a short time, I intend to show how they lost it in an equally short time by their own crimes."[64] It is scarcely surprising that he thought the rot started with Constantine.[65] Zosimus was not unconcerned with prophecy, but he interpreted ancient oracles; he understood the sybils not as foretelling the End of the World but as asserting that while the regular rhythm of pagan festivals was sustained, Roman power would continue.[66] His increasingly was a lone voice.

Notes

1 W. Wright, ed. and trans., *The Chronicle of Joshua the Stylite* (Cambridge, 1882; reprint Amsterdam, Philo Press, 1968) gives the fullest account. Famine is also mentioned by F. J. Hamilton and E. W. Brooks, trans., *The Chronicle of Zachariah of Mitylene* (London, 1899), 7.2. Both Joshua (*Chron.* 54) and Zachariah (*Chron.* 7.2) refer to the writings on the subject of Jacob of Sarugh. For the extent of the famine, "from Antioch as far as Nisibis," Josh. Styl. *Chron.* 44.

2 Josh. Styl. *Chron.* 33 (eggs laid), 38 ("the very air was vomiting them against us"); Zac. Mit. *Chron.* 7.2.

3 Josh. Styl. *Chron.* 38 (country people), 41 (sleeping in the streets), cf. 42-43. Zac. Mit. *Chron.* 7.2 and Evagrius *Hist. Eccl.* 3.36 refer to incursions of Arabs into Roman territory from Palestine to Mesopotamia; these were presumably occasioned by hunger.

4 Josh. Styl. *Chron.* 42.

5 Josh. Styl. *Chron.* 40 (cabbages), 41 (vegetable stalks).

6 Josh. Styl. *Chron.* 44.

7 Josh. Styl. *Chron.* 44.

8 Josh. Styl. *Chron.* 45.

9 Josh. Styl. *Chron.* 47, who mentions also the destruction of the synagogue at Berytus. Zac. Mit. *Chron.* 7.2 also refers to an earthquake, though this may be that recorded in Josh. Styl. for 499 (*Chron.* 34). The African bishop Victor Tonnennensis *Chron.* ad ann. 502 A.D. (*Chronica Minora* ed. Mommsen 2.193) mentions "ingens terrae motus," and Theodore Lector *Hist. Eccl.* 2. frag. 54 refers to an earthquake at Neocaesarea in Pontus about this time. I have not been able to see the article on three earthquakes in the East under Anastasius (494, 497, and 502) in B. Helly and A. Pollino, eds. *Tremblements de terre: histoire et archéologie* (4ème rencontre internationale d'archéologie et d'histoire of 2-4th November 1983, Valbonne, 1984).

10 For the Nicomedia earthquake of 358 A.D., Ammianus Marcellinus 17.7, 1, Jerome *Chron.* ad ann. 358 A.D. (= 241a Helm), etc.; of 362 A.D., Amm. Marc. 22.13, 5.

11 Josh. Styl. *Chron.* 47; Joshua might have known of threnodies on the Nicomedia earthquakes of the fourth century by Ephrem Syrus (mentioned Gennadius *De viris illustribus* 67; Marcellinus Comes *Chron.* ad ann. 459).

12 Josh. Styl. *Chron.* 47. Joshua (*Chron.* 49) records that "many thought and said . . . that the end of the world was come," but himself reflected that it was more likely that the disasters were sent as a chastisement for sin. Severus of Antioch (*Homily* 19 *On the Drought*) was equally wary of those who leaped to eschatological conclusions (Patr. Orient. 37/1, p. 27, lines 20-25).

13 Josh. Styl. *Chron.* 48.

14 Josh. Styl. *Chron.* 48; Zac. Mit. *Chron.* 7.3; Procopius *Aedif.* 3.5, 3; cf. *Bell. Pers.* 1.7, 3; Evagrius *Hist. Eccl.* 3.37. Theodosiopolis has not had the same degree of recent archaeological attention as frontier-cities further south, but see F. de' Maffei, "Fortificazioni di Giustiniano sul limes orientale: monumenti e fonti," *Proceedings of the 17th International Byzantine Congress* (Washington, D.C., August 1986), pp. 253-56.

15 Josh. Styl. *Chron.* 50ff.; Zac. Mit. *Chron.* 7.3-4; Procopius *Bell. Pers.* 1.7, 3-32; *Aedif.* 3.2, 8; cf. *Anecd.* 23.7; Marc. Comes *Chron.* ad ann. 502.

16 For summaries of Roman-Persian relations, Josh. Styl. *Chron.* 7-11, 18-25; Procopius *Bell. Pers.* 1.2-6. Recently, Z. Rubin, "Diplomacy and War in the Relations between Byzantium and Sassanids in the 5th Century A.D.," in P. Freeman and D. Kennedy, eds., *The Defense of the Roman and Byzantine East: Proceedings of a colloquium held at the Uni-*

versity of Sheffield in April 1986 (Brit. Inst. Arch. at Ankara monograph 8 = B.A.R. Int. series 297, Oxford, 1986), 2:677-95.

17 P. J. Alexander, ed., *The Oracle of Baalbek* (Washington, D.C., Dumbarton Oaks studies 10, 1967), lines 170-73.

18 *Oracle of Baalbek*, lines 183-84.

19 *Oracle of Baalbek*, lines 217ff.

20 *Armenian Apocalypse of Daniel*, in F. Macler, ed., *Les apocalypses apocryphes de Daniel* (Thesis, Univ. de Paris, 1895), p. 88. On this text, P. J. Alexander in his *Oracle of Baalbek*, p. 118.

21 H. Erbse, ed., *Fragmente griechischer Theosophien* (Hamburg, 1941); also K. Buresch, ed., *Klaros* (Leipzig, 1889), pp. 95-126. Recent discussion and bibliography, R. van den Broek, "Four Coptic Fragments of a Greek Theosophy," *Vigiliae Christianae* 32 (1978): 118-42; S. P. Brock, "Some Syriac Excerpts from Greek Collections of Pagan Prophecies," *Vig. Christ.* 38 (1984): 77-90.

22 *Tübingen Theosophy* 2 shows that Book 11 of the original *Theosophia* included a chronicle from the time of Adam to the emperor Zeno. The scheme of world history is laid out in *Tüb. Theos.* 3. "The exact date depended, of course, on the system of computation that was adopted" (C. Mango, *Byzantium: the Empire of New Rome* [London, 1980], p. 204).

23 R. Bauckham, "The Martyrdom of Enoch and Elijah: Jewish or Christian?" *Journal of Biblical Literature* 95 (1976): 447-58 provides a useful table (447-49); cf. J. Nützel, "Zum Schicksal der eschatologischen Propheten," *Biblische Zeitschrift* 20 (1976): 59-94; K. Berger, *Die Auferstehung des Propheten und die Erhöhung des Menschensohnes* (Göttingen, 1976).

24 *Oracle of Baalbek*, lines 94-95, on which pages 53ff.

25 P. J. Alexander, *Amer. Hist. Rev.* 73 (1968): 1001-2.

26 *Tüb. Theos.* 3. For an introduction to this strain in Early Christian thought J. Daniélou "La typologie millénnariste de la semaine," *Vig. Christ.* 2 (1948): 1-16; cf. also P. J. Alexander, *Oracle of Baalbek*, pp. 119-20 and note 44 below.

27 N. K. Sandars, *The Sea Peoples* (London, 1978), pp. 20-21 and 24.

28 Horace *Odes* 4.7, 1-2—on spring. On the seasons in Roman life and art G. M. A. Hanfmann, *The Seasons Sarcophagus at Dumbarton Oaks* (Washington, D.C., 1951). On the Golden Age as a literary motif Bodo Gatz, *Weitalter, Goldene Zeit und Sinnverwandte Vorstellungen* (Hildesheim, Spudasmata, 1967). In the Golden Age there was eternal spring: Ovid *Metamorphoses* 1.107.

29 *Historia Augusta* vita Elgabali 35, 4; for the possibility that passages in Lactantius' *Divine Institutes* may reflect adversely on a claim by Diocletian to be bringing back the Golden Age, Oliver Nicholson, "The Wild Man of the Tetrarchy: A Divine Companion for the Emperor Galerius," *Byzantion* 54 (1984):

266-67, esp. note 62.

30 *Latin Panegyric* 5.(9.)18, 4-5. A. D. Nock, *Journal of Roman Studies* 37 (1947): 107, note 57 notes that a herm published by H. Fuhrmann, "Zum Bildnis des Kaisers Diocletian," *Romische Mitteilungen* 53 (1938): 35-45 implies "that Diocletian has brought back 'Saturnia regna.'"

31 Vergil *Eclogue* 4.6.

32 Vergil *Eclogue* 4.40-44, in the translation of John Dryden.

33 Delphi: e.g., Pausanias 10.16, 2 (the note of P. Levi *ad loc.* refers to an illustration on an Apulian vase of the stone that marked the spot at Delphi "which makes it look like a five-foot Easter egg budding like an acorn from a carved and coloured base"); for further references Liddel and Scott s.v. Ομφλος. Jerusalem: E. D. Hunt, *Holy Land Pilgrimage in the Later Roman Empire 312-460* (Oxford, 1982), pp. 18-20; to which add Josephus *Bell. Jud.* 3.52; *Book of Jubilees* 8.19; Ezekiel 38:12; and Psalm 48:2 for background.

34 On which most recently Brian Croke, "Porphyry's Anti-Christian Chronology," *Journal of Theological Studies* 32 n.s. (1986): 168-85.

35 P. M. Casey, "Porphyry and the Origins of the Book of Daniel," *Journal of Theological Studies*, n.s. 27 (1976): 15-33.

36 E.g., Cyprian *de lapsis* 31. Scenes from Daniel regularly recur in the Roman catacomb paintings: A. G. Martimort, "L'iconographie des catacombes et la catachèse antique," *Rivista di Archeologia Cristiana* 25 (1949): 107, counts nineteen of the Three Children, thirty-nine of Daniel himself, and six of Susannah and the Elders, and argues that they reflect the normal basic Christianity of catechetical classes. For Constantine's admiration of Daniel, *Oratio ad sanctum coetum* 17 (and for a monument he erected at Constantinople of the prophet Eusebius, *Vita Constantini* 3.49).

37 Cyril of Jerusalem (*Catechetical Lecture* 15.16) may be taken as typical in his estimate of Daniel's authority: "We speak not from apocryphal books, but from Daniel. . . ." K. Berger, *Die griechische Daniel-Diegese* (Leiden, 1976), pp. xi-xxiii, gives a handy list of 188 apocalypses.

38 For the refutation of Methodius of Olympus, who perished in the Great Persecution, Jerome, *de viris illustribus* 83; for that of Apollinaris Philostorgius, *Hist. Eccl.* 8.14. On that of Eusebius, *de vir. illustr.* 81; and on all three Jerome, *Comm. in Danielem*, prologue, which states that Porphyry's attack on Daniel ran to a whole book, Eusebius' defense to three, and Apollinaris' to one large book.

39 Jerome *de vir. illustr.* 80.

40 Jerome *Chron.* ad ann. 317 A.D. (Helm 230e), *de vir. illustr.* 80. On the dating of Lactantius' life and works, see succinctly T. D. Barnes, *Constantine and*

Eusebius (Cambridge, Mass., 1981), p. 291.

41   *Divine Institutes* (hereinafter *Inst.*) 7.15-26, summarized, with variations, in *Epitome* 66-68. For a summary L. Atzberger, *Geschichte der Christlichen Eschatologie* (Freiburg im Bresgau, 1896), pp. 601-11. V. Fabrega, "Die chiliastische Lehre des Laktanz," *Jahrbuch für Antike und Christentum* 17 (1974): 126-46 emphasizes Lactantius' use of Revelation.

42   *Inst.* 7.14, 9. For Lactantius' scheme of world history, O. P. Nicholson, "The Sources of the Dates in Lactantius *Divine Institutes*," *Journal of Theological Studies* 36 n.s. (1985): 291-310.

43   *Inst.* 7.14, 16; cf. *Inst.* 7.15, 14-19.

44   For the dates *Inst.* 7.14, 7ff.; for a summary of God's purpose *Inst.* 7.6, 1-2. For a comprehensive collection of Lactantius' observations on righteousness V. Loi, "I concetto di 'justitia' e i fattori culturali dell' etica di Lattanzio," *Salesianum* 28 (1966): 583-624. Also V. Buchheit, "Die Definition der Gerechtigkeit bei Laktanz und seinen Vorgängern," *Vigiliae Christianae* 33 (1979): 356-76. *Inst.* 5.14, 9 divides "justitia" into "pietas" and "aequitas"; for further anatomy of these virtues *Inst.* 6.10.

45   For the date, *Inst.* 1.23. *Inst.* 1.11, 6-1.14, 12 are concerned in general with the doings of the three generations of rulers later worshipped by the Greeks as gods; *Inst.* 5.5-7 describes the end of Golden Age of Saturn ("justus in regno fuit": *Inst.* 1.12, 1). The most exhaustive study of the Golden Age in Lactantius is V. Buchheit, "Goldene Zeit und Paradies auf Erden (Laktanz Inst. 5.5-8)," *Würzburger Jahrbuch* 4 N.F. (1978): 161-85 and 5 N.F. (1979): 219-35. L. J. Swift, "Lactantius and the Golden Age," *American Journal of Philology* 89 (1968): 144-56 fails to distinguish the Golden Age from the Garden of Eden and so detects nonexistent "inconsistencies in Lactantius' varied descriptions of man's primaeval state" (147); cf. J. C. Frédouille "Lactance historien des religions," in J. Fontaine and M. Perrin, eds. *Lactance et son temps* (Paris, 1978), pp. 237-52 and O. P. Nicholson, "The Sources of the Dates," p. 292.

46   *Inst.* 5.5-6; 1.10, 10ff.; 1.13-14; 1.21, 22-28; cf. 1.11-12. "'Tum belli rabies et amor successit habendi' . . . Sublata enim dei religione": *Inst.* 5.5, 12-13, quoting Vergil *Aen.* 8.327.

47   *Inst.* 5.6, 7.

48   *Inst.* 5.5, 8 and 7, quoting Ovid *Metamorphoses* 1.111.

49   *Inst.* 7.24, 11, quoting (here in Dryden's translation) Vergil *Ecl.* 4.38-39. The same passage is quoted by Constantine, note 57 below. For further references P. Courcelle, "Les exégèses chrétiennes de la quatrième églogue," *Revue des études anciennes* 59 (1957): 294-319.

50   For the metaphor *Inst.* 5.1, 14 (echoing Lucretius 1.936-50). Lactantius deliberately emphasized the non-Christian testimonies to his predictions (e.g., *Inst.* 7.18), but this was because they would be more persuasive than Christian prophecies "uno spiritu similia dicentibus" (*Inst.* 7.25, 1). For the shape of Lactantius' prophecy, the works referred to in note 41.

51   *Inst.* 7.25, 6.

52   *Inst.* 7.15, 11. G. Alföldy "The Crisis of the Third Century as seen by Contemporaries," *Greek, Roman and Byzantine Studies* 15 (1974): 89-111 and B. Kötting "Endzeitsprognosen zwischen Lactantius und Augustinus," *Historisches Jahrbuch* 77 (1958): 125-39 perhaps overestimate the importance of the vagaries of personal feeling in the formation of apocalyptic.

53   *Inst.* 7.25, 8. Lactantius, of course, did not know the day nor the hour of the end; the uncertainty is essential to the generation of prophecy.

54   On the oath of Diocletian and Maximian in the Temple of Jupiter Capitolinus, mentioned in *Panegyric* 6.(7.)15, 6, C. E. V. Nixon, "The Panegyric of 307 and Maximian's Visits to Rome," *Phoenix* 35 (1981): 70-76. In a dedication erected at the time of the conference held in 308 to reconcile their differences, the emperors describe Mithras as "fautor imperii sui" (*Corp. Inscr. Lat.* 3.4413). Had Mithras guaranteed the agreement they had reached? He had a long history as a god who sanctioned contracts: M. Leglay "La Δεξιωσις dans les mystères de Mithra," *Acta Iranica* 4 (1978) = *Etudes mithraïques, actes du 2ème congrès internat.*, esp. 282-83.

55   Eusebius *Hist. Eccl.* 9.3; cf. *Prep. Ev.* 4.2.

56   *Panegyric* 6.(7.)21, 4; Lactantius *Mort.* 44, 5 with Eusebius *Vit. Con.* 1.28.

57   Constantine *Orat. ad sanct. coet.* 20.

58   It is impossible to estimate numbers, though R. Lane Fox, *Pagans and Christians* (London, 1986) 586 emphasizes the comparative numerical weakness of Christianity c. 300 A.D. There was more to the conversion of the Empire than the counting of hearts. For T. D. Barnes (*Constantine and Eusebius* [Cambridge, Mass., 1981], p. 191) Christianity at the start of the fourth century was already "powerful and respectable"; even if this is accepted, the Church was nothing like so powerful and respectable as the ancient religion. The conversion of the urban landscape took centuries; the first temple in central Rome to become a church, the Pantheon, was not converted until the sixth century (*Liber Pontificalis*, vol. 1, p. 317, Boniface IV).

59   *Codex Theodosianus* 16.10, 2 with T. D. Barnes, *Constantine and Eusebius*, pp. 210, 247.

60   For P. Athanassiadi-Fowden, *Julian and Hellenism* (Oxford, 1981), pp. 166-67, Julian was the first Byzantine emperor because of his attempt to impose a normative faith on the Empire from above.

61   Zac. Mitt. *Chron.* 8.4 mentions that the "Temple of Solomon" at Ba'albek was struck by lightning in 526, and a church constructed there later. P. J. Alexander, *Oracle of Baalbek*, p. 43ff. emphasizes

the seer's local interests.

62 Zac. Mitt. *Vita Severi*, p. 40, Kuegener = Patrol. Orient. 2, 1 (Paris, 1907).

63 E.g., in 408 A.D. a pagan festival at Calama led to rioting and deaths. Augustine hoped that the result of the traumatic events would be a rich gain of souls for the Church (Augustine *Epistle* 91, 8-10).

64 Zosimus *Historia Nova* 1.57, 1. On Zosimus and Polybius, F. Paschoud, *Cinq études sur Zosime* (Paris, 1975), pp. 184-206. For the date of Zosimus' work, Alan Cameron, "The Date of Zosimus' *New History*," *Philologus* 113 (1969): 106-10; W. Goffart, "Zosimus, the First Historian of Rome's Fall," *American Historical Review* 76 (1971): 412-41 places the historian in the context of his time.

65 Zosimus *Hist. Nov.* 2.7; 2.29-39.

66 Zosimus *Hist. Nov.* 2.6-7. For further interpretations of ancient oracles 1.57, 4; 2.6; 2.36. A younger imperial servant thought sibyls too ambiguous and their interpretation too hazardous to make them any use as prophecies: Procopius *Bell. Goth.* 5.24, 34-37.

Two Early Anecdotes Concerning Gregory the Great from the Greek Tradition[1]

Ivan Havener, O.S.B.

Despite his stormy relationship with John IV, "the Faster," Patriarch of Constantinople from 582 to 595, and his occasional interference with the affairs of the Patriarchal See of Constantinople,[2] Gregory the Great, Pope of Rome, is nonetheless one of the most highly revered Latin saints among the Greeks.[3] The extant literary beginnings of this Greek veneration of Gregory can be traced to two early anecdotes, stories that are instructive both for the early dating of this veneration and for their emphasis on moral edification. We shall review these anecdotes, seeking what they reveal about the relations between the Eastern and Western churches at the time of their composition, what they tell us from a sociological perspective about the early medieval Mediterranean world, what we learn about the Greek estimation of a key Latin figure, and what the literary and religious functions of such miracle stories are.

Gregory the Great was born ca. 540 and was Pope of Rome from 590 to 604. His life has been recorded in two important Latin works, one by Paul the Deacon[4] in the eighth century and another by John the Deacon of Rome,[5] who wrote a century later than Paul. Of these two "lives" only that of John the Deacon is at all related to the traditions about Gregory that have survived in Greek; in fact, it is quite clear that John the Deacon has borrowed parts of his narrative about Gregory from Greek sources, twice citing anecdotes that he acknowledges have come from the Greeks. In the case of one of these anecdotes, John the Deacon names the Greek source as the *Leimon,* which is a reference to the *Spiritual Meadow* [=*Pratum Spirituale*] of John Moschus.[6] Indeed, both anecdotes are found in several important manuscripts of the *Spiritual Meadow.*[7]

The putative author of these anecdotes, John Moschus, was a monk of the monastery of St. Theodosius near Jerusalem who, after living as a hermit for a period of time, caught a not-uncommon monastic illness, namely, "travel fever." He traveled throughout the Mediterranean world visiting Palestine, Egypt, Sinai, Cyprus, Samos, Syria, and several other places, all the while gathering the anecdotal narratives about saintly bishops and monastics that were to make up the content of his *Spiritual Meadow.* In 604, the year of Gregory's death, John Moschus and his younger traveling companion Sophronius fled from the Persians and went to Antioch and then to Egypt.[8] Finally they went "to the great city of the Romans" in 614. Whether this reference means Rome, or Constantinople as the "New Rome," is now a matter of scholarly dispute. Likewise, the date of John Moschus' death remains uncertain—either 619 or 634.[9] In any case, if the Gregory anecdotes really go back to John Moschus, they probably were written down sometime between 604 and 634 and possibly before 619, that is, no later than fifteen to thirty years after Gregory's death and much earlier than the Latin "lives" of Gregory.

The Prostration Anecdote

One of these Gregory anecdotes appears, to my knowledge, only in John Moschus' work among Greek writings. It reads as follows:

We visited Abba John the Persian at the Monidia, and he told us about the great Gregory, the most blessed Bishop of Rome, saying, "I went to worship in Rome at the tombs of the holy apostles Peter and Paul, and one day, as I stood in the midst of the city, I saw that Pope Gregory was about to pass by me. So I decided to prostrate before him. But when his retinue saw me, each of them began to tell me, 'Abba, do not prostrate yourself.' But I did not realize that they were saying this to me; besides, I thought it to be out of place not to prostrate before him. Then as the pope came near me and had seen that I had begun to prostrate myself, as the Lord is my witness, brothers, he prostrated himself on the ground first and did not rise until after I had arisen. And after he

ff 19

greeted me with much humility, by his hand he gave me three coins and also ordered that a cloak and all my needs be given to me. Then I glorified God who had bestowed on him such humility, mercy, and love toward all."[10]

The style, form, content, and even the opening words of this anecdote are entirely consistent with other stories found in the *Spiritual Meadow,* and the Greek text agrees very closely with John the Deacon's Latin rendering of the story, though John the Deacon apparently has left out a couple of extraneous lines.[11] John Moschus also includes stories about other saintly Latins in his work, such as Pope Leo the Great, the Roman abbot Theodore, and others whom he designates as coming from Roman families,[12] so that inclusion of this material about Gregory is not at all foreign to his thought.

Of special interest in this anecdote about Gregory is the figure of Abba John the Persian, known to us from the *Sayings of the Desert Fathers and Mothers.*[13] According to John Moschus, John the Persian was visiting at a place called "Monidia," a *lavra* that was part of a group of monasteries of Scetis in lower Egypt. Although the *Desert Sayings* tradition says that John the Persian "abided in Arabia of Egypt"[14] rather than in Egypt proper, John Moschus is probably referring to the same person—not an impossibility, since, according to John Moschus' own story, John the Persian was a traveler. If we were to assume some historical credibility to a visit of John Moschus with John the Persian in Egypt, then John the Persian must have belonged to the very latest level of the *Desert Sayings* tradition, since the collection of these sayings came to its present form at the end of the sixth century,[15] around the time of Gregory's pontificate.

Given the legendary character of the story, however, it does not seem wise to press its historicity. Far more significant, perhaps, is the attitude of openness between Eastern Christianity and the Latin church so clearly expressed in this story. That much is certainly accurate historically. John Moschus appreciated holiness wherever he found it, whether it was present in a Greek or a Latin. We find a complete absence of antagonism on the part of this Greek writer toward the Latin church and no indication of the bitterness and strife between the Latin and Greek churches that eventually led to the great rupture between the churches in the eleventh century. Indeed, the story reveals that at that time Rome continued to be a place of religious pilgrimage for both Greeks and other Eastern Christians. Rome was revered as the burial place of Peter and Paul, saints who were the objects of veneration

by all Christians. We note also that travel from one place in the empire to another is simply assumed to be possible, even for poor monks of the desert and for others like John Moschus himself.[16]

Another fascinating feature of this anecdote about Gregory is his designation as "great." Although this adjective became popular as a way to refer to Gregory in the Latin West, it was not often used in the Greek-speaking world. The most frequently used Greek expression is "the Dialogist" (*ho Dialogos*), a way of distinguishing this Gregory from such other famous Greek Gregories as Gregory Nazianus "the Theologian" (*ho Theologos*) and Gregory "the Thaumaturge" (*ho Thaumatourgos*). But "the Dialogist" designation seems to have been used to describe Gregory only after his *Dialogues* were translated into Greek during the reign of Pope Zacharias (741-752), the last of the Greek popes of Rome.[17] There is some irony, then, that a Greek writer was either the first or among the first to use the term "great" as a designation for Pope Gregory.

Finally, the central feature of this edifying narrative is the virtue of humility as demonstrated by Gregory's prostration before the humble Desert Father, John the Persian. This humility is accompanied by mercy and love, as shown by Gregory's generosity in almsgiving and in looking after John's needs. The concluding lesson of the story focuses on the response of Father John, glorifying God who has blessed Gregory with this humility, mercy, and love. In other words, through the examples of this towering figure of Latin Christianity and the lowly figure of a Persian desert monk, the listener or reader is encouraged to be humble, merciful, and loving, recognizing these virtuous attributes as gifts from God who, in turn, is to be praised for bestowing them on humanity.

The Excommunication Anecdote

The second anecdote about Gregory the Great has a far more complex textual history, because it circulated as an independent unit of tradition quite apart from its presence in the version of John Moschus' *Spiritual Meadow* that John the Deacon had at his disposal.[18] Appearing in other works, this anecdote in a slightly longer form also has been attributed variously to Anastasius, Patriarch of Antioch,[19] to Anastasius of Mount Sinai,[20] and in some manuscripts simply to Anastasius without any further identification. It is also found in a truncated form in the *Chronicon* of George the Monk (also called *Harmartolos*)[21] who wrote ca. 867; he does not name the author of the anecdote.

Before sorting out these attributions in an attempt

to find the original author of the story, I will first give a translation of this anecdote from what appears to be the most complete and reliable printed Greek text available:[22]

A certain presbyter by the name of Peter who came from Rome related to us about Gregory the Dialogist, Pope of the same city, who is numbered among the saints, that while being pope, he founded a great monastery of men and gave orders that none of the monks should ever possess anything for himself, not even a penny.

Once, a certain brother from the monastery had a secular brother and asked him, saying, "I do not have a shirt, but do me a favor; buy one for me." The secular brother said to him, "Brother, here are three coins; take them then; buy whatever you want." Then taking the three coins, the brother kept them for himself.

But another brother saw that he possessed the three coins, and he went and told the hegumen [= abbot], and the hegumen told the saintly pope. After he had learned of it, the blessed Gregory banned him from communion, since he had broken the rule of the monastery. Then after a short time, the brother who had been excommunicated died, without the pope learning of it. But after two or three days, the hegumen went and told him that the brother had died. Then at this information, he [= Gregory] was not a little grieved, because he did not release him [= the brother] from the penalty before he had departed from life. And after writing a prayer on the tablet, he gave it to the archdeacon and ordered him to go and read it over the tomb of the brother. And the wording was as follows: "The brother who has died is released from the excommunication." Then the archdeacon left, as he was bidden, and over the tomb of the brother, he read the tablet that contained the prayer.

And on the same night the hegumen saw the brother who had died and said to him, "Didn't you die, brother?" And he replied to him, "Yes." And again he asked him, "And where have you been till today?" The brother answered him, "Truly, I was in prison even until yesterday, and until that hour I was not released."

Then it became known to all that in the very hour the archdeacon said the prayer over his tomb, in that hour he was released from the excommunication, and his soul was freed from condemnation, and they gave praise to God forever. Amen.[23]

This text is more refined than that attributed to John Moschus and has a conclusion that is missing from the John Moschus version.[24] Since the response of the crowd to the wondrous effect of Gregory's prayer corresponds to a regular feature of most miracle stories,[25] its absence in John Moschus' version suggests that his is an abridgment and, therefore, a secondary rendering of the text.[26] As a result, we must look elsewhere than to John Moschus for the origin.

The attribution of this anecdote in several manuscripts to an Anastasius who was Patriarch of Antioch is especially intriguing since there were two Greek patriarchs by that name who were contemporaries and friends of Pope Gregory. Of these two, Anastasius I was the better known and a more controversial figure, but the anecdote about Gregory was clearly written after Gregory's death (according to the anecdote, Gregory's term as pope, which ended with his death, is viewed as a past event), and since Anastasius I died five years before Gregory, he could not have authored this story. The situation is quite different, however, for his immediate successor, Anastasius II.

Reigning as Patriarch of Antioch from 599 to 609, Anastasius II undertook the translation of Gregory's lengthy *Pastoral Rule* [= *Regula pastoralis*] into Greek. Although this translation seems to have vanished without a trace,[27] Gregory himself makes reference to it in a letter to John, Subdeacon of Ravenna:

Certainly while I am in this flesh, I do not want it to happen that those things I may have said become easily known to people. For I took it amiss that the deacon Anatolius of most loving memory gave the lord emperor, at his request and command, the book of the *Pastoral Rule*, which my most holy brother and fellow bishop, Anastasius of Antioch, translated into the Greek language. And according to what was written to me, it pleased him very much; yet it displeased me very much that those who have what is better should be occupied with what is least.[28]

As far as our anecdote is concerned, Anastasius II could well have had as a motive of composing it the preservation of a fascinating story about an admired fellow bishop. It is significant, perhaps, that Anastasius II, a Greek, also was able to translate from Latin, because this anecdote about Gregory is an abbreviated version of a story in Book IV of the *Dialogues* of Gregory.[29] On the other hand, he may have actually heard the story from a Roman presbyter named Peter, possibly the same person as the deacon Peter in Gregory's Latin text.

The tantalizing possibility also exists that there was a direct interrelation between Anastasius II and John Moschus; for in 604, the year of Gregory's death, John Moschus came to Antioch and Anastasius II was the reigning patriarch. If John Moschus obtained this anecdote from Anastasius II, its twofold Greek textual tradition could be accounted for easily: The story existed first as an isolated narrative composed by Anastasius II; then John Moschus, who was seeking out such stories for his *Spiritual*

Meadow, took it over but slightly altered it in the process.[30]

Conceivably, then, this anecdote was written within a few months of Gregory's death, [31] or no later than 609, the year of Anastasius' death. John Moschus also could have obtained his story, of course, at a later time but no later than 619 or 634, the two possible dates of his death.[32]

One other possibility for the authorship of this Gregory anecdote is a renowned theologian and hegumen whose name has come down to us as Anastasius of Mount Sinai, who died shortly after 700. A set of anecdotal material that contains this Gregory story is attributed to him as well, but how he may have obtained this story is unclear,[33] and its attribution to him is, in fact, poorly attested in the manuscripts. If he is, indeed, its original author, this would mean that the story was added to the *Spiritual Meadow* long after the death of John Moschus[34] and forty to fifty years before the complete edition of Gregory's *Dialogues* was translated into Greek.

Although the question of authorship of this anecdote about excommunication cannot be settled with any certainty, its investigation confirms the rich interaction between the Latin West and the Greek East at this period of history. But the anecdote itself, its own message and merit, is partly responsible for its cross-cultural survival.

The portrait of Gregory in this last anecdote is one of an active, dynamic church leader. As Pope of Rome he founds a monastery and writes the rule of the monastery, and its hegumen is directly responsible to him. Gregory intervenes in the disciplining of a disobedient monk; it is he who bans the brother from communion and is deeply grieved on hearing of the brother's untimely death—not because he died, but because he died still under the penalty Gregory imposed. Gregory's power is so great that the release from the penalty can be effected by an archdeacon merely reading Gregory's written words. Ultimately, however, this story is not primarily about Gregory, but about the power of God working through the church and its leaders; the concluding words indicate that the people who witness this incident give praise, not to Gregory, but to God forever. These words parallel the conclusion of our first anecdote. God is praised for his action through human beings such as Gregory.

Reverence for Gregory the Great in these Greek anecdotes is given because he acts as God's agent, making use of God's gifts; he serves as an example to the readers or hearers of these anecdotes. He is a Latin Christian who, according to the Greek authors of these stories, is worthy of veneration by Greek Christians. The miracle stories serve, therefore, a didactic function. But these anecdotes reveal some other important facets of life in the early medieval Mediterranean world, as well. Travel from one part of this world to another was apparently not uncommon, even for monastics. Religious pilgrimage and monasticism itself were part and parcel of Christian life at that time, as was a certain harmony among Christians—Latin, Greek, and Persian—despite their cultural and linguistic differences.

Notes

1   I am grateful for a National Endowment for the Humanities Travel to Collections grant in 1984 that enabled the research for this article to be undertaken.

2   See Jeffrey Richards, *Consul of God: The Life and Times of Gregory the Great* (London, Boston and Henley: Routledge & Kegan Paul, 1980), pp. 217-21.

3   See esp. Hippolyte Delehaye, "S. Grégoire le Grand dans l'hagiographie grecque," *Analecta Bollandiana* 23 (1904): 449-54 and François Halkin, "Le pape S. Grégoire le Grand dans l'hagiographie byzantine," *Orientalia Christiana Periodica* 21 (1955): 109-14. Until Pope Paul VI's apostolic constitution, "Missale Romanum," of April 3, 1969, Gregory's feast day in both the Latin and Greek calendars was March 12. Since the revision of the Roman missal, however, Latins now celebrate his feast on September 3.

4   Migne, *PL* 75.41-60.

5   Migne, *PL* 75.61-242.

6   Migne, *PL* 75.100 [= book 2.45]; cf. col. 213 [= book 4.63].

7   The critical edition of the Greek text of the *Spiritual Meadow*, being prepared by Philip Pattenden, has not yet, to my knowledge, appeared in print. He discusses the manuscript tradition of this work as part of the prolegomena to this new edition in an article entitled, "The Text of the *Pratum Spirituale*," *The Journal of Theological Studies*, n.s. 26 (1975): 38-54. Although the two Gregory anecdotes are firmly attested in some important manuscripts of the *Spiritual Meadow*, they are missing in others.

8   See Hans-Georg Beck, *Kirche und theologische Literatur im byzantinischen Reich*, vol. 2/1 of the *Byzantinisches Handbuch*, vol. 12 of the *Handbuch der Altertumswissenschaft* (Munich: C. H. Beck, 1959),

p. 412 and Henry Chadwick, "John Moschus and His Friend Sophronius the Sophist," *The Journal of Theological Studies*, n.s. 25 (1974): 55-59.

9 See the discussion of the complicated issues surrounding these two questions by Chadwick, pp. 41-74, esp. 49-55, 58; Keetje Rozemond, "Jean Mosch, Patriarche de Jérusalem en exil (614-34)," *Vigiliae Christianae* 31 (1977): 60-67; Elpidio Mioni, "Jean Moschus," *Dictionnaire de spiritualité*, vol. 8 (Paris: Beauchesne, 1974), cols. 632-33; and Jean-Marie Sansterre, *Les moines grecs et orientaux à Rome aux époques byzantine et carolingienne (milieu du VIe s.— fin du IXe s.)*, Académie Royale de Belgique. Mémoires de la Classe des Lettres, 2nd series, vol. 66, no. 1 (Brussels: Palais des Académies, 1983), I. *Texte*, pp. 57-61, and II. *Bibliographie, notes*, pp. 110-14.

10 Migne, *PG* 87/3.3015-18 [= *Spiritual Meadow*, chap. 151]. The translation is my own.

11 The Latin translator of John the Deacon's text of the anecdote is not named, though as Pattenden, 38 n. 3, suggests, he may have been Anastasius Bibliothecarius, quoted elsewhere in John the Deacon's life of Gregory. An eleventh-century Latin translation of this anecdote appeared in the *Liber de Miraculis* of John the Monk, an Amalfitan, who selected forty-two tales from John Moschus, Daniel of Scetis, and Anastasius of Mount Sinai and translated them at the monastery of Panagia of Balukli at Constantinople. The Latin text of Moschus printed in Migne, *PG* 87/3, which includes both Gregory anecdotes, was translated by the Camaldulese monk and humanist Ambrogio Traversari in 1423; see Chadwick, pp. 41-45.

12 E.g., Migne, *PG* 87/3.3011-16 [= *Spiritual Meadow*, chaps. 147-50]; also cols. 2959-60 [= chap. 101], cols. 2961-62 [= chap. 105], etc. Claude Dagens, "Grégoire le Grand et le monde oriental," *Rivista di Storia e Letteratura Religiosa*, 17 (1981): 248, suggests that Moschus may have learned of the two Gregory anecdotes from Eulogius, Patriarch of Alexandria from 581 to 607, who was a personal friend of Gregory; see also Beck, p. 381.

13 Migne, *PG* 65.235-40. There is, however, a possibility that Father John's designation as "the Persian" [Greek = *Persēs*] has been confused with the Greek word for an Egyptian sycamore tree, called *persis*. The only difference between these Greek words in the nominative case is an *eta* and an *iota*, which are often pronounced the same and often are used interchangeably in Greek manuscripts. It would have been easy, therefore, to confuse these two words and thus identify John Persis with John the Persian, a well-known figure from the *Desert Sayings* tradition. A reason for suggesting this confusion of identities is that according to the *Ecclesiastical History* of Sozomen (Migne, *PG* 67.1281 = book 5, chap. 21), the Egyptian *persis* tree is said to have bowed down in adoration of Christ at his flight into Egypt. By using this term *persis* as a second name for Father John, the original anecdote may have been underscoring John's predilection for prostrations. If this is the case, then John the Persian has been wrongly confused with John Persis, who is otherwise unknown to us.

14 Migne, *PG* 65.235-40.

15 See Benedicta Ward, ed., *The Sayings of the Desert Fathers: The Alphabetical Collection* (London and Oxford: Mowbrays, 1975), p. xiv. This Gregory anecdote does not appear among the *Desert Sayings* collections.

16 See Chadwick, p. 58. He points out that the see of Rome was the great defender of the Council of Chalcedon, and John Moschus was himself "a zealous Chalcedonian" and, therefore, had good reason to have had an attachment to Rome.

17 The classic biography remains that of Domenico Bartolini, *Di S. Zaccaria Papa e degli anni del suo pontificato* (Ratisbona [= Regensburg]: Friedrich Pustet, 1879).

18 The printed Greek text of John Moschus in Migne, *PG* 87/3.3072, which is based on one manuscript, is defective in several places; the accompanying Latin translation by Ambrogio Traversari [col. 3071] is based on a better Greek text, as is John the Deacon's text in Migne, *PL* 75.106. A very good Greek text is to be found in the eleventh- to twelfth-century Venice codex, Bibl. Marc. Gr. 2.70 [fol. 223v].

19 The Greek text is that of Ioannes Baptista Pitra, *Iuris ecclesiatici graecorum historia et monumenta*, vol. 2. *A VI ad IX saeculum* (Rome: Typis S. Congregationis de Propaganda Fide, 1868), 276-77. It is based on two manuscripts housed in Rome: Vatican Gr. 720 [fol. 77rv] and Bibl. Vallicelliana F 47 [fols. 256v-57v].

20 The Greek text is edited by F. Nau, "Le texte grec des récits utiles à l'âme d'Anastase (le Sinaïte)," *Oriens Christianus* 3 (1903): 84-85. It reproduces a single codex, namely, London, Brit. Mus. Add. 28, 270 [fols. 88v-90r], dated C.E. 1111.

21 The critical Greek text, based on several manuscripts, is that of *Georgii Monachi Chronicon*, ed. Carolus de Boor and Peter Wirth (Stuttgart: B. G. Teubner, 1978), 2: 748-49; see also Migne, *PG* 110.929, 932. The conclusion of this anecdote in the *Chronicon* shows that the text is based on a version that is closer to one ascribed to Anastasius rather than to John Moschus, for the John Moschus manuscripts always omit these concluding words.

22 As mentioned in n. 18 above, the printed Greek text of this anecdote in John Moschus' *Spiritual Meadow* (Migne, *PG* 87/3.3072) is defective. A complete text of this anecdote in a version attributed to John Moschus has not yet appeared in print. The version of the anecdote attributed to Anastasius of Sinai and printed by F. Nau (see note 20) contains numerous embellishments that are certainly not original.

The text of Pitra, 276-77, however, contains what is lacking from the printed John Moschus text, while having none of the numerous extraneous embellishments of the text printed by Nau. The Pitra text, therefore, is the best printed Greek text currently available.

23 The translation is my own. The naming of Gregory as "the Dialogist," as one "who is numbered among the saints," and the concluding "Amen" probably are later additions to the text.

24 See Nau, p. 84 note 4; p. 85 notes 1, 2, 4.

25 Cf. Rudolf Bultmann, *The History of the Synoptic Tradition*, trans. John Marsh, rev. ed. (New York and Evanston: Harper and Row, Publishers, 1968), pp. 225-26.

26 This is also the conclusion of Nau, pp. 59-60.

27 Beck, p. 401.

28 Gregory the Great, *Epistolarum 12, Epistola 24* (Migne, *PL* 77.1234). The translation is my own. There is also one letter from Gregory to Anastasius that has been preserved (*Epistolarum Liber 12, Epistola 48* [Migne, *PL* 77.980-81]), evidently a response to Anastasius' declaration of orthodoxy on assuming the patriarchal throne of Antioch. See also Beck, p. 401.

29 Migne, *PL* 77.420-21. The Greek version of this incident shows clear signs of being a revision of the Latin story: (1) In the Greek version, a presbyter named Peter related the story, whereas in the *Dialogues*, Gregory related these events to the deacon Peter. Why would a later Latin version reduce Peter's hierarchical status? (2) More important, Gregory did not, in fact, found a monastery in Rome during his pontificate, as the Greek version claims, but he founded the monastery of St. Andrew on his family property in Rome and was its abbot before becoming pope. The Latin version does not conflict with the facts. (3) One wonders why the hegumen in the Greek version was not able to handle this matter of discipline without going to the pope. The Latin version does not have this problem. (4) The Greek version once again inflates the hierarchical status of its participants, speaking of an archdeacon (or archdeacons in some manuscripts) who does the deed that gains release for the brother, whereas in the Latin version, it is the prior who acts. Therefore, despite the Latin version's greater detail, its account is more sober in general and harsher and must be seen as the older, original version. The Greek version follows the basic outline of the Latin text but is less specific (e.g., only Gregory and Peter are named) and the miraculous is heightened by the reduction of time for the remedy to take effect.

These observations are diametrically opposed to the position of Francis Clark, *The Pseudo-Gregorian Dialogues*, Studies in the History of Christian Thought, vol. 37 (Leiden: E. J. Brill, 1987), 1:15, 104-6. Clark holds that this anecdote by John Moschus was written before the *Dialogues* were composed under the pseudonym of Gregory the Great.

30 Moschus records a story that he heard from one of the presbyters at Antioch, who, in turn, was relating a story told by Anastasius, the patriarch; see Migne, *PG* 87/3.2889-92.

31 If this could be proven, questions concerning the authenticity of the Latin *Dialogues* could be set aside, for the Latin text must have been extant during Gregory's lifetime; cf. note 29 above.

32 See note 9 above.

33 Perhaps the monks of Sinai preserved such a story about Gregory in the light of the cordial relations that Gregory maintained with that community. Two letters of Gregory to members of the Sinai community are extant: *Epistolarum Liber 11, Epistolae 1 & 2* (Migne, *PL* 77.1117-21); cf. Chadwick, p. 58.

34 So Nau, pp. 59-60. Against Nau's position, however, it should be noted that he cites only one manuscript to support the authorship by Anastasius of Mount Sinai (see note 20 above) but is completely silent about the numerous codices that ascribe this story to Anastasius, Patriarch of Antioch: e.g., Rome, Bibl. Vallicelliana F 47 [fols. 255v, 256v-57v]; Vienna, Nationalbibl. Theol. Gr. 184 [fols. 118v, 119v] and Hist. Gr. 56 [fols. 184v, 185v]; and especially Paris, Coislin 238 [fol. 181rv], a manuscript that Nau cites for other passages ascribed to Anastasius of Mount Sinai but one that clearly ascribes the Gregory anecdote, instead, to the patriarch. Perhaps Anastasius of Mount Sinai borrowed his text of the Gregory story from the earlier work of Anastasius of Antioch, much like John Moschus may have done several years earlier.

A special word of thanks is in order to Dr. Julian Plante and the staff of the Hill Monastic Microfilm Library of Saint John's University, Collegeville, MN, for their many kindnesses and the opportunity to see the Vienna manuscripts on microfilm.

The Public Baths of Medieval Spain: An Architectural Study

Catherine B. Asher

Of the Mediterranean monuments reflecting interaction among Christians, Jews, and Muslims, perhaps the public baths are most instructive. They represent a largely secular institution, with less potential for the formal constraints that religious and ritual use impose on a building. Muslims initially built the public baths of medieval Spain to satisfy the religious requirement for washing prior to prayer, but the baths became a major social forum and as such were popular with Jews and Christians as well. These groups often used the same baths as Muslims, but at different times or days. Although most of the public baths of medieval Spain were built by Muslims, some were constructed by Jews or Christians. All the surviving public baths built before the Christian Reconquest suggest that a single form was used; after the Reconquest, however, a different picture emerges.[1]

Characteristic of the public baths of medieval Spain is one constructed during the eleventh century in Granada (Fig. 1);[2] revenue from it supported the city's most important mosque. In plan the bath is a narrow lateral structure divided into two main areas: the entrance, composed of a patio, latrines, and a dressing room, and the actual baths, with the *tepidarium* (warm area) being the largest of the three rooms (Fig. 2). The *frigidarium* (cold area) is a narrow barrel-vaulted rectangular room divided at either end by double horseshoe arches on columns (Fig. 3). The *tepidarium* features a slightly asymmetrical rectangular central chamber bordered on three sides by an arcade. The central and largest portion of this room is vaulted with a groin supported by a horseshoe-arched arcade on three of the room's four sides; aisles created by this arcade are barrel-vaulted. The *caldarium* (hot area) repeats the *frigidarium* in elevation and plan. Star-shaped and octagonal skylights pierce the vaults of these three rooms. The walls and vaults are of brick, and the capitals are drill-worked marble.

The basic plan of this type of Spanish public bath, in which the bather encounters a cold, a warm, and a hot area, was fully developed by the Romans well before the first century A.D. By 360, in the region of Rome, some 865 baths were recorded in an official survey,[3] and the ruins of public baths are found in every Roman province and colony, including Spain, for example, at Barcelona, Tarragona, and Gerona.[4] These baths, however, in spite of their presence on Spanish soil, seemed to exert little, if any, influence on the types of public baths, that is *hammam*, constructed after the Muslim Umayyad conquest of Spain in the eighth century. This lack of influence may be because the Christian rulers, who held power in Spain between the end of Roman authority and the Umayyad conquest, apparently built no public baths of this type. Thus, when the tradition of constructing baths resumed under the Muslim Umayyad caliphs, the forms that stimulated the architecture were not Roman but, apparently, those from other parts of the Muslim world.

Imperially sponsored Roman baths were elaborate structures characterized by vast and numerous rooms, extremely complex and bearing little relationship to the form of any Spanish medieval public bath.[5] Similarly, the thermal baths of Roman Spain, whose water flowed from natural hot springs and which were used for health purposes, have little connection to the public baths of medieval Spain. These thermal baths, such as the Caldas of Malavella in Gerona,[6] most often have a single central pool flanked by columns or piers.

Spanish medieval baths apparently were modeled directly on those built by the Arab Umayyads, in an area corresponding to modern Jordan, prior to this dynasty's conquest of Spain.[7] Among the baths the Umayyads constructed, the layout of the three principal rooms—the *frigidarium*, the *tepidarium*, and the *caldarium*—is nearly uniform. For example, at Qusayr Amrah,[8] in Jordan, the bath is entered through a large hall leading to single chambers for each of the three principal bath rooms. In Roman baths, as noted above, the hot, warm, and cold portions each occupy multiple rooms. Although some provincial Roman baths, such as one at St. Rémy in France[9] and one at Kempten in Germany,[10] have a single chamber each for the cold, warm, and hot areas, these are located too far from Qusayr Amrah and the other desert palaces to have been a likely source of influence. More likely, the Umayyad bath, with its concise organization of the three rooms, was derived from some of the baths built for the North Syrian early Christian communities such as at Brad.[11] These baths had been modeled on local Roman provincial ones. The bath at Brad featured only five rooms, probably followed by a hall. The Umayyad baths at Djebel Seis[12] and Qusayr Amrah, as do their Spanish heirs, follow this same pattern, in some cases with a further reduction in the number of rooms, housing only three rooms, the *frigidarium*, *tepidarium*, and *caldarium*.

The superstructures of the Spanish baths have a similar lineage (Fig. 4). In structure, they are domed and vaulted both externally and internally. This form is quite unlike the early Christian baths of Syria, domed and vaulted internally but covered with timber roofs.[13] The Spanish baths adhere closely to the Umayyad ones, for example, at Qusayr Amrah in Jordan, where no roof covers the exterior domed and vaulted forms. A specific pattern develops for the vaulting of Umayyad baths built before their conquest of Spain, namely that the *frigidarium* is barrel-vaulted, the *tepidarium* is groin-vaulted, and the *caldarium* is domed. The baths of Islamic Spain do not hold rigidly to this pattern of vaulting, but they show a fascination with various roofing systems, the variety becoming almost a trademark of Spanish baths.

Thus, though Roman baths had been built in Spain, the immediate source for the public bath in medieval Spain was not the Roman bath. Rather, the source was earlier Umayyad baths in Jordan, which were, in turn, based on the Roman and early Christian baths of Syria. The Roman bath form

Fig. 1. Plan of Granada bath (courtesy of François-Auguste de Montequin).

apparently was abandoned in Spain before the Umayyad conquest. In medieval Spain, then, the first public baths were constructed by the Umayyads, now settled there. Since they identified closely with their earlier Arab Umayyad ancestors, the construction initially served as a link to the earlier Umayyad dynasty. Its continued popularity was testimony to the highly functional nature of this building type.

Public baths were constructed throughout the period of Islamic domination in Spain and even into the twelfth through fourteenth centuries, when Christian powers increasingly dominated. From the Spanish Umayyad period, only one bath remains, the one of the Caliphal Palace at Córdobá,[14] although this city once had several in each of its twenty-one suburbs.[15] Some chroniclers claim Córdobá had as many as three to six hundred baths.[16] So important were public baths in Umayyad Spain that the number of baths, among other statistics, showed the relative importance of an Islamic Span-ish city. This ninth-century bath of the Caliphal Palace, although not a public bath but one for the royal residents, is included here for it is the earliest surviving Arab bath in Spain and serves as the prototype for subsequent baths. Because it is not yet fully excavated, only the *caldarium* has been identified with certainty (Fig. 5).[17] However, this room serves as a model for both the *caldarium* and *frigidarium* of other Spanish baths. It is a narrow rectangular room, divided horizontally into three bays by a horseshoe arch on pillars, anticipating the tripartite division of the narrow chambers of virtually all subsequent medieval baths in Spain, for example, the eleventh-century one at Baza,[18] the thirteenth- or fourteenth-century one in Ronda,[19] and even the thirteenth-century Christian bath of Gerona. Although Visigothic ecclesiastic architecture already had made use of horseshoe arches on pillars to divide a thin rectangular room into small end bays,[20] the concept of dividing a room in this manner is common in earlier Islamic architecture. Examples include the hypostyle Umayyad mosques of Damascus[21] and Córdobá.[22]

The division of a large room into many smaller units becomes an increasing preoccupation of the architects of later baths. Thus, although the basic format of the *caldarium* and *frigidarium* may reflect Spanish Visigothic technique or derive from an Islamic predilection for the division of space, the widespread prevalence of this type of room in Spanish Medieval architecture is of greater significance. This brick-constructed, narrow barrel-vaulted room pierced with skylights and divided by horseshoe arches into three bays was a room type used in domestic architecture of the time.[23] The barrel-vaulted *caldarium* of the Bath in the Palace of Córdobá is representative of a standard versatile and utilitarian

Fig. 2. *Frigidarium* of the bath at Granada.

Fig. 3. *Tepidarium* of the bath at Granada.

form that architects used for the next several centuries in Spain.

In the Umayyad bath of Córdobá, one room is groin-vaulted, the others covered by barrel vaults, recalling the earlier Umayyad play with various vaulting systems. Further links with the earlier Umayyad baths such as the one at Qusayr Amrah may be seen in the star-shaped and square apertures in the vaults, a feature also of all subsequent Spanish baths.

Six known baths date to the eleventh and twelfth centuries.[24] Of these, the eleventh-century bath in Baza is situated in the Jewish quarter and thus may have been constructed by Jewish patrons.[25] The one of Barcelona, likely built in the twelfth century, was reputedly a Christian bath, although Cadafalch notes that documents show that at one time it was under Jewish maintenance.[26] These two, however, adhere closely to the format of the other known Islamic baths of the period in Palma,[27] Granada, Toledo,[28] and Valencia.[29] Moreover, there is little indication that they were built for a specific clientele. Although towns were divided into Muslim, Jewish, and Christian quarters, the division was loose, and the adherents of each faith used the baths of the other religion. For example, Christians patronized the Arab-owned bath in Tarragona, and only after the Reconquest, when the usage of baths increasingly was regulated along sectarian lines, were Christians not allowed to use it on Friday, when it served as a mosque.[30]

Beginning in the eleventh century, the *tepidarium* becomes notably larger than the other two rooms, a departure from all earlier baths—Roman, early Christian, and Middle Eastern Umayyad—in which the forechamber is the largest room. The *tepidarium*, a room of relaxation and leisure, usually has a large central area with galleries on two, three, or even all four sides, thus assuming the form of a large room divided into bays in the manner of contemporary mosques such as that of Bab Mardoum[31] in Toledo, dated 999.

During this period, the *tepidaria* are divided into bays by horseshoe arches. For example, at the baths in Granada and in Baza, the *tepidarium*'s central bay is covered by a groin vault resting on horseshoe

Fig. 4. Exterior, bath at Ronda.

arches supported by piers or columns. The corresponding bay in the baths at Palma, Valencia, and Barcelona is covered with a lobed dome resting on horseshoe arches. The flanking galleries in these baths are either barrel-vaulted or both groin- and barrel-vaulted. In each instance, the central bay is higher than the side bays and is well lighted by skylights, often in the shape of stars, whereas the side galleries are lower and more dimly illuminated.

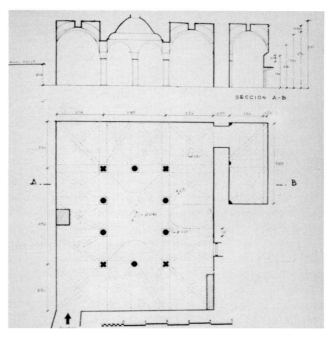

Fig. 6. Plan of the bath at Zaragoza (courtesy of Al-Andalus).

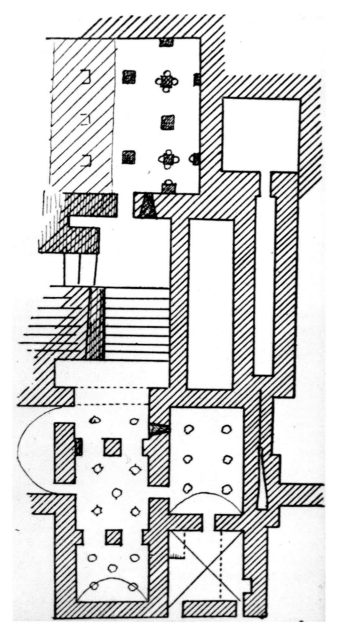

Fig. 5. Plan of the bath of the Caliphal Palace in Córdoba (courtesy of François-Auguste de Montequin).

Fig. 7. Marble capital in the *tepidarium* of the bath at Granada.

The visible effect of the division of the room into bays by horseshoe arches is that of an increasingly obscured and nondirectional space. In Spain this effect is exemplified in the mosque of Bab Mardoum. Here, too, a room is divided into small bays by horseshoe arches supported on columns; the central one is higher than the others and illuminated by clerestories.[32] Thus, during the eleventh and twelfth centuries, many of the devices seen in the plans and elevations of the small private mosques also were used in the baths, although in a simplified form.

Several more public baths were constructed in Islamic dominated areas during the thirteenth and fourteenth centuries.[33] These baths in large measure adhere closely to types developed earlier in Spain. Thus, the *tepidarium* continues to be the largest and most carefully articulated room of the three. In some baths, for example those of Gibraltar,[34] the domed central bay becomes larger and the side galleries assume lesser importance. In other baths, for example, the one at Zaragoza,[35] the central bay remains, but the surrounding galleries become increasingly complex (Fig. 6). In the Zaragoza *tepidarium* the galleries are divided into fourteen bays, each covered with a dome or groin vault supported by horseshoe arches on columns. Thus the effect of a limited nondirectional space seen in the eleventh- and twelfth-century baths of Toledo, Palma, and Barcelona is more fully developed here, creating an effect very much like that of a hypostyle mosque such as the Mosque of Córdoba, where the forest of columns prevents a specific visual orientation.

The bath of Zaragoza is also particularly interesting in that, unlike almost all other Spanish medieval baths, the arches are semicircular, not the customary horseshoe type. Thus, although the division of the gallery may resemble to a certain extent, a hypostyle mosque, the fluid lines of the transverse rib of the vault form circular arches that suggest the arched vaults of eleventh-century church crypts.[36]

As the simplicity of the central bay is emphasized in the baths of Zaragoza and Ronda by contrast to the complexity of the surrounding galleries, so the central bay in the baths of Gibraltar and Murcia[37] is emphasized by the large dome that covers it. At the Gibraltar bath, the dome remains dominant, but the mode of embellishment, with simple triangular *muqarnas*, is different. The Gibraltar bath, like the Palma one, served as an important model for some North African baths, for example, the Hamman al-Mokhfiya in Fez,[38] different principally in its more elaborately embellished complex *muqarnas* formations.[39] The embellishments are perhaps an indication of the greater wealth of a dynasty that was not contending with the economic drains of the Christian invasions.

Most of the public baths in Spain are civic structures created to fulfill public needs. Those that remain are made from inexpensive, yet durable materials, such as brick and rubble masonry, by contrast to the ashlar masonry or ornamental brick generally used for Spanish religious architecture. In al-Makkari's reference to a bath near Seville with a beautiful lifelike sculpture of a woman and a boy, the author's tone of amazement suggests that such decoration was most unusual.[40] The extant baths lack elaborate ornamentation.[41] Elegantly carved stucco work has been found in the bath in Zaragoza,[42] but this sort of high quality work is exceptional. Kufic inscriptions embellish the Granada bath;[43] such inscriptions are found only here and may be a reflection of this bath's importance, since its income supported the major mosque in the city. Although many of the pillar capitals in baths are carved, the carving is generally crude and at best mediocre (Fig. 7). For example, the marble capitals in the Granada bath are drill-worked, but they are inferior to those finely executed capitals in the Mosque of Córdoba.

This discussion medieval Spanish baths has included no mention of the façades. Unlike most buildings, the baths do not have façades as such; rather, they appear to be sandwiched between stores, mosques, and other buildings.[44] In the baths it is the interior, not the exterior, that is significant— the architecture of a major social institution designed to be functional. As a result, such architecture shuns extraneous ornamentation.

After the Christian Reconquest, an increasing number of regulations were instituted that segregated the usage of baths along sectarian lines; although these rules varied from province to province, official distrust of public baths was pronounced.[45] Possibly reflecting different responses to these regulations are the two extant baths of the period, the bath of Doña Leonor de Guzman in the Palace of Tordesilles[46] and the public bath in Gerona.[47]

The bath of Doña Leonor de Guzman was built as a private bath by Alfonzo XI for his mistress.[48] Although the patron was a Christian, the bath is a type developed in Islamic dominated areas. The *tepidarium*, or main room, is divided into nine groin-vaulted bays that are supported by horseshoe arches. The concept of directionless space further obscured by horseshoe arches is even more fully exploited here than it was in the thirteenth-century bath of Zaragoza. Little in the format or decoration suggests a Christian patron. In fact, the bath, with its

Islamic-derived geometric ornamentation, suggests a luxurious setting surpassing that of any public bath. In short, although officially the public bath was not favored, this building type was constructed for at least one private patron, with no attempt to disguise its origins.

In constrast to this bath, essentially an embellished version of an Arab bath, the public one of Gerona appears to take on decidedly Christian overtones, possibly a response to official pressure (Figs. 8-9). This bath was rebuilt between 1294 and 1296 at the request of James II of Aragon after the original bath was destroyed in a battle by Philip III.[49] The *tepidarium* still remains the most important room, but in layout it differs from any other *tepidarium* in Spain. This room is a large square that, unlike all earlier models, is not divided into bays. In the center of the room is an octagonal pool bordered by eight columns supporting an octagonal horseshoe-arched arcade. On the exterior, a colonnaded lantern with a pointed dome falls on the arcade, allowing light to flood the central pool. The room, in contrast to earlier baths, is also well illuminated by arched windows fitted with perforated screens in one side wall. As there are no other columns or surrounding galleries, the central pool remains the dominant feature of the room.

C. Martinell has suggested a resemblance between the *tepidarium* of this Gerona bath and Spanish Christian baptisteries.[50] Indeed, several similarities are striking. Stone construction often associated with Christian architecture, and not the brick and/or rubble masonry generally used for Arab baths, is used in the bath of Gerona as well as in the Baptistery at Tarrasa.[51] Both structures feature a central octagonal pool flanked by eight columns, above which is a centrally placed dome. Such baptisteries represent a standard type whose origins are found in the architecture of Christian martyria and Roman *heroa*. This same device of an octagonal pool with eight columns crowned by a dome is found in illustrations of the Fountain of Life,[52] a patently Christian theme. Thus, construction techniques and architectural devices[53] commonly found in a Christian religious context are used in a public bath— a building whose function and structure usually is associated in Spain with Muslims. As J. F. Powers has indicated, in Reconquest Spain, officials in-

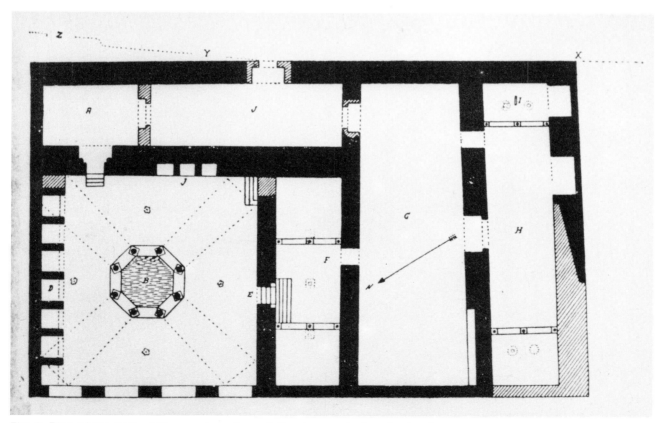

Fig. 8. Plan of the bath at Gerona (courtesy of Cuadernos de Arquitectura).

creasingly uncomfortable with the institution of the public bath, of whose Muslim origins they were acutely aware, instituted rules and regulations governing the use of the baths by Christians, Muslims, and Jews. This regulation was advanced, in large part, to encourage segregation among the sects.[54] In the same manner, it seems possible that the use of these specifically Christian forms in a decidedly Islamic building type was an attempt on the part of the patron to make the structure appear less Islamic and, ultimately, to legitimize the use of the public bath by Christians.

Fig. 9. Central pool in the tepidarium of the bath at Gerona.

Notes

1   I would like to express my gratitude to Professor Jerrilyn D. Dodds for her interest in this topic. This paper is concerned only with public baths used in large part as a social forum, and not with any aspect of Christian or Jewish ritual baths.

2   M. Gomez Moreno, *Ars Hispaniae* (Madrid: Editorial Plus Ultra, 1951), 3:171. Hereafter, *Ars Hispaniae* will be known as *AH*. François de Montequin, *Compendium of Hispano-Islamic Art and Architecture* (St. Paul: Hamline University, 1976), p. 80. Marques de Lozoya, *Historia del Arte Hispanico*, (Barcelona: Salvate Editores, 1931), 1, Fig. 310.

3   Guilio Giannelli, *The World of Ancient Rome* (London: Macdonald and Co., 1967), p. 94.

4   Blas Taracena, "Arte Romano," in *AH* (1947), 2: 58-60; Fig. 40.

5   For an example, see D. Krencker, *Die Trier Kaiserthermen* (Augsburg: Filser Verlag, 1929), 1, 1:15, Fig. 19.

6   J. de C. Serra Rafols, "Las Termas Romanas de Caldas de Malacella (Gerona)," *Archivo Espanol de Arqueologia* 14 (1940-41): 305.

7   M. Sourdel-Thomine, "Hammam," *Encyclopaedia of Islam*, 3rd ed. (London: Luzac and Co., 1966), 3:141, states that although the early Umayyad baths are derived clearly from Roman sources, they lack the large galleries, gymnasiums, and swimming pools of the Ancient Roman baths. These features are to a large part found in the imperial baths and not generally in the smaller provincial ones. As the following discussion will show, these smaller baths are probably the more direct ancestors of the Umayyad bath. Sourdel-Thomine also states that the large forecourt of the Umayyad bath closely resembles that of the Roman public bath especially in terms of decoration, frescoes, and sculpture. However, it must be understood that these extant Umayyad baths are private baths and reflect personal tastes. It is unlikely that the Umayyad public baths would feature such decoration, especially as the use of the public bath was closely associated with Muslim ritual ablutions prior to prayer.

8   Oleg Grabar, *The Formation of Islamic Art* (New Haven: Yale University Press, 1973), Fig. 59.

9   Axel Böethius and J. B. Ward-Perkins, *Etruscan and Roman Architecture* (Baltimore: Penguin Books, 1970), Fig. 134.

10 Krencker, p. 238, Fig. 356.

11 Howard Crosby Butler, *Ancient Architecture in Syria, Publications of the Princeton University Archaeological Expedition to Syria, 1904-05* (Leyden: E. J. Brill, 1920), Section B, Part 6, Fig. 331. For more examples, see Butler, *Ancient Architecture*, B:3 (1909), Fig. 134, and B:4 (1909), Fig. 180.

12 J. Sauvaget, "Les Ruines Omeyyades du Djebel Seis," *Syria* 20, 3 (1939), Fig. 7.

13 Butler, *Ancient Architecture,* B:6, 331.

14 M. Gomez Moreno, p. 171, Fig. 226.

15 Ahmed Ibn Mohammed al-Makkari, *The History of the Mohammedan Dynasties in Spain,* trans. Pascual de Gayangos (reprint ed., New York: Johnson Re-Print Corp., 1964), 1:206.

16 Robert Ignatius Burns, "Baths and Caravanserais in Crusader Valencia," *Speculum* 46, 3 (July, 1971): 454.

17 Gomez Moreno, p. 171, and de Montequin, p. 46, express differing opinions about the identity of most of these rooms.

18 Gomez Moreno, p. 225. M. Gomez Moreno, "Baño de la Juderia en Baza," *Al Andulus* 12 (1947): 151-55; de Montequin, p. 80.

19 de Montequin, pp. 158-59. Leopoldo Torres Balbas, "La Acropolis Musulmana de Ronda," *Al Andulus* 9 (1944), Plate facing p. 476. Fernando Chueca Goitia, *Historia de la Arquitectura de la Espanola: Edad Antiqua y Edad Media* (Madrid: Editorial Dosset, 1965), p. 453.

20 For example, the rock-cut church, the Virgen de la Pena at Faido in H. Schlunk and T. Hauschild, "Die Holenkirche beim Cortijo de Valdecanes," *Madirder Mitteillungen* 11 (1970), Plate 1.

21 John Hoag, *Islamic Architecture* (New York: Harry N. Abrams, 1973), Fig. 14.

22 Ibid., Figs. 82; 84.

23 See, for example, the eleventh-century Palace of Aljahez in Zaragoza in Chueca Goitia, Plate 60, Fig. a.

24 These include the baths at Baza, Barcelona, Palma, Granada, Toledo, and Valencia.

25 For its location, see Gomez Moreno, "Baño de la Juderia en Baza," p. 153.

26 Roderigo Amador de los Rios, "Casas de Baños de los Musulmanes en Espagna," *Hojas Selectas* 3 (1904): 681. Cesar Martinell, "Los Baños Medievales en el Levante Español," *Cuadernos de Arquitectura* 1, ii (November, 1944): 10-12. Elias Tormo, "Los Baños Arabes del Almirante, en Valencia," *Boletin de la Academie de la Historia* 113, ii (1943): 245-47; Plates facing 262 and 264. Puig i Cadafalch, "Els Banys de Girone i la Influencia Moresca a Catalunya," *Institute d'Estudis Catalans, Anuari* 5, part i (1913-14): 696-97.

27 Gomez Moreno, *AH,* p. 271; de Montequin, p. 84; Cadafalch, pp. 694-95; Martinell, pp. 15-17; 19; G. Rosello-Bardoy, *Sobra los "Baños Arabes" de Palma de Mallorca* (Palma: Imprenta Atlante, 1956), Plates 1-12.

28 de Montequin, p. 46, dates this bath to the tenth century, but offers no justification for this position. Gomez Moreno, *AH,* p. 212, dates the bath to the early thirteenth century on the grounds that the horseshoe groin-vault is unique to this period.

29 de Montequin, p. 79; Tormo, p. 244; Martinell, pp. 12-15; Cadafalch, pp. 612-13; Lozoya, p. 240.

30 José Ma Sanz Artibucilla, "Los Baños Moros de Tarragona," *Al Andulus* 9 (1944): 226; James F. Powers, "Frontier Municipal Baths and Social Interaction in Thirteenth-Century Spain," *The American Historical Review* 84, iii (June 1979): 661-67.

31 Hoag, Figs. 99-109. A second example is the mosque of Las Tornerias in Gomez Moreno, *AH,* Figs. 264, 267-68.

32 Hoag, Fig. 99.

33 This paper focuses on the public baths of the medieval period, and hence the well-known baths of the Alhambra are excluded here.

34 de Montequin, pp. 158-59. Leopoldo Torres Balbas, "Gibraltar, Llave Y Guarda de España," *Al Andulus* 7 (1942), Plates 6-7; Plate facing p. 207.

35 Leopoldo Torres Balbas, "La Juderia de Zaragoza y su Baño," *Al Andulus* 21 (1956), Plate facing p. 174; Plate 7, p. 187.

36 The crypt of Castillo in Cardona, unfortunately not published, is a good example. In addition, in the bath of Zaragoza, as in this crypt, the capitals are completely plain, not carved as they are usually in the baths.

37 Leopoldo Torres Balbas, "El Baño Musulman de Murcia y Su Conservation," *Al Andulus* 17 (1952): 436; Amador de los Rios, p. 677; A. F. Calvert, *Valencia and Murcia* (New York: John Lane and Co., 1911), Plate 224.

38 Henri Terrasse, "Trois Bains Merinides du Maroc," *Mélanges William Marcais* (Paris: G. P. Maisonneuve et Cie, 1950), Fig. 5.

39 Ibid., Plates I and II.

40 al-Makkari, p. 60.

41 Leopoldo Torres Balbas, "El Baño de Torres-Torres (Valencia) Y Otras Levantinos," *Al Andulus* 17 (1952): 180-82, Plates 1 and 2.

42 Ibid., Plate 60c.

43 See Cheuca Goitia, Plate 60b, d.

44 Gomez Moreno, *AH,* p. 250.

45 Powers, pp. 661-67.

46 Leopoldo Torres Balbas, "El Baño de Doña Leonor de Guzman en El Palicio de Tordesillas," *Al Andulus* 24 (1959): 415-18; Plates 24-26, Plates facing p. 414.

47 Roderigo Amador de los Rios, "Errores Inveterados: Los Supuestos 'Baños Arabes' de Gerona," *Revista de Archivos, Bibliotecas y Museos* 32, v-vi (May-June, 1915), Plates XVIII-XIX; Tormo, Plate facing page 264; Cadafalch, p. 698; 701-7; Martinell, pp. 4; 6-11; Marcel Durliat, *Art Catalan* (Paris: Arthaud, 1963), Plate 106.

48 Torres Balbas, "El Baño de Doña Leonor de Guzman," p. 411.

49 Durliat, p. 156.

50 Martinell, p. 10.

51 Jacques Fontain, *L'Art Pré-Roman Hispanique* ([Yonne]: Zodiaque, 1973), Plates 158-61.

52 John Beckwith, *Early Medieval Art* (New York: Frederick A. Praeger, 1964), Plates 23-24.

53 Another parallel device used in the Gerona bath and in Christian churches, but not in Arab baths, is finely carved capitals. The capitals in churches of this period are well executed, for example, those at Santiago de Compostela. See Thomas W. Lyman, "The Pilgrimage Roads Revisited," *Gesta* 8, 2 (1969), Fig. 1, p. 30 and the Cloister of Sant Benet de Bages in Duriat, Plate 102. The capitals, too, in the Gerona bath are finely carved. Contrasting examples are the crudely carved capitals of the Palma bath.

54 Powers, pp. 649-67.

The Revival of Early Islamic Architecture by the Umayyads of Spain

Jonathan M. Bloom

Muslims first arrived in Córdobá in 711; they made it the provincial capital a few years later.[1] Although they must have had a place for communal prayer from the beginning, the present congregational mosque was begun only in 784-85 by 'Abd al-Rahman I, who was the sole member of the Umayyad family in Syria to escape massacre by the Abbasids in 750. He arrived in Córdobá six years later, but did not begin the mosque until the last years of his life. The building, completed in 786-87, consisted of an open courtyard preceding a hypostyle prayer hall whose roof was supported by an inventive system of double-tiered supports. This building, the Great Mosque of Córdobá, is one of the most important and best known monuments of medieval architecture (Fig. 1).[2] Careful study of the building not only illustrates its subsequent stages of construction, but also explains its architectural iconography and its use in the tenth century in advancing the ideological claims of Córdobá's rulers.

During the ninth and tenth centuries, the rulers of Córdobá repeatedly enlarged and embellished the mosque. 'Abd al-Rahman's son and successor, Hisham, added a structure from which the call to prayer could be given. In the second quarter of the ninth century the mosque became too small for the congregation, so 'Abd al-Rahman II broke through the *qibla* wall[3] and enlarged the mosque by continuing the original system over eighty additional supports. Over a century later, 'Abd al-Rahman III expanded the mosque's courtyard and simultaneously built the immense tower that still stands encased in the masonry of today's bell tower. A few years later, al-Hakam II, the son and successor of 'Abd al-Rahman III, expanded the mosque's prayer hall a second time by breaking through the *qibla* wall again and extended the eleven naves to the south by maintaining the original two-tiered columnar system supporting a gabled wooden roof. This time, however, the first central bay in the addition was domed

and the new bays culminated in an ensemble of three more domed bays surrounding the *miḥrāb*. Not only were these areas distinguished on the horizontal plane by elaborate screens of intersecting cusped arches, but the three bays surrounding the *miḥrāb* also were revetted with finely carved marbles and gold mosaic. This latter area was the *maqsūra*, an area of the mosque reserved for the ruler's use. Finally, in 987-88, the chamberlain al-Mansur expanded the mosque to the east, increasing its size by a third and giving it its present overall dimensions.

Certain features of the mosque have provoked the interest of historians of Islamic and medieval architecture alike, who have debated the origin of the mosque's forms and their role in medieval architecture. The horseshoe arch, the forest of columns, the alternating voussoirs of brick and limestone, the parallel gable roofs over arcades perpendicular to the *qibla* wall, and the design of the Puerta de San Esteban—the only surviving portal from the ninth century—all are thought to show Syrian influence, for similar forms are found in Umayyad architecture there. The two-tiered system of supports is thought to be the result of local influence, for some see in it the aqueduct of Segovia.[4] The mosaic decoration of the three bays in front of the *miḥrāb* is thought to stem from Byzantine influence, especially since medieval texts specify that a Byzantine master came to supervise the work. Only the ribbed vaults and intersecting cusped arches are thought to be original inventions. The vaults antedate any example known from Europe or the Middle East and have fueled the fruitless debate about the role of Córdobá and Islamic architecture in the formation of Gothic. The intersecting cusped arches became one of the hallmarks of Spanish Islamic architecture.

The concept of influence, be it local, Syrian, or Byzantine, is poorly conceived, for it confuses the role of agent and patient.[5] Not the architecture

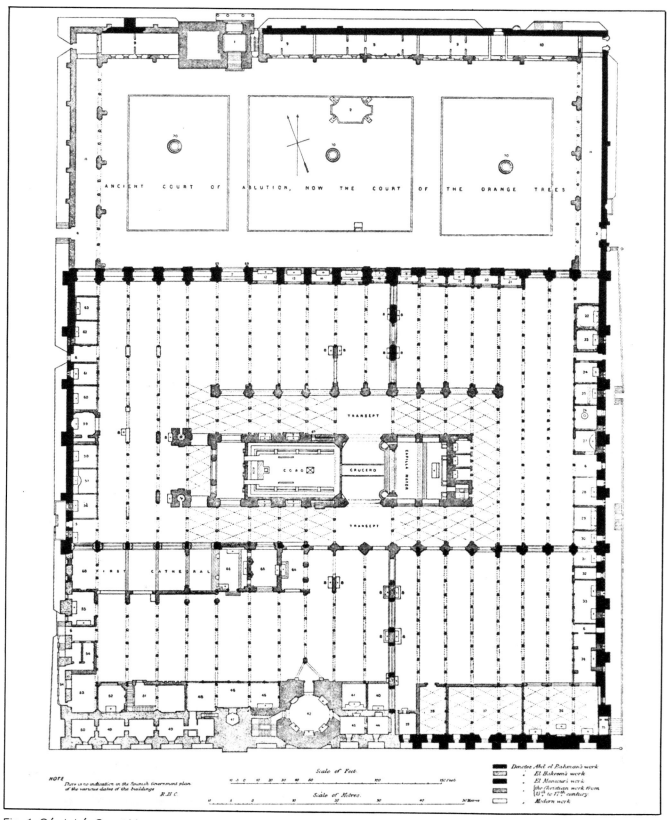

Fig. 1. Córdobá, Great Mosque, plan, eighth through tenth centuries.

of Syria, nor the aqueduct of Segovia, nor the mosaics of Constantinople, nor Armenian vaults was able to exert any influence on the mosque, for buildings are incapable of influence. Rather, the builders of the mosque copied or emulated select features of these architectural traditions. To identify Syrian, Byzantine, or Armenian features in Cordoban architecture is then pointless; the real problem is explaining why the builders chose to build what they did. The penultimate stage of the mosque's creation—when al-Hakam II expanded and decorated it with mosaics, ribbed domes, and intersecting arches—is particularly fruitful for investigating the builders' intent and the meaning of medieval architectural form.

Arabic histories say that the caliph al-Hakam II sent an ambassador to the Byzantine emperor, requesting him to send a workman to decorate the mosque. The Byzantine emperor complied and the ambassador returned with a master-craftsman and 320 *qinârs* (approximately 16,000 kg.) of mosaic cubes as a gift from the emperor. The caliph provided the master with a house and Mamluks who were apprenticed to learn his craft. He completed the mosaics on the dome in front of the *miḥrāb* in June 965 (Fig. 2).[6] Scholars have tried to categorize the mosaic decoration, calling it purely Byzantine, Byzantine with Hispano-Umayyad elements, or even Byzantine with Iranian ornamental motifs, in an effort to differentiate the work of the master from his indigenous pupils.[7] Henri Stern undertook the first careful study of the mosaics and demonstrated that the story of the Byzantine master might well be true, for the technique hardly differs from contemporary Byzantine practice: White limestone, gray marble, seventeen colors of glass paste, and gold tesserae were manufactured and used in the usual Byzantine way. The only technical oddity is an underglaze-painted ceramic cornice separating the gadrooned dome from its octagonal base, which Stern believed was produced by workers who had never made anything like it before.[8] The decoration also shared features with contemporary Byzantine art, although the mosque's singular forms generated unusual surfaces for mosaic revetment and the aniconic nature of mosque decoration would have taxed the imagination of a Byzantine master-mosaicist used to figural and narrative representations.

Fig. 2. Córdobá, Great Mosque, interior of the dome in front of the *miḥrāb*.

Only the part of the story in which the Byzantine master mosaicist trained pupils does not ring true. Whatever courses he may have offered went unattended because mosaics were not used again in Umayyad Spain. No school of mosaicists was founded, and the technique had no issue in the Islamic architecture of Spain. Why then were mosaics used?

Mosaic was a luxurious technique universally associated in medieval times with the Byzantines, but Byzantine associations were secondary in the Mosque of Córdobá. For the Muslims of Córdobá, their primary associations were with early Islamic architecture. The historian Ibn 'Idhārī is explicit: The caliph wished to imitate the Umayyad caliph al-Walîd b. 'Abd al-Malik who, early in the eighth century, had built the Great Mosque of Damascus and decorated it with mosaics. Al-Hakam II identified with his Syrian Umayyad forebears and wished his mosque to emulate theirs.

The Cordoban caliph never saw the mosque of Damascus because he was isolated in Spain, thousands of miles from what he believed to be his ancestral homeland, so he had to rely on verbal descriptions of it. In the middle of the ninth century, the litterateur al-Jahiz had described the mosque as one of the most beautiful things of this earth, "built on marble columns in two tiers, the lower tier of large columns, the upper of small ones. Elsewhere every city and tree in the world are depicted in gold, green and yellow mosaic. In the *qibla* of the mosque is a dome known as the Dome of the Eagle. Nothing in Damascus is higher than it, nor is there a more beautiful view from anywhere else."[9] He also noted that the Damascus mosque was decorated with kufic inscriptions written in gold on a blue ground.[10]

Al-Hakam II or his advisers must have had access to these or similar descriptions. That the Cordoban copy was in the same technique as the original was sufficient; the subject matter did not have to be similar, although all of the inscriptions at Córdobá were written in gold, and most of them on a blue ground.

Yet the identification with Damascus goes further. Other Arabic sources state that in the early eighth century the Umayyad caliph al-Walîd had requested the "king" of the Byzantines to provide help building and decorating the Mosque of the Prophet in Medina, which was once similarly decorated with mosaics, and similar stories are told about the mosque in Damascus.[11] Sir K. A. C. Creswell, the great scholar of early Islamic architecture, proved, however, that these stories were untrue. Why should the caliph need to ask for Byzantine help when, a decade

earlier, his father had built and decorated the Dome of the Rock in Jerusalem without their help? Furthermore, the stories first appear only in twelfth-century sources.[12]

Whether Byzantine workmen actually decorated the mosque of Damascus is immaterial in this context, but most people in the medieval Islamic world believed they had, and that belief is essential for understanding the mosaics of the mosque of Córdobá. Not only did the Spanish caliph wish to have mosaics like those the Syrian caliph had ordered for Damascus, but he had to order them from the same source, the king of Rum. Thus the Cordoban caliph emulated both the techniques of Umayyad art and their source.

Throughout the ninth century, the Umayyad emirate had been a strictly regional power, ignored by the Abbasid caliph in distant Baghdad, but tacitly allied with the Byzantines against the neighboring Franks. In the tenth century 'Abd al-Rahman III transformed the Umayyad emirate into a major Mediterranean power, and, in 929, proclaimed himself Commander of the Believers, the title reserved for caliphs. Although the Umayyads of Spain had not accepted the Abbasids' right to rule as caliphs, they had tolerated it for the 173 years since 'Abd al-Rahman I established an Umayyad emirate in the Iberian peninsula. But the Umayyads were forced to respond when the Fatimids proclaimed their Shi'ite caliphate two decades earlier in North Africa. If the world could tolerate two caliphs, it could just as well tolerate three. 'Abd al-Rahman III soon began Madinat al-Zahra, a new palace complex outside of Córdobá that undoubtedly was meant to symbolize his imperial ambitions. The heir apparent al-Hakam II supervised the work. Now that al-Andalus was the greatest power in Europe, his order to expand and decorate the mosque in Córdobá immediately after his accession is another element in a broad pattern of the western Umayyads, expressing their imperial pretensions by identifying with their forebears, the Umayyad caliphs of Damascus.

That the Spanish Umayyads consciously recapitulated the real or imagined Umayyad past in Syria suggests that other aspects of the mosque of Córdobá may have paralleled the mosque of Damascus. The standard sources state that the Muslims arrived in Córdobá, took half of the cathedral church of Saint Vincent, and used it as a mosque.[13] When it proved too small, a vestibule was added, and then another, until it was too difficult to get in and around the church. Finally, in 784-85, after thirty years of haggling, 'Abd al-Rahman I and the bishop agreed on a price for the church and its land. Demolition began the following year and the new mosque was finished in 786-87.

No Christian source mentions a Church of St. Vincent, however, and the Muslim sources are universally late. Ibn al-Athir, the historian who wrote in the middle of the thirteenth century, is the earliest but geographically distant; Ibn 'Idhâri, a local source, is even later, but he quotes al-Razi, a minor tenth-century source whose works are now lost; al-Makkari, the authority who wrote most about the mosque, wrote in the mid-seventeenth century. Thus, the earliest written sources for the mosque's history are contemporary not with its foundation, but with its later expansion and decoration. It is no accident that these sources contain material that parallels information about the Great Mosque of Damascus, originally the cathedral church of St. John and shared by the Christians and Muslims of the city after the conquest. Waqidi (748-823), an early source, says that tradition records that the church was divided between the Christians and Muslims, although he did not know the source of the rumor and found no mention of it in contemporary sources.[14] The Muslims of medieval Córdobá, therefore, might well have thought that the Damascus church had been divided, although in modern times Creswell was to show that the Muslims used the ancient temple enclosure, not the church itself.[15]

Another remarkable feature of al-Hakam II's work at Córdobá is the series of four ribbed domes that cover significant areas of the mosque, three over the *maqsūra* (Fig. 3), and one in the middle of the new prayer hall. Nothing like them is known in Spain, and architectural historians have searched far and wide for their source. Although a single dome over the bay in front of the *mihrāb* had been known since the early eighth century, the multiplication of domes at Córdobá is without precedent. The recurrent evocation of Umayyad Damascus in this stage of the mosque, however, suggests that a source might be found there. Indeed, one of the notable features of the Damascus mosque was its dome, called the "Dome of the Eagle."[16] Although this dome was replaced by another in 1082-83, Creswell proved that the earliest dome was of wood and rested on great cross-beams. No early source describes the original dome in detail, but Ibn al-Jubayr, who saw the replacement in 1184, said that there were actually three domes, which must have been supported by transverse wooden beams. The central dome was actually double; the exterior one was covered with lead, and the interior one was round like a sphere, strengthened with stout wooden ribs bound with iron. The ribs curved over the dome and met at the summit in a round circle of wood.

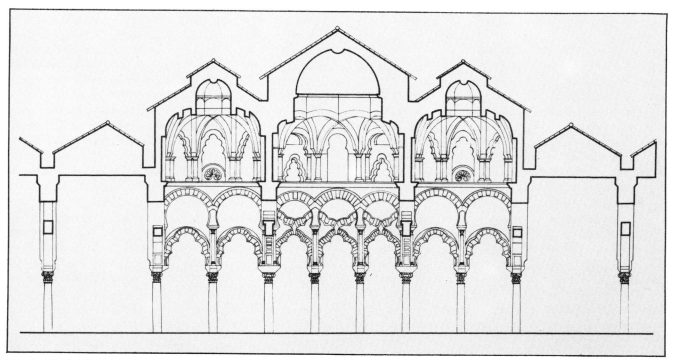

Fig. 3. Córdobá, Great Mosque, plan of the *maqsūra* area.

From the interior, the inner dome was inlaid with carved, colored, and beautifully gilded wooden panels.[17]

We cannot determine whether the domes Ibn al-Jubayr saw copied the Umayyad originals. If the style of decoration may have changed considerably, the basic scheme—three ribbed wooden domes, the central one larger than those flanking it, and all decorated on the interior with gold and colored panel decoration—probably remained the same. Without any further textual evidence, one can only imagine in what terms the original domes might have been described, but a literary description may have played some role in the generation of the three-bayed *maqsūra* as well as the mosque's singular ribbed domes.

No evidence exists that any of the earlier Cordoban mosques had an area reserved for the ruler, although the idea of a *maqsūra* goes back to Umayyad times. Indeed, medieval Muslims thought it a distinctly Damascene and Umayyad idea. It was well known that the first *maqsūra* was made by Mu'awiyah, the founder of the Umayyads, after a foiled assassination attempt in the Damascus mosque. According to another account, however, it was Marwan b. al-Hakam, his cousin and eventual successor, who built the first one.[18] In any event, ninth- and tenth-century historians, such as Baladhuri, Ya'qubi, and Tabari, all agree that the *maqsūra* was an Umayyad invention. The Abbasid caliph al-Ma'mun even attempted to abolish the custom because it was contrary to the traditions of the Prophet. Once again, the trail leads to Damascus.

A final aspect is even more intriguing. For the first time in the twelfth century—nearly 200 years after al-Hakam II—sources note fragments of an early Koran preserved in the Mosque of Córdobá. The four pages were said to have been copied by the caliph 'Uthman himself, who had prepared a new recension of the Koran and sent copies of it to Mekkah, Basra, Kufa, and Damascus. The Cordoban example was said to have been stained with his blood when he was assassinated in Medina. Again, there is no way of knowing when the leaves first appeared in Córdobá, and the same relic is claimed in widely scattered regions of the Islamic world.[19] Yet the tenth century is the most likely date: 'Uthman was not only one of four Orthodox caliphs accepted by all Muslims, but was also the first caliph of the family of Umayya. Mu'awiyah seized power from 'Uthman's successor 'Ali to revenge his death and eventually established the Umayyad dynasty in Damascus. A relic of these events would have been the perfect prop for the newly proclaimed Umayyad caliphs of Spain.

Whatever its religion, the medieval world shared modes of thought. Not only was the present lived in terms of the past, but the past was remembered in terms of the present. Architecture was no exception, for revivals are one of the constant features of medieval Mediterranean architecture. The subtleties of the process in the Christian West were first elucidated by Richard Krautheimer in a well-known series of articles on the Carolingian revival of early Christian architecture.[20] He suggested that churches with continuous transepts copied St. Peter's in Rome, because the continuous transept was a feature identified with the church of an apostle. As Constantine had built a church to honor the apostle of Rome, Charlemagne wished to build churches to honor the apostles to the Franks and the Germans and align himself with the first Christian emperor.

Although these examples of transmission rely on a visual familiarity with the prototype—Charlemagne had been to Ravenna and must have known San Vitale; St. Peter's in Rome was familiar to hordes of pilgrims—it was Krautheimer again who identified a more abstract means of artistic transmission, in which the similarity between buildings was expressed numerically. A series of buildings said to be copies or replicas of the Rotunda of the Holy Sepulchre in Jerusalem shared no common features except roundness or the number of supports, for the Rotunda was supported by twelve columns and four piers. It was Krautheimer who succinctly expressed the nature of medieval perception in suggesting that any building with more than four sides was round.[21] Even a square building with the requisite supports might have been considered a replica of the church in Jerusalem.

It should be no surprise, therefore, that the Muslims of Córdobá thought about their Great Mosque in ways identical to those of Christians in northern Europe. In the tenth century the mosque was redesigned to copy—in medieval terms, of course—the Great Mosque of Damascus that the Umayyad caliphs had built several hundred years before. Just as the Carolingians had used architecture to align themselves with Constantine when they revived the empire in the West, the Umayyads of Spain—only a century or so later and a thousand miles to the southwest—used architecture to align themselves with the Umayyads of Syria when they revived the caliphate in the West.

Notes

1 *The Encyclopaedia of Islam,* 2nd ed. (Leiden: E. J. Brill, 1954), s.v. "Kurtuba."

2 The most accessible source for the history and development of the mosque is K. A. C. Creswell, *Early Muslim Architecture* (Oxford, 1932-40; 2nd ed. of vol. 1, 1969), 2:138-66. More recent work is summarized in Christian Ewert and Jens-Peter Wisshak, *Forschungen zur almohadischen Moschee,* (Mainz, 1981), 1:56-94; many of the authors' conclusions, however, remain unproven.

3 *Qibla* is the direction of Mekkah, which a Muslim should face when praying. A *miḥrāb* is a niche placed in the center of the *qibla* wall to show the direction of prayer.

4 See, for example, Creswell, pp. 156-57.

5 For a particularly lucid exploration of this issue, see Michael Baxandall, *Patterns of Intention* (New Haven: Yale University Press, 1986).

6 Ibn 'Idhârî al-Marrâkushî, *al-Bayân al-Mughrib,* ed. G. S. Colin and E. Lévi-Provençal (repr. Beirut, n.d.), 2:237-38.

7 Henri Stern, *Les mosaïques de la Grande Mosquée de Cordoue* (Berlin, 1976), p. 22.

8 Stern, p. 14.

9 The original text of al-Jahiz is no longer extant, but parts of it are quoted by Ya'qût, *Mu'jam al-Buldân,* ed. F. Wüstenfeld (Leipzig, 1866-73), 2:593.

10 Barbara Finster, "Die Mosaiken der umayyaden Moschee von Damaskus," *Kunst des Orients* 7 (1970-71): 119.

11 Hamilton A. R. Gibb, "Arab-Byzantine Relations under the Umayyad Caliphate," *Dumbarton Oaks Papers* 12 (1958): 219-33.

12 Creswell, 1:153ff.

13 Creswell, 2:138-40.

14 Creswell, 1:187.

15 Creswell, 1:156-96.

16 It results from a mistranslation from the Greek word *aetos* that can mean either "eagle" or "gable," the latter being correct (Creswell, 1:169).

17 Creswell, 1:168-69.

18 Creswell, 1:42.

19 Ibn Battuta claimed to have seen a copy in the Basra mosque (Ibn Battuta, *Voyages,* trans. C. Defremery and B. R. Sanguinetti [Paris, 1982], 1:377).

20 Richard Krautheimer, "Introduction to an 'Iconography of Medieval Architecture,'" *Journal of the Warburg and Courtauld Institutes* 5 (1942): 1-33; and idem., "The Carolingian Revival of Early Christian Architecture," (1942); rev. ed. in W. Eugene Kleinbauer, ed. *Modern Perspectives in Western Art History* (New York, 1971), pp. 349-96.

21 Richard Krautheimer, "Sancta Maria Rotunda," *Arte del primo millennio* (Atti del IIo convegno per lo studio dell' arte dell' alto medioveo, Pavia, 1950) (Turin, 1953), pp. 23-27.

Scenario for a Roman Provenance
for the Mosque of Córdobá

Marvin Mills

To question the provenance of the Mosque of Córdobá is to challenge the essence of Spanish architectural history. Islamic historians, including al-Razi in the tenth, el Idrisi in the twelfth, Ibn 'Idhâri in the thirteenth, and al-Makkari in the seventeenth century, have based their writings about the mosque on the bedrock assumption of its Islamic origin, though conceding at times that parts of the structure may have still older remains. However, an alternative original function and date is possible for the building; I suggest as one possible scenario that it originally may have been designed and constructed for use as a Roman warehouse, perhaps in the first century A.D., and later, following the Islamic conquest of Spain, it may have been converted with relatively minor changes to a mosque.

Córdobá was a great Roman political, intellectual, and economic center that exported much needed metals and grain throughout the Empire. In the fifth century A.D., Roman Córdobá fell to the Christian Visigoths, who in turn succumbed to Muslim conquerers in 711 A.D. The Muslims, led by 'Abd al-Rahman I, established an independent Umayyad kingdom in Spain and proclaimed Córdobá their capital. 'Abd al-Rahman I is said to have founded and built the first stage of the Great Mosque of Córdobá in 786 A.D. (Fig. 1).[1]

Unfortunately, no extant documents of the eighth century allude to the mosque's construction. It was not until two hundred years later, in the tenth century, that writings on the subject appear of which the works of Isa ibn Ahmad al-Razi are the most important. However, we know of his writings only from quotations appearing in works by later writers, principally al-Makkari in the seventeenth century.[2] Al-Razi relates how 'Abd al-Rahman I dismantled the church of St. Vincent located on the bank of the Guadalquivir River to clear a site for the building of the Great Mosque. According to al-Razi, the church had replaced an earlier Roman temple. This story has been challenged by some leading scholars.[3] Creswell argues that the story was devised to parallel the legend of the origin of the Mosque of Damascus in Syria built in 715 A.D., which al-Razi called the source of inspiration for the Mosque of Córdobá. (See Jonathan Bloom's paper, p. 39.) Terrasse, citing research of Felix Hernandez, states that the church of Saint Vincent must have been demolished, because no reliable evidence exists of its foundations.[4] Gomez-Moreno finds no evidence of any previous church.[5] But the lack of evidence could also suggest that the church of Saint Vincent was never built as new construction. Complicating the issue further is that during 756-788, Córdobá witnessed a period of continuous bloody uprisings and murderous intrigues, reducing the likelihood of massive financial allocations for an elaborate mosque at that time.[6]

It is not the absence of historical data alone that raises questions regarding the provenance of the Mosque of Córdobá. Certain architectural and decorative features associated with the mosque cannot be explained adequately within the context of what is known about the development of Islamic art and architecture. Apparently no precedent existed in Islamic Spain for a mosque of that scale;[7] it is doubtful that the Arab and Berber invaders, nomadic peoples, were capable of producing anything in Spain on the technical level of the mosque.[8] Furthermore, there is no evidence of a crescendo of development leading up to its construction, nor was there any spread of nondynastic works following its completion.[9] An additional reason to question the reliability of the Arab sources is the short span of time they allow for the construction of the mosque's first stage. The Stage I prayer hall was 79 meters wide by 42 meters deep, covering 3,330 square meters; in addition, there were 1,590 square meters of courtyard. The prayer hall was the largest of any mosque built in the West at the time, but al-Razi reports that the construction was completed in one year and al-Makkari suggests it took two years. Lambert, however, argues that it would have taken closer to fifteen years to complete a hall of that size.[10] Remodeling of an existing building, however, could have been done comfortably in the year or two cited by the two Arab historians.

It is known that Roman Córdobá had many great buildings, including villas, temples, baths, an encircling wall, and most important for my proposed scenario, warehouses. Often the docks and warehouses of a Roman city were elaborate, as can be seen in this quote:

> I wish the reader could see the beauty of the docks and warehouses of Porto, the perfection of their reticulated masonry, their cornices and entablatures, carved and moulded in terra-cotta, their mosaic pavements, their system of drainage and ventilation![11]

The warehouse scenario also would explain the unusual alignment of the mosque. According to Islamic tradition, a *mihrāb,* or niche, placed in the center of the wall usually facing toward Mekkah (called the *qibla* wall), indicates the direction of prayer. The *qibla* wall of the Mosque of Córdobá does not face Mekkah; it is oriented 60 degrees south of east; Mekkah is 10 degrees south of east from Córdobá. Explanations have been offered for this deviation from the norm, but none are satisfactory.[12]

The mosque's location on the periphery of the city in a prime commercial area is also unusual. Congregational mosques are generally integral with the fabric of the city and accessible to as many people as possible; thus, the advantage of a central location. This building's location on the Guadalquivir River next to a Roman bridge, adjacent to the Roman quay and docks, and accessible to fine Roman roads extending in four directions, would appear to support the warehouse hypothesis.

According to scholars who have studied the mosque, it underwent four stages of development dating from 786-1002;[13] all the stages were said to be Islamic, dating from the building's origin in the eighth century. It is my contention that the structure's first three stages are Roman, and only its fourth stage, dating to 987, may be Islamic. According to the accepted scenario for the mosque, Stage II was added from 822-951 and included a 23.75-meter expansion of the court to the north during the reign of 'Abd al-Rahman III in 951; however, as noted above regarding the original construction of the mosque, this addition, too, receives no mention in any contemporary documents. In 1984, I had the opportunity to study the mosque; my own on-site investigations did not uncover any construction joint or discontinuity in materials in the wall at the western side (Fig. 2).[14] As an architect, I am particularly cognizant of these types of construction features; the apparent lack of such a joint raises an important question regarding the validity of the theory of a 23.75-meter expansion northward in the tenth century. A future close examination for construction joints in all alleged expansions is recommended.

The theory for a four-stage expansion over two hundred years is further weakened by the overall continuity of style over the entire period. In addition, the alleged additions of Stages II and III would have required the rebuilding of the *mihrāb* twice and the pedestrian bridge over the street to the Alcazar once. Assuming an Islamic origin, a more logical sequence of staging for the building would have been to start at the river and work northward; then the *mihrāb* and the bridge over the street need only to have been built once. If, however, my warehouse

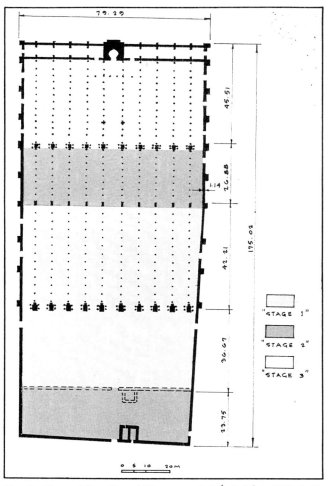

Fig. 1. Plan of the Great Mosque of Córdobá in 961 A.D.

scenario is accepted, and the first three stages of the building are Roman and not Islamic, then the building's unusual elongated plan could be explained by its function. The warehouse would have allowed goods to be stored close to what seems to have been the adjacent road to the east, located under what was later assumed to be Stage IV. The *miḥrāb* may have been originally a Roman shrine or altar, not unusual in a warehouse;[15] the court was suited to be a staging area for products that, if necessary, could have been kept under cover in the surrounding porticoes (Pl. 1).

If the first three stages of the building are Roman, it could be compared with the famous Porticus Aemilia built outside Rome in the second century B.C. According to William MacDonald the Porticus Aemilia was:

> a vast warehouse on the east bank of the Tiber . . . composed of some 200 barrel-vaulted chambers set in

long tiered rows, it covered an area 60 × 487 meters. The vaults did not rest upon solid walls but rather upon perforated supports resembling pier arcades so that each chamber was open laterally as well as axially to its neighbors. The result was a practical, fire-resistant building of ordered clarity, well-suited to warehousing and trans-shipping goods (Fig. 3).[16]

The Mosque of Córdobá's hypostyle hall of columns, its two-way circulation, its vast enclosed space would serve well as a warehouse. The inconsistency in the width of the end aisles being narrower than all other aisles of the first three stages raises further unanswered questions as to its function as a mosque, which normally has uniformly wide aisles. As a warehouse, however, it may have responded to special administrative or storage needs along the perimeter. What have been assumed to be discontinuities in construction between the stages may have been no more than separations designed for fire

Fig. 2. Córdobá, Great Mosque, joint on west wall.

Fig. 3. Rome, Horrea Galbana, Porticus Aemilia, Severan Marble Plan, fragments 23 and 24 (courtesy Cambridge University Press).

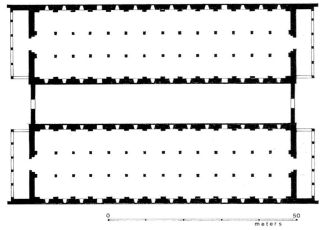

Fig. 4. Trier, plan of Roman *horrea*.

protection, or as separate areas to store different materials.

Yet another feature that contributes to my questioning the origin of the Mosque of Córdobá is evidence that unlike most other mosques, it may not have been built on one level. Excavations under the mosque reveal rooms and probably a street some four to five meters below floor level, down to the level of Roman Córdobá.[17] The rooms are paved with mosaics that to my observation appear to be Roman; room A, for example, reached by ladder through a removable piece of stone flooring from Stage I, was paved with orange, dark red, black, and white tesserae laid in geometric patterns; in one section was depicted an amphora. The mosaic pavement continued under the wall on one side, suggesting that the surrounding brick wall may have been a later construction. The room apparently coincided with a single structural bay above, and had a ceiling about three meters high.

Fig. 5. Córdobá, view from roof of Great Mosque showing entry arch and bridge.

Fig. 6. Córdobá, Great Mosque, entry showing buttress and crenelated roof.

Fig. 7. Córdobá, view of Roman bridge.

Fig. 8. Mérida, Roman aqueduct *(courtesy of Espasa-Calpe, S.A.).*

𝒥 45

A second underground area was reached from Stage IV adjacent to Stage I; this is area B. It was larger than room A, comprising several bays running north and south along what appeared to be a former roadway; if this indeed was a roadway, it would confirm that this area is at the level of Roman Córdobá. Masonry steps connect the roadway with the upper level of the mosque.

I would suggest that a detailed study of areas A and B would prove very helpful in gaining a more precise understanding of the building's history; it is essential that the full extent of the lower level be determined. It may be that this level is coextensive with at least the first three building stages. Since the columns have been reliably judged to be point supports, the column loads from the mosque level could carry down to an original lower level of columns or piers of the same layout. Walls that exist below could be non-load bearing and of post-Roman construction.[18]

Whereas a mosque would not have been built on two levels, a warehouse might have been so constructed. If grain were stored on the upper level it would have benefited from the drying effect of the circulating air beneath the floor. The Roman double warehouse at Trier in Germany (Fig. 4), built in the early fourth century, consisted of a pair of two-storied warehouses, each about 70.1 meters long and 19.8 meters wide. The loading yard passed through the two buildings. The floor of the upper story was carried on two longitudinal rows of stone piers.

> The traveller from Gaul, reaching the city by the [Roman] bridge would have an impressive view of the ornate east gate, the massive baths beside it, and the double-warehouse, symbol of prosperity. . . .[19]

It is possible that the same relationship of bridge, archway, and warehouse may have prevailed at Córdobá (Fig. 5).

Roman warehouses were fortified to provide security for the valuable goods stored within. The popular Roman building method of using alternating headers and stretchers to add strength to the wall also is used for the exterior walls of the Mosque of Córdobá. This feature, along with its crenelated roof and heavy piers, gives the mosque the general appearance of being fortified (Fig. 6). The building's piers, or buttresses, probably are not needed to

Fig. 9. Pompeii, arch in La Casa del Citarista, before 79 A.D.

support the well-built masonry walls and wood roof framing; rather, they may have been intended to withstand the lateral thrust of stored merchandise, such as grain, that would have been piled up loose against the exterior walls on the upper level. The marble grilles in the walls would have provided proper ventilation; the lower level would have been suitable for heavy metals. Scholars have argued that the Muslims who built the mosque imitated Roman masonry techniques, possibly using as a model the nearby Roman bridge (Fig. 7). An alternative explanation may be that both the mosque and the bridge were Roman and built at the same time, during the Augustan Era, the first century B.C. to first century A.D.

The mosque's rectangular buttresses are not a tradition of the East, where they are typically semiround; rather, they are Roman in style. They are similar to the buttresses of the Roman warehouses at Bonn, Germany and at Housteads in Roman Britain.

The famous interior double arches made up of bracing horseshoe-shaped lower arches and semicircular upper arches have been attributed to the creative ingenuity of the Spanish Muslims, but, I contend, this attribution is made only for lack of an alternative explanation.[20] To my knowledge, this particular motif has no apparent predecessor. These double arches serve a practical purpose. The advantage of the approximately ten-meter-high ceiling is maintained while using two levels of relatively short columns, which are easier to obtain than long ones. The arches also avoid using undesirable horizontal ties and enclosed upper spaces as in the Mosque of Kairouan. It could be argued that a precedent for this technique may be found in the Mosque of Damascus built in 715 by al-Walīd; it has both multiple levels of arches in its prayer hall façade and porticoes surrounding the court. The arcade arches of its prayer hall façade are slightly horseshoe-shaped.[21] However, I would like to suggest another possible source.

The Romans had a history of using multiple level arch construction as seen at the Pont du Gard at Nîmes in France and the aqueducts at Segovia and Mérida in Spain, possibly dating to the Augustan Age (Fig. 8). The piers of the Roman Los Milagros aqueduct at Mérida have alternating red bricks and white stone coursing, as do the arches of the Casa de la Citarista in Pompeii, dated to the first century A.D. (Fig. 9). This decorative scheme also was used extensively in the Mosque of Córdobá (Fig. 6). The Roman arches, however, are not horseshoe-shaped; the precedents for that form may be

traced to the Sasanian Palace at Ctesiphon in Iraq, built by Shapur I in the third century A.D.; an earlier example can be found in the caves of Ajanta in India dating from the second century B.C., and the monasteries at Masik, also in India, built in the second or first centuries B.C. This is not to suggest, however, that the arches found at these sites are the ultimate source for the horseshoe arches found in the Mosque of Córdobá: that issue is yet to be adequately resolved.

Another unresolved question regarding the mosque is the origin of its interior columns. The prevailing view is that those columns dating from Stage I are Classic and Visigothic, plundered from abandoned sites. The capitals and shafts are of different heights and appearance, although the combined height of base, shaft, and capital are all about the same (as one would expect they would be to serve their load-carrying function). The columns of the first three stages all may have been Classic with the exception of some later Visigothic and Muslim replacements. According to R. Thouvenot, Roman capitals were designed to vary from the true Classic orders to accommodate to indigenous influences.[22] Thus, what has been interpreted to be reused Classic and Visigothic, or Islamic interpretations of Classic capitals, may in fact be the Iberian-Roman variation of Classic. Considering the unusually high degree of integration of the Romans into Iberian culture, it would be reasonable to expect Roman architecture to have become modified in its Spanish context.

The only stage of the mosque that I believe to be Islamic is Stage IV. This conclusion is based on personal observations made in 1984 in the course of investigating the mosque with the permission

Fig. 10. Córdobá, Great Mosque, roof beams within gable.

and cooperation of the Spanish government. While seeking to extract samples of brick from the voussoirs of the arches of the interior bays of Stage IV, I found

Fig. 11. Córdobá, Great Mosque, sample of wood beam taken from storage room.

that what appeared to be alternating bands of brick and stone were in fact all stone, with the brick only simulated by means of a coating of painted plaster.[23] In the course of drilling for powder samples of the brick to take back for thermoluminescence analysis, only white dust rained down. Even the contractor in charge of restoration was unaware of this decorative deception. I concluded that if this stage was Roman, their structural expertise would probably have been displayed by exposing real masonry construction, not simulating it as was the case here. This detail suggests a non-Roman source for this stage.

The thermoluminescence technique of analyzing the powder samples proved not to be successful.[24] Unfortunately, the samples I obtained suffered from "optical bleaching," a measure of high light sensitivity that reduced the accuracy of the measurement. Another technique employed was carbon-14 dating of several wood structural members. A fragment of wood taken from a roof beam at the eastern edge of Stage III was dated ca. 1030-580 B.C. suggest-

Fig. 12. Córdobá, Great Mosque, exterior wall showing interlaced lobed arches over blind niches.

ing the beam may date from as early as the Carthaginian period (Fig. 10).[25] Another wood sample taken from beams stored in the mosque produced quite different results; it dated between 645-915 A.D. (Fig. 11). This would be consistent with an Islamic origin of the mosque. Unfortunately it is impossible to say what part of the mosque these stored beams were from, or to know with certainty that they were part of the mosque at all. As can be noted from this brief survey, our attempts to use scientific dating methods to solve some of the questions regarding the mosque's origins were inconclusive. However, we did, apparently, establish a precedent in the application of archaeometry to the dating of Muslim medieval buildings. As these scientific techniques become increasingly refined, they will be valuable tools available to scholars of Islamic architecture, to be added to the traditional methods of stylistic analysis, epigraphic evidence, and literary references.

Having built an argument for a possible Roman provenance for the first three stages of the Mosque of Córdobá, I must point out that certain features

Fig. 13. Córdobá, Great Mosque, interior view of *miḥrāb* showing blind niches and shell-domed ceiling.

do not comfortably relate to either Muslim or Roman sources: the interlaced and lobated arches in the *maqsūra* (the prayer hall area close to the *miḥrāb*); the interlaced arches over some exterior doorways (Fig. 12); the intersecting ribbed vaulting of the cupola in front of the *miḥrāb* (Pl. 2); the *miḥrāb*'s six-sided form, shell ceiling, and trilobed blind niches; and cross-bracing of the columns by means of horseshoe arches (Fig. 13). Do these features point to a possible earlier provenance for the building?

In any case, the argument for a Roman provenance is obviously worthy of further investigation. The

Roman presence is manifest in the disposition of huge spaces, the squared ashlar stonework, the profusely decorated entries, the Roman order of columns, the porticoed court, the alternating brick and stone voussoirs, and the double arches. Curiously, Roman writers like Pliny and Strabo do not seem to have asked the question: Where was the main Roman warehouse in Córdobá? Nor have modern investigators been deeply concerned. There had to have been at least one large warehouse near the river; Córdobá was too important a commercial center for it to have been otherwise. Perhaps, then, it was there all along and never destroyed. We may owe a debt of gratitude to Islamic Spain for having repaired, extended, and even enhanced the imperial Roman warehouse of Córdobá.[26]

Notes

1 O. Grabar, *The Formation of Islamic Art* (New Haven: Yale University Press, 1973), p. 20.

2 Al-Makkari, *The History of Mohammedan Dynasties in Spain,* trans. Pascual de Gayangos, vols. 1 and 2 (London, 1843).

3 K. A. C. Creswell, *A Short Account of Early Muslim Architecture* (Beirut: Librairie du Liban, 1968), p. 213. H. Terrasse, *L'Art Hispano-Mauresque des Origines au XIIIe Siècle* (Paris: Editions G. Van Oest, 1932), p. 59.

4 Terrasse, *L'Art Hispano-Mauresque*, p. 59.

5 M. Gomez-Moreno, *Ars Hispaniae* (Madrid: Editorial Plus-ultra, 1951), 3:19.

6 A. Lowe, *The Spanish* (Anchor Press Ltd., 1975), p. 63.

7 Grabar, *Islamic Art*, p. 20.

8 Terrasse, *L'Art Hispano-Mauresque*, p. 52.

9 Terrasse, *L'Art Hispano-Mauresque*, p. 69.

10 E. Lambert, *Etudes Médiévales*, Tome 3 (Privat-Didier, 1956), p. 55.

11 R. Lanciani, *Ancient Rome* (New York: Benjamin Blom, 1967), p. 248.

12 The Mosque of Córdobá could have had an orientation of north-south, which would have been a reasonable *qibla* direction by corresponding to the Medina-Mekkah geographical relationship. A third possibility has been suggested by David A. King, "Some Medieval Values of the Qibla at Cordoba," *Journal of the History of Arab Science* 2 (1978): 370-87, in which he notes that the axis of the mosque is parallel to one side of the Ka'abah in Mekkah. This would make the Ka'abah and the Great Mosque parallel along

their great axis. But neither contemporary writers nor medieval writers relate any such motivation in construction. King also suggests that the Ka'abah may have been astronomically aligned to the star Canopus, to the midsummer sunrise, or to the southernmost setting of the moon at the winter solstice ("Faces of the Kaaba," *The Sciences* [May/June, 1982]: 19-20). This raises the possibility that the building in question was not necessarily built to relate to the Ka'abah but that both mosque and Ka'abah were built for similar astronomical considerations. In any case, a thorough study of the mosque's possible astronomical orientations should be undertaken.

13 Creswell, *Early Muslim Architecture*, pp. 213-16.

14 L. Golvin, *Essai sur l'Architecture Religieuse Musulmane*, tome 4, *L'Art Hispano-Musulman* (Paris: Editions Klincksieck, 1979), p. 59.

15 G. E. Rickman, *Roman Granaries and Store Buildings* (Cambridge: University Press, 1971), p. 52. Rickman describes a niche in the Grand Horrea in Ostia: "A small square niche is preserved in the front wall of one of these northern rooms; it is framed by small pilasters in the brickwork and probably held the statue of some tutelary deity."

16 W. MacDonald, *The Architecture of the Roman Empire, An Introductory Study*, rev. ed., publications in the History of Art, no. 17 (Yale University Press, 1982), pp. 5-6.

17 P. Mackendrick, *Romans on the Rhine* (New York: Funk and Wagnalls, 1970), p. 221.

18 E. Hole, *Andalus- (Spain under the Moslems)* (London: Robert Hale Ltd., 1958), p. 37. Hole quotes Don Rafael Castejon: ". . . below the floor of the mosque each column stands on isolated foundations of masonry. . . ."

19 P. Mackendrick, *Romans on the Rhine*, p. 221.

20 Rafael Moneo Valles, "La Vida de los Edificios, las Ampliacones de la Mezquita de Cordoba," *Arquitectura* 66 (Sept./Oct. 1985): 26-36. In this recent analysis the author makes the interesting observation that the rows of columns perpendicular to the *qibla* wall show the application of the principle of the Roman aqueduct to the interior construction complete with roof channels for water drainage and multiple level arches in the interior. He refers to the structural system of the mosque as ". . . un sistema formada por muros-acueductos" (p. 29).

21 G. T. Rivoira, *Moslem Architecture* (New York: Hacker Art Books, 1975), pp. 86-91.

22 R. Thouvenot, *Essai sur la Province Romaine de Bétique*, 2nd ed., (1940; reprint ed., Paris, 1973), p. 384.

23 Golvin, *Essai sur l'Architecture*, p. 87. Golvin noted the same phenomenon: "Les arcades reprennant assez curieusement le dispositif ancien (Abd al-Rahman I): arcs superposés à claveaux bicolores (rouges et blancs), mais cette bichromie est obtenue par la peinture la plupart des temps (sans doute partout?). . . ."

24 Archaeometry is the science of determining the age of ancient materials by analysis of their physical and chemical properties. Thermoluminescence is a specific technique of archaeometry that developed in the 1960s that concerns itself with dating ancient baked clay products, principally pottery and fired brick, by analyzing and quantifying the remains of radioactive qualities since the last firing. Baked clay accumulates a radioactive dose from its last firing at 600 degrees C or above at a predictable constant rate. This natural dose is composed of the external radiation of gamma rays plus cosmic rays and an internal dose rate from beta and alpha particles. The uncertainty in age determination is estimated at six to fifteen percent plus or minus. See S. Fleming, *Thermoluminescence Techniques in Archaeology* (Oxford: Clarendon Press, 1979).

25 Carbon-14 dating of wood structural members is a less sophisticated and intimidating procedure than thermoluminescence. This in situ example was dated by the Beta Analytic, Inc. laboratories of Coral Gables, Florida. The results have an estimated ninety-five percent probability including correction for the Devries effect. Assuming the possibility that the sample had been contaminated by preservatives, the date could have been affected by five hundred years. But even accepting this extreme possibility, the beam dates between the Carthaginian and Roman periods. However, there is also the possibility that the beam could have been reused from older construction.

26 A future paper is being prepared on the interpretation of what has been uniformly regarded as a minaret. There is good reason to believe that it was a Roman lighthouse, used to receive and signal information about freighters along the Guadalquivir River all the way to the ancient Phoenician city of Cadiz at the mouth of the river. Thus, the signal tower could have functioned as a useful adjunct to the warehouse. It would have been similar to the still extant tower lighthouse at La Coruña in the northwest corner of the Iberian peninsula which was built in the age of Trajan in the second century A.D. and is the only surviving lighthouse of the Roman world.

The Carpet Pages of the
Spanish-Hebrew Farhi Bible

Sybil Mintz

Medieval Spain's rich blend of cultures can be demonstrated in the decorated pages of the fourteenth-century Hebrew manuscript, the *Farhi Bible*.[1] Its thirty carpet pages reflect the calligraphy and traditions of earlier and contemporary Hebrew manuscripts, the complex geometric patterns of Islamic art, and the fantastic imagery and decorative details of the illuminated manuscripts of Christian Spain, as well as of France and Italy. The Farhi Bible, named for its Syrian-Jewish owner, is a culmination of the absorption of the Islamic and Spanish-Christian culture by the Jews of Spain.

Dating perhaps to the Phoenician settlement of the Iberian peninsula, but definitely to the Roman occupation, the Jews of Spain lived through the Visigothic invasion, the Islamic takeover, and the Christian Reconquest. For the Jews, periods of persecution and forced conversions alternated with times of peaceful coexistence, high positions, and creative and intellectual growth. In the fourteenth century in Catalonia and Aragon, the enlightened ruler Pedro IV protected the Jews and hired them as astronomers, mapmakers, translators, and craftsmen. During his reign from 1336 to 1387, Barcelona became an intellectual and artistic center. Here, too, the Spanish Hebrew codex reached the height of its development.

Yet, for Spain, the fourteenth century was one filled with sporadic anti-Semitic outbursts, reaching a peak with the persecution of 1391. Copied in the years just before that onslaught, the Farhi Bible reveals a religious fervor and a yearning for the Messianic Age. According to its colophon, the owner-scribe Elisha Crescas devoted sixteen years, from 1366 to 1382, to the self-imposed task of copying the Bible for his personal use. Like other Spanish Jewish scribes of that period, he referred to the Bible as *mikdashiyah*, or the Temple. Just as they prayed daily for the restoration of the Temple, the Jewish scribes and illuminators placed images of the vessels of the sanctuary in their Bibles, as Crescas did in his.[2] Moreover, they richly decorated its pages as they would adorn their sanctuary.[3]

Although Crescas stated that he "created" or "produced" this manuscript, he, as this paper will show, had one or more artists do at least part of the decoration. According to custom, the names of the artists often were omitted. The same "very careful square Sephardic hand of the fourteenth century,"[4] used throughout both volumes of his two-volume, 1,046-page[5] manuscript, however, establishes Crescas as the only scribe.

The first volume, a grammatical treatise and dictionary,[6] is lavishly decorated, with 192 of its 193 pages illuminated; in the second volume, the biblical text itself, only the headings of each book, except Lamentations, and the first word of each *pericope* (*parasha* or paragraph) have ornamentation. Starting on page 42 of the nonbiblical first volume are thirty consecutively placed carpet pages (ornamental pages).

The typical Farhi carpet page (Pl. 3) has a vertical panel containing a square filled with a geometric pattern of interwoven bands. Above and below the square are horizontal bands, in which large, gold or purple Hebrew letters against a filigree background make up continuous Biblical quotations referring to the Torah (five books of Moses). Surrounding the vertical panel is a decorative border. In each outer corner of the page is an ornamental leaf accompanied by one or more gold-filled circles. In the upper, lower and outer margins are three to six lines of the *masoretic* text written in miniscule Hebrew script. The initial words of each sentence of the text are enlarged and backed by a red filigree background.

This *masoretic* text, containing in the margin additional remarks regarding the correct spelling, writing, and reading of the Hebrew Bible, dates back to very early Hebrew manuscripts. For example, its arrangement in the margin of the Farhi page is related to earlier Hebrew Bibles such as the Burgos *Damascus Keter* (crown) of 1260 (Fig. 1), but also to early Spanish Latin manuscripts, such as the *Codex Vigilanus* of 976.[7] Yet this practice may be related to the decorative text around doorways of Spanish synagogues[8] and, ultimately, to mosque doorways in Spain and other Islamic countries.

Some of the features—the texts, the script, the use of marginal decoration—are traditional in illuminated Hebrew manuscripts. However, other features, such as the geometric motif, developed parallel to those in non-Hebrew codices. That is, while the sources of the specific geometric formations within the central squares can be found in contemporary Islamic art, geometrics already decorate the earliest extant illuminated Hebrew manuscript, the *Moshe ben Asher Codex* of 895,[9] which predates the earliest extant illuminated Koran.[10] Moreover, the circular designs such as the one on Farhi page 52 (Pl. 3) can be compared to the intricate geometric circular illustrations of *matzah* (unleavened bread) in *haggadahs* (prayer books from which prayers, psalms, and midrashic commentaries are recited during the ritual meal of Passover), which date back to the ninth and tenth centuries, up to contemporary *haggadahs*,[11] such as the fourteenth-century *Golden Haggadah* of Barcelona (Fig. 2).

Hebrew codices with geometrics were created within Islamic cultures; this was the result not only of artistic interaction but of religious influence.[12]

Specific geometric configurations within the central squares can be traced to Islamic manuscripts and Islamic and Mudéjar crafts, especially silk weaving, metalwork, bookbinding, ceramics, wall tiles, and woodcarving. Geometric patterns are found in the earliest Islamic decorative arts, as the mid-eighth-century floor mosaics at the palace of Khirbat al-Mafjar, Jordan.[13] In the middle of the twelfth century, Egypt developed a "compartmental geometric style primarily of star configurations."[14] It spread

Fig. 1. Carpet page, *Damascus Keter*, Jerusalem, Jewish National and University Library, MS Heb. 4°790, fol. 114, Burgos, 1260 (courtesy of Jewish National and University Library).

Fig. 2. Matzah, *Golden Haggadah*, London, British Library, Add. 27210, fol. 44v, Barcelona, fourteenth century (courtesy of British Library).

to Anatolia, North Africa, and Spain. These designs became more complex and intricate.[15] By the middle of the fourteenth century, geometric decoration, especially the star formation, was at the height of its development and popularity.[16] Variations of the star motif appear on most of the Farhi carpet pages. The same sixteen-pointed star configuration on both Farhi page 42 (Pl. 4) and the exactly contemporary Egyptian *Arghun Shah Qu'rān* carpet page (Fig. 3) is evidence of its popularity.

Further comparison of these two pages demonstrates that the layout of the Farhi carpet pages was related to Koran illumination. In each, a vertical panel contains an upper and lower horizontal inscription, a square filled with a geometric configuration of white interlaced bands and a decorative border, single in the Bible and triple in the Koran. Farhi page 42 (Pl. 4), unlike the following twenty-nine pages, has two additional features in common with the Arghun Shah folio, namely spiky projections from the vertical panel and the *palmette ansa* (a standard feature of Koran carpet pages that stems from the Roman *tabulae ansa*, handles used for attaching a rectangular writing tablet to the wall).

Still another motif from Islamic art is the *arabesque*, which fills the spandrels and the background spaces on a number of the Farhi pages, as in the spandrels of page 52 (Pl. 3). The arabesque, too, was abundant in contemporary Islamic and Mudéjar art. Thus, the Farhi Bible can be stylistically and iconographically associated with the art of Islam as well as with earlier and contemporary Jewish art.

Yet artistic comparisons also tie the Bible's illumination to the art of Christian Spain, especially Barcelona. Within the borders of the vertical panels and in the outer corners are motifs derived from Latin manuscripts of Spain, France, and Italy. The tight interweaving in some of the borders, for example on page 70 (Pl. 5), can be compared to the eleventh-century *Beatus Apocalypse* of Madrid[17] or to the mid-eleventh-century *Saint-Sever of Aquitaine Beatus*.[18] Such plaitwork was influenced by the Carolingian Renaissance,[19] by Insular traditions as well as by a Visigothic carryover, plus a possible Coptic input.[20] Foliate forms, such as running, branching vine scrolls and spiraling leaves that decorate a number of the borders, can be traced to French, German, English, and Italian manuscripts. The leaves twisting around a rod in the border on Farhi page 54 (Pl. 6) are similar to border ornamentation in the slightly later Italian *Visconti Hours*.[21]

It is the corner ornamentation of the carpet pages, the full fleshy, yet spiky acanthus leaves accom-

panied by gold-filled circles with linear projections, that ties this manuscript to Barcelona, specifically to the workshop or the school of the Master of Saint Mark. The manuscripts, both Christian and Jewish, that this school produced demonstrate the Italian influence in Barcelona in the second half of the fourteenth century.[22] Manuscripts produced by this workshop include the Latin *Libro de Privilegios* (or *Llibre Verd*) of Barcelona (1361-1385)[23] and the Hebrew *Maimonides' Moreh HaNevukhim* (Fig. 4).

Other Farhi features related to this Barcelona style are the occasional hidden animals and human and animal heads. Although Spanish Hebrew Bibles were generally non-representational, animals and grotesques occasionally appear, primarily in the separate first volume, which was, in fact, a fourteenth-century innovation.[24] Human heads without a body also appear, perhaps because of the ruling of Rabbi Asher ben Yekiel and his son Rabbi ben

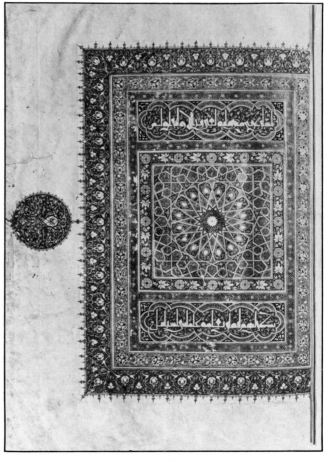

Fig. 3. Carpet page, *Arghun Shah Qu'rān*, Cairo National Library, MS 54, Egypt, ca. 1368-88 (courtesy of National Library, Cairo).

Fig. 4. Frontispiece, *Moreh HaNevukhim,* Copenhagen, Royal Library, Cod. Hebr. 37, fol. 202, Barcelona, 1348 (courtesy of Royal Library of Copenhagen).

Asher Baal ha-Turin, who lived in Barcelona and in Toledo at the beginning of the fourteenth century. The ruling circumvented the Second Commandment, saying it was permissible to depict a head without a body or a body without a head.[25]

Human and animal heads, as well as dragons, were deftly worked into the border corners on a few of the Farhi pages, such as page 42 (Pl. 4) and page 54 (Pl. 6). These features can be compared with the heads in the border corners of folio 202 in the St. Mark Workshop *Moreh HaNevukhim* (Fig. 4). Cartoon faces, animals, and grotesques were hidden in some of the Farhi corner leaves. The concealed creatures in the leaves on pages 42 and 54, as well as in the lower one on page 70 (Pl. 5), can be compared with the hidden figure in the lower row of foliate forms in the fourteenth-century Latin *Historia Escolastica* by Pedro Comestor of Catalonia.[26] The sole exposed animate form of the carpet pages, the dog resting lightly on the upper corner leaf of page 70 (Pl. 5), ties this manuscript to another contemporary Barcelona codex, the *Barcelona Haggadah*, especially on folio 20v.[27]

Thus, the Farhi artist of the corner and border was part of, or influenced by, the Barcelona school which produced both Christian and Hebrew manuscripts. This artist was not, however, the designer of the central square geometrics nor was he the scribe Crescas. First, the leaves are painted in a much looser style than that of the sharply delineated outlined forms of the central square design. Furthermore, the leaves are carelessly attached to the vertical panels; they spread into the margins and crowd the lettering. Crescas would have never let the leaves abut the script, as they do on several of the carpet pages, as on page 52 (Pl. 3).

Therefore, although Crescas might have drawn the orderly, exacting configurations within the central squares, in that their Islamic character is in keeping with the Koran-like layout, which he as scribe would have done, the Barcelona illuminator appears to be a second hand. In the pages that follow the carpet pages is further evidence of a second hand (Fig. 5). Freely placed ornamentation, painted in the manner of the corner leaves, fills in spaces left open by the scribe. Additional evidence of a second hand is the tightly designed *palmette ansa* on page 42 (Pl. 4), which is incorporated into the vertical panel by a blue penned line and is placed into an opening of the text, provided by the scribe Crescas, in contrast to the placement of the leaves on the same page and their lack of this blue outline. This feature also suggests that the leaves were added later.

Yet the art work cannot be divided easily between two artists, for the same colors and some of the same painting techniques and forms appear in both the leaves and the backgrounds of the vertical panels, as on page 52 (Pl. 3). These similarities suggest one of two possibilities:

1. Crescas only laid out the page. An artist, perhaps Mudéjar, did the geometrics, and another, of the Barcelona school, painted the interspatial details and the borders and added the leaves.

2. Crescas laid out the page, designed the geometrics, following Islamic and Hebrew manuscripts as well as Islamic craft patterns, and drew the interspatial forms and those in the border. Then the Barcelona artist painted the decorative details within the central square and the border, perhaps adding the heads, as well as the dragon on page 42 (Pl. 4), and finally added the corner leaves.

Fig. 5. *Farhi Bible*, Sassoon Collection, MS 367, p. 52, detail upper left (courtesy of R. David Sassoon).

Nevertheless, the result is an intricate and successful fusion of motifs from earlier and contemporary Christian and Hebrew manuscripts with the layout and designs from Islamic manuscripts and crafts. The Bible's rich artistic vocabulary places it at a crossroads when "the last phase of the decisive encounter took place between the Latin Middle Ages and the great inheritance of the Islamic world."[28] Moreover, Crescas' *mikdashiyah*, which now belongs to the Sassoon family of Jerusalem, is tangible evidence of an age of rich cultural involvement for the Jews of Spain, an age that, soon after the Bible's completion, ended abruptly.

Notes

1   Sassoon Collection, MS 369.

2   *Farhi Bible*, Sanctuary Vessels, p. 182.

3   Joseph Gutmann, *The Temple of Solomon* (Missoula, Mont., 1976), p. 132.

4   David S. Sassoon, *Ohel Dawid: Descriptive Catalogue of the Hebrew and Samaritan Manuscripts in the Sassoon Library* (London, 1932), p. 13.

5   Each side of every folio has been numbered.

6   The text is taken from the Hebrew lexicons, each entitled *Sepher Ha-Shoreshim*, one by B. Jonah ibn Ganah, eleventh-century Spain, and the other by David Kimkhi (ca. 1160-1235) of Narbonne, Languedoc. Sassoon, p. 7.

7   Escorial, Library of the Royal Monastery, f.16v, Jesus Dominguez-Bordona, *Spanish Illumination* (New York, 1969), Plate 25.

8   Leila Avrin, "Micrography as Art," *Etudes de Paléographie Hébraïque* (Jerusalem, 1981), p. 42.

9   Cairo, Ben Ezra Synagogue.

10 Richard Ettinghausen, *Arab Painting* (New York, 1977), p. 120.

11 Bezalel Narkiss, "Matzah," *Encyclopedia Judaica* (1971).

12 Joseph Gutmann, *Hebrew Manuscript Painting* (New York, 1978), p. 16.

13 Oleg Grabar, *The Formation of Islamic Art* (New Haven/London, 1973), Fig. 71.

14 Richard Ettinghausen, "Muslim Decorative Arts and Painting," *Islam and the Medieval West 1*, ed. Stanley Ferber (Binghamton, N.Y., 1975), p. 6.

15 Ibid.

16 Eva Baer, *Metalwork in Medieval Islamic Art* (Albany, 1983), pp. 84-85.

17 Madrid, Biblioteca Nacional, B31, f.6. Dominguez-Bordona, Plate 31.

18 Paris, Bibliothèque Nationale, MS lat 8878. Pedro de Palol Salellas and Max Hirmer, *Early Medieval Art in Spain* (London, 1967), Plate 83.

19 John Williams, *Early Spanish Manuscript Illumination* (New York, 1977), pp. 21-22.

20 Jacques Guilmain, "Interlace Decoration and the Influence of the North on Mozarabic Illumination," *Art Bulletin* 42, 3 (Sept., 1960): 213.

21 Millard Meiss, *Visconti Hours* (New York, 1972), f. BR 112v.

22 Millard Meiss, "Italian Style in Catalonia and a Fourteenth Century Catalan Workshop," *Journal of the Walters Art Gallery* 4 (1941): 45-87.

23 f. 205, Meiss, "Italian," Fig. 36.

24 Jacob Leveen, *The Hebrew Bible in Art* (New York, 1974), p. 106.

25 Bezalel Narkiss, "Zoocephalic Phenomenon," *Norms and Variations in Art* (Jerusalem, 1983), p. 63.

26 Madrid, Bibliotheca Nacional, Sign. Ri99. Dominguez-Bordona, Plate 49.

27 Bezalel Narkiss, *Hebrew Illuminated Manuscripts in the British Isles 1: The Spanish and Portuguese Manuscripts* (Jerusalem/London, 1982), Plate 51, Fig. 211.

28 Rudolph Schnyder, "Islamic Ceramics, a Source of Inspiration for Medieval European Art," *Islam and the Medieval West*, ed. Stanley Ferber (Binghamton, N.Y., 1975), 1:33.

The Three Hebrew Children in the Fiery Furnace: A Study in Christian Iconography

Ann Walton

Then was Nebuchadnezzar full of fury and the expression of his face was changed against Shadrach, Meshach, and Abed'nego. He ordered the furnace heated seven times more than it was wont to be heated.

And he ordered certain mighty men of his army to bind Shadrach, Meshach and Abed'nego, and to cast them into the burning fiery furnace.

Then these men were bound in their mantles, their tunics, their hats, and their other garments, and they were cast into the burning fiery furnace.

Because the King's order was strict and the furnace very hot, the flame of the fire slew these men who took

up Shadrach, Meshach, and Abed'nego.

And these men, Shadrach, Meshach and Abed'nego fell bound into the burning fiery furnace.

Then King Nebuchadnezzar was astonished and rose up in haste. He said to his counselors, 'Did we not cast three men bound into the fire?' They answered the king, 'True, O King.'

He answered, 'But I see four men loose, walking in the midst of the fire, and they are not hurt; and the appearance of the fourth is like a son of the gods (Daniel 3:21-25).

One of the earliest pictorial representations that can be identified as Christian iconography shows three young men standing amid flames, the three Hebrew children in the fiery furnace whose story is related in the book of Daniel.[1] Although the story did not occupy a position of major importance in Early Christian representational art, it nonetheless remained a persistent subordinate theme throughout the Middle Ages and into our own time.

Using fifteen representative examples from the second through the thirteenth centuries, this paper explores this iconography.[2] Two distinctive types of configuration exist concurrently during the thousand-year period: a linear grouping (Type A) and a pyramidal construction, which can be traced from the second-century Catacomb of Priscilla (Fig. 1) through to the twelfth-century capital at Autun (Fig. 2) (Type B).

The earliest extant representations of the three Hebrew children in the fiery furnace occur in frescoes decorating the walls of the Roman Catacomb of Priscilla. One of these, in the Capella Greca, can be dated to the second century.[3] Another, in the Cubiculum Velatio, is dated a century later. In both,

the three children, dressed in Persian costumes, are shown standing in an orant position (their hands raised in prayer) amid flames (Figs. 1 and 3). In the later fresco, a large bird carrying a branch hovers above two of the children. These two types of composition, Type A (Fig. 3), which is linear, and Type B (Fig. 1), pyramidal, become standard throughout the Mediterranean basin during the thousand-year period under discussion.

The context of these iconographic images in both locations is funerary and the theme, salvation. The association of these images with burial practices can be seen in Rome for at least four centuries. It spread to other parts of the Roman world, especially through the programs found on sarcophagi.[4] Examples other than the catacomb frescoes include a sarcophagus from Rome dated to the fifth-sixth centuries. Although such representations are mainly found in and around Rome, the theme also occurs elsewhere, particularly in France. However, on the sarcophagi, the three Hebrew children are never the main focus of the overall program; they usually are relegated to the upper register of the presentation cycle on the short end of the sarcophagus while figures of Christ and the apostles occupy the focal point on the front (Fig. 4).

With the acceptance of Christianity as a tolerated and then official religion of Rome in the fourth century, Christian iconography rapidly outgrew its tentative beginnings. Covert meanings become fixed in elaborate cycles of Biblical repertoire.[5] At the same time, the transference of iconographic schemes from one medium to another becomes common in Christian art, as can be seen in the Type A composition of the Three Hebrew Children on a gold glass dated to the fourth century (Fig. 5).

A later example of such elaborate programs can be seen in fresco; a fourth figure, a winged angel holding a staff, is introduced; he stands alongside the children. A similar fourth figure can also be noted in other Type A representations of the scene, including a silver reliquary casket from San Nazaro Maggiore and the gold glass noted earlier (Figs. 6 and 5). The fourth figure in the Type B representations is always placed above the children (Figs. 1, 2, 7, and Pl. 7).

The intervention of God through the agency of a messenger such as an angel parallels similar biblical stories of intervention. Old Testament events were often paired with New Testament lessons in such cycles as proof of the fulfillment of prophecies.

One such repertoire of Christian iconographic programs, the so-called "Help of God," has its source in the *Ordo Commendationis Animae* (the office of the dead).[6] The *Ordo* contains names of Old Testament and Apocrypha figures saved by God's miraculous intervention, and includes the three Hebrew children in the fiery furnace. Their inclusion in the *Ordo* could account for the presence of the story among salvation episodes in decorations for burial chambers.

However, as early as the fourth century, examples exclusive of the association with death can also be found. The eucharistic connotations of an ivory pyxis link the theme to salvation through the sacrament of the mass (Fig. 8). An unusual juxtaposition of the story with the tale of Joseph fleeing from Potiphar's wife occurs in a red earthenware bowl

Fig. 1. Catacomb of Priscilla, Cubiculum Velatio, 2nd half of 3rd c. (courtesy of Pontificia Commissione di Archeologia Sacra, Città del Vaticano).

from Tunisia (see Fig. no. 415, p. 464 of *Age of Spirituality* [New York: The Metropolitan Museum of Art, 1979]).[7] This bowl illustrates not only the widespread popularity of the theme of three Hebrew children, but also yet another interpretation of its iconography. Here, the salvation by God from fiery lust may be comparable to the protection from the heat of the fiery furnace.[8]

The Type A composition occurs in a seventh-century Mount Sinai icon that is stylistically comparable to the sixth-century Murano Diptych (Pl. 8 and Fig. 9). However, the icon lacks the story cycle and parallel themes seen in the diptych. In both objects, the fourth man standing alongside the children is an angel holding a cruciform staff.[9] In the ninth-century Faras fresco from North Africa, the fourth figure, a winged angel holding a cruciform staff, is shown amid as well as towering above the children (see Fig. no. 328 in Kurt Weitzmann, *Studies in the Arts at Sinai* [Princeton, N.J.: Princeton University Press, 1982]). What is also of interest here is that for the first time the angel is shown larger than the children.

Fig. 2. Capital, "Trois Hébreux dans la Fournaise," Autun (courtesy of Editions Trianon).

Fig. 3. Catacomb of Priscilla, Cappella Greca, Rome, 2nd c. (courtesy of Pontificia Commissione di Archeologia Sacra, Città del Vaticano).

The development of the pyramidal, Type B composition can be seen in three examples: the mosaic from Hosios Loukas (Fig. 7), an enamel painting possibly from Maastricht (Pl. 7), and a carved capital from Autun (Fig. 2). In all three the fourth figure of an angel is unmistakably above the three children and protects them with outspread wings.

The two carved capitals from twelfth-century French churches (Fig. 2 and 10) exemplify two different approaches to the same problem—how to integrate the iconography of the three Hebrew children into the decoration of a column.[10] At Autun the angel is suspended above the three, while at Moissac (Fig. 10), the four figures are spread around the basket of the column marking the four corners and separated by spikes of flame.

From this brief overview it can be seen that two distinctive types of configuration existed during the thousand-year period: The first configuration, seen in the Catacomb of Priscilla (Fig. 3) through the capital at Moissac (Fig. 10), can be described as linear, since the three or four figures stand in a row; the second, a pyramidal construction, can be traced from the second century at the Catacomb of Priscilla (Fig. 1) through to the twelfth-century capital at Autun (Fig. 2). In this formation, a hovering winged angel or bird[11] is suspended above the three Hebrew children.

The elements that constitute the iconographic program of the three Hebrew children can be identified as follows:

The three children. The youthful visage of the three Hebrew children is unchanged throughout the entire period under investigation. St. Jerome observed that the reason for this may have been cas-

tration.[12] This supposition is not specifically confirmed in the text of Daniel; however, the youthfulness of the three is easily accounted for by Nebuchadnezzar's charge to Ashpenaz (Daniel 1:3-4), ". . . to take certain of the Israelite exiles, of the blood royal and of the nobility, who were to be young men of good looks and bodily without fault. . . ." The book of Daniel contains other accounts of the three Hebrew children that are earlier and later than their experience in the fiery furnace.[13] According to the Biblical accounts of the three, their youthful appearance is appropriate for their age at the time of this episode.

In both Type A and B images, the position of the children is frontal, whether their bodies are fully (Figs. 1 and 3) or only partially shown (Figs. 2, 4, and 7). Their glances vary from straight ahead (Figs. 3 and 8) to inward toward each other (Figs. 4, 7, and 9).

Nimbi become part of the iconography in the seventh century (Pl. 8) and also can be seen in Fig. 7, Pl. 7, and the Faras fresco. In all four examples, the fourth figure of an angel with a nimbus is present, possibly indicating equal reverence toward all four figures. The use of the nimbus does not appear much earlier than the sixth or seventh century and does not seem to be the exclusive property of one geographic area since it can be found in the Middle East as well as in the West.

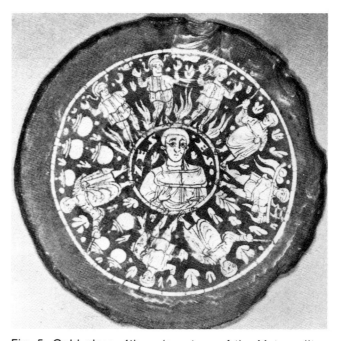

Fig. 5. Gold glass, 4th c. (courtesy of the Metropolitan Museum of Art, New York).

Fig. 4. Sarcophagus, 5-6th c.

A peculiar nob protrudes from the curly head of each child in Fig. 7, from Hosios Loukas in Phocis. Perhaps this is a misunderstanding of a distinctive feature of the Persian costume, namely the bonnet or Phrygian cap.[14]

Costume. The Biblical account in Daniel 3:21 states, ". . . then these men were bound in their mantles, their tunics, their hats and their other garments, and they were cast into the burning fiery furnace." The Persian clothing of the children denotes their adopted country of origin. The earliest interpretation of the literary description can be seen in Figs. 1 and 3 where the Phrygian cap, belted tunic, and trousers can easily be identified.[15] When a mantle is worn, it is fastened in front with a fibula (Figs. 4, 6, 7, 8, and Pl. 8). This formula for clothing changed little over the centuries, from its earliest manifestation as the costume Roman artisans conventionally used to depict Persians.[16] The use of Persian dress to identify the three Hebrew children may have led later artisans to confuse them with the three Magi, whose origins also were indicated by Persian costume.[17] This accident may account, in part, for the increasing inclusion of the three Magi and subsequent exclusion of the three Hebrew children in decorative programs after the fourth century. This is not to say that they faded entirely from iconographic programs; rather, that they continued to be a minor but persistent feature of Christian art.

Occasionally, slight variations in the Persian costume showed local adaptation. For example, a broad vertical band extending from the neck to the hem of the tunic that was not part of the traditional Persian costume can be seen in Fig. 5. This garment resembled the *megaloschema* worn by monks, which may be its source.[18] That this type of apparel appears in several examples from areas geographically far apart may support an argument for diffusion of the typology.

The tucking up of the tunic is another example of a deviation from the prototype established in Figs. 1 and 3. The tunic in the earliest examples is clearly belted somewhere near the waist and hangs freely over the trousers (Figs. 1, 3, 4, and 9). Fig. 6 shows the tunic on two figures tucked up into the belt above both legs. The tucking up of the tunic sometimes coincides with a slight variation in the orant position of the hands: The combination of these two elements lends a rhythmic pattern to the composition. This combination was by no means a part of all presentations or even consistent within the same example (Fig. 6 and Pl. 8). It is seen primarily in Type A, occasionally in Type B. Obviously the

truncating of the figure would limit this line of inquiry.

The Furnace. Daniel 3:26 states that, "King Nebuchadnezzar came near to the door of the burning fiery furnace and said Shadrach, Meshach and Abed'nego, servants of the Most High God, come forth and come here!" When the furnace is actually a part of the program and not merely implied, two distinctive types appear, the rectangular furnace seen in Figs. 1 and 4, which is a feature of Type A, and the beehive furnace of the Tunisian bowl and associated with Type B.[19] The rectangular furnace of Type A is a schematic convention used to represent a furnace large enough for four men to walk around inside while the semicircular furnace of Type B (Figs. 2, 7, and the Tunisian bowl) is proportionately more convincing. The rectangular furnace may have any number of semicircular stoke holes between one and five (Figs. 3 and 4). The wood for the fire is included in Figs. 2 and 4.

Often the furnace is not specifically shown but is implied (Figs. 3, 6, 7, 8, 9, Pls. 7 and 8, and the Faras fresco). It would appear that when the artist had the option of showing the figures inside of the furnace, as opposed to atop the furnace, he did not need to identify graphically the type of furnace (Figs. 5, 6, 8, 9, 10, Pl. 8, and the Faras fresco). In these instances, it was sufficient to indicate the interior of the furnace by curls of flame (Pl. 8) or spikes of flame (Figs. 8, 9, 10, and the Faras fresco) or a masonry background (Fig. 8).

In many respects, Fig. 3 is an enigma in its present form. The lunette configuration suggests the interior of a beehive type of furnace seen in Type B; however,

Fig. 6. Silver reliquary casket, San Nazaro Maggiore, San Ambrogio, Milan.

there once may have been a Type A box furnace beneath the children, which has been destroyed by a later tomb cut into the wall beneath them.[20]

The Fourth Man. Daniel 3:25 states ". . . But I see four men loose, walking in the midst of the fire, and they are not hurt; and the appearance of the fourth is like a son of the gods." The fourth man in the Type A presentation appears both as a man (Fig. 6) and as a winged angel (Figs. 8, 9, and Pl. 8). Because the fourth man does not enter the narrative until after the children have been cast into the oven, the artist and/or his patron could exercise some discretion about which part of the story to illustrate. The iconography, therefore, does not always include a fourth figure.

The Type B configuration differs from Type A in that the winged angel is a compositional necessity, since the wings of the angel form a protective arc above the heads of the children (Figs. 2, 7, and Pl. 7). The Faras fresco would seem to be a transition between Types A and B; the four figures stand in a row with the wings of an angel forming an arc above the heads of the children. The spikes of fire suggest the beehive oven associated with a Type B composition.

In two instances, the fourth figure is not an angel. A dove carrying an olive branch represents the Holy Spirit in Fig. 3, and in Fig. 5, Christ himself appears

to the left of the children, attired as a teacher or prophet in a long tunic. He raises a *Virga thaumaturga* ("Wonder-working wand") in the direction of the children as though to calm the fire. In Fig. 6, the fourth man also extends such a wand diagonally across his body. Type A angels more commonly hold a diagonal staff that terminates in a cross, symbolizing and anticipating the saving act of Christ (Fig. 9 and Pl. 8).

Inscriptions. Inscriptions are sometimes included in the composition (Figs. 7, 10, and Pls. 7 and 8) to identify the subject or to instruct the observer of certain teachings. Fig. 10, Pl. 8, and the Faras fresco identify the three by name. Fig 10 goes so far as to identify each of the children by both their Babylonian and Hebrew names and further identifies the Angel of God and the fiery furnace.[21]

The inscription around the beaded border of Pl. 7 relates to a parallel of the three children in the fiery furnace as prototypes and exempla of the Virgin and Christ.[22] The inscription "nec pueros ledit vesania regis et ignis, nec matris natu disolvit claustra pudoris" can be interpreted "neither the fury of the king (i.e., Nebuchadnezzar) and the fire could harm the youths, nor birth destroy the seal of virginity of the Mother." Further inscriptions around their heads identify the three as Anaias, Azarias, and Misael. They hold a scroll bearing

Fig. 7. Mosaic, Church of Hosios Loukas, Phocis, Greece from *Great Ages of Man: Byzantium* (Alexandria, Virginia: Time-Life Books, Inc., 1966), photograph by Erich Lessing (courtesy of Time-Life Books, Inc.).

Pl. 1. Córdobá, Great Mosque, front view of *maqṣūra* and *miḥrāb*.

[Pl-1]

Pl. 2. Córdobá, Great Mosque, inside view of cupola in front of *miḥrāb*.

[Pl-2]

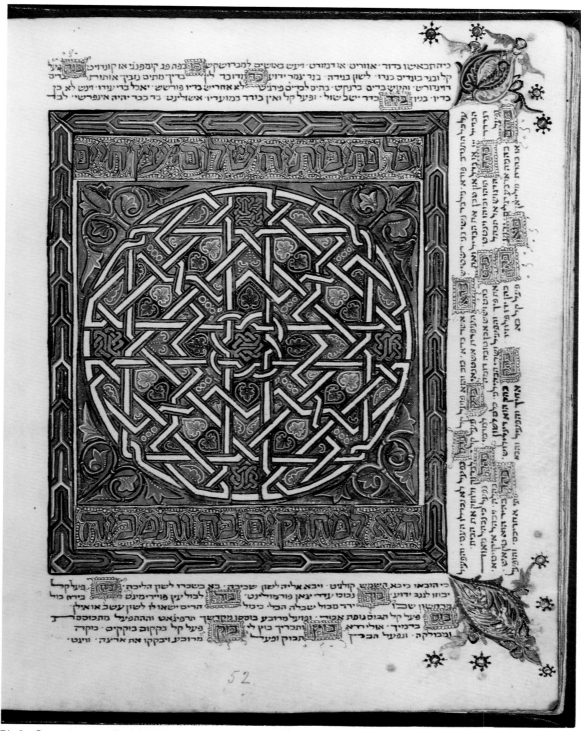

Pl. 3. Carpet page, *Farhi Bible*, Sassoon Collection, MS 367, p. 52 (courtesy of R. David Sassoon).

[Pl-3]

Pl. 4. Carpet page, *Farhi Bible*, Sassoon Collection, MS 367, p. 42 (courtesy of R. David Sassoon).

[Pl-4]

Pl. 5. Carpet page, *Farhi Bible*, Sassoon Collection, MS 367, p. 70 (courtesy of R. David Sassoon).

[Pl-5]

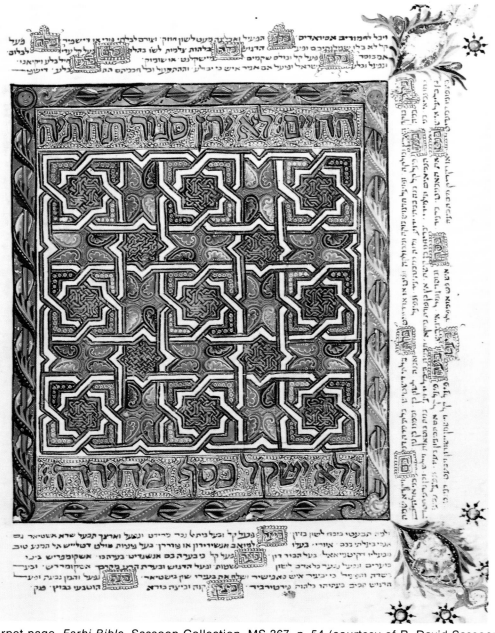

Pl. 6. Carpet page, *Farhi Bible*, Sassoon Collection, MS 367, p. 54 (courtesy of R. David Sassoon).

[Pl-6]

Pl. 7. "Plaque with Three Worthies in the fiery furnace," Meuse, Maastricht (?), 3rd quarter 12th c., Champlevé enamel and gilding on copper (courtesy of the Museum of Fine Arts, Boston: William Francis Warden Fund).

[Pl-7]

Pl. 8. Encaustic icon, 7th c., Mt. Sinai (courtesy of Princeton University Press).

[Pl-8]

a quotation from the Apocrypha Vulgate text addition to Daniel 3:23, called *The Song of the Hebrew Children*, "Benedict(us) es D(omi)ni d(eu)s patru(m) nostror(um) et laudabilis (e)t glorios(us) in s(e)c(u)la" "Blessed art thou, O Lord, thou God of our fathers and to be praised and exalted above all forever."[23]

We have observed that during the thousand-year period, both Types A and B occur in various locations around the Mediterranean Sea. Initially this subject was identified with the "Help of God" cycle that adorned objects for Christian burial. By the fourth century the image was found on nonburial objects as well: objects such as the pyxis and paten. Both Type A and Type B configurations were identified in a variety of materials, from fresco to glass, stone, ivory, and silver. The Mt. Sinai icon of the three Hebrew children (Pl. 8), stands alone, without parallel stories of faith, and as such may be regarded as an object worthy of exclusive consideration, not a supporting part of a cycle.

These few examples serve to illustrate the persistence of this iconographic theme throughout the Christian world. For over one thousand years, the three children in Persian dress praise God with their hands raised in an orant position. The iconography of the two Roman catacomb paintings of Type A and Type B extends from second-century Rome (Figs. 1 and 3) to the capitals of twelfth-century French churches (Figs. 2 and 10). The literary parallel to the artistic representation of the three Hebrew children in the fiery furnace, namely the *Ordo*, remains in use in the liturgy of the Christian church unto this day. Although the theme reflects

the desire to depict assurance of salvation during the service for the dead, I believe that it can signify more than that. When this representation spread from the service of the dead, by the fourth century if not earlier, to adorn the life-giving paten and pyxis, the three Hebrew children came to be seen as symbols of God's salvation of the living.

The prayer of the three Hebrew children found in the Vulgate text of the Apocrypha, where it is entitled *The Song of the Three Hebrew Children*, can be found in the Liturgy of the Greek and Roman church, in the Canticles of the Psalms, in the Roman Missal, Martyrologium, and Breviary; it is read at the feast of the Martyrs as well as at the Commendation of the Dead, as noted above. It is also found in the Pseudo-Augustinian Sermon used in the Christmas Mass and in liturgical drama.[24]

We may find an explanation for the continued appearance of Type B in the liturgical drama. During the Middle Ages the liturgical drama of the three Hebrew children in the fiery furnace was enacted as part of the Office of Matins (morning prayers) on the Sunday before Christmas in both the Church of the East and the Church of the West.[25] Three youths from the congregation were led into an enclosure, which represented the furnace, and either a picture of an angel, or a human being suspended

Fig. 8. Ivory pyxis, 2nd half of 5th c.

Fig. 9. Murano ivory diptych, 6th c.

in air representing the angel, was raised and lowered above the heads of the children by means of pulleys.[26] The close proximity of this liturgical drama to Christmas, which recalls the birth of Christ, points up the medieval parallel between the three Hebrew children and the Virgin and Child.

After the twelfth century, the depiction of the three Hebrew children in the fiery furnace continued to be a part of the iconographic canons of Eastern Orthodox church decoration. Although it did not entirely disappear from the Latin Church, it became increasingly rare. Regardless of its form, the iconographic program of the three Hebrew children, clad in their mantles and tunics, their hats and hosen, continued to have meaning for Christians in the Middle Ages, both in the Latin West and the Orthodox East.

Notes

1   The three Hebrew children are variously referred to as the three worthies, the three Babylonians, the three youths, the three confessors, the three men, the three Hebrew princes, the three Jews, and the three Israelites. By far the most common name used

is the three Hebrew children and that is the name I will use. Individually they are named Shadrach, Meshach and Abed'nego in Babylonian, and Hananiah, Mishael, and Azariah in Hebrew.

The Book of Daniel is thought to have been written around 200 B.C. about events of the sixth century B.C. It was included by the seventy Jewish scholars in Alexandria as writings and not prophecy in the Septuagint, presumably because of the late date for recording the text. There is, however, considerable confusion over the exact date of composition. Three copies of the Book of Daniel were found among the Dead Sea Scrolls. Daniel is divided into the stories and the prophecies and is written partly in Greek and partly in Aramaic. The story of the three Hebrew children in the fiery furnace is in the earlier Aramic section. S. B. Frost, G. A. Buttrick, *et al.*, *The Interpreter's Dictionary of the Bible* (Nashville: Abingdon Press, 1984), 1:763.

2   Over two hundred examples of this subject are recorded in the Princeton Iconographic Index. In the course of my research, I have uncovered several hitherto unrecorded additions to the Index.

3   P. Styger, *Die Romischen Katakomben: Archäologische Forschungen über den Ursprung und die Bedeutung der altchristlichen Grabstatten* (Berlin, 1933).

4   Edmond Le Blant (*Etude sur les sarcophages chrétiens antiques de la ville d'Arles* [Paris, 1878]), in connection with his work on the Arles sarcophagi, observed that the same symbolic scheme had been used extensively in the context of the "Help of God" to the dying. Later work by Karl Michel developed this

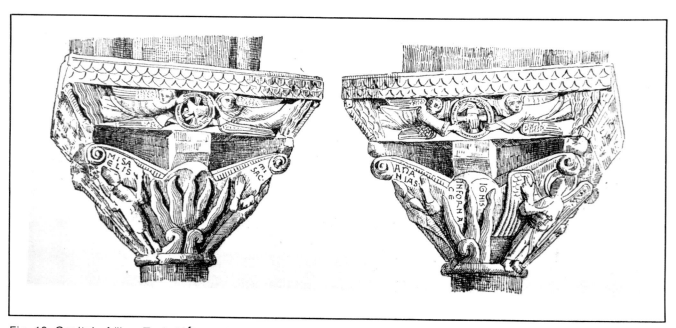

Fig. 10. Capital of "Les Trois Hébreux," Moissac (courtesy of Editions les Monédières).

study (see Karl Michel, *Gebet und Bild in Früh-christlichen Zeit* [Leipzig: Dieterich'sche Verlags, 1902]; and Françoise Henry, *Irish Art* [Ithaca: Cornell University Press, 1967] 1: 142), which has been disputed by Odo Casel, who regarded all of the decorative expression of primitive Christianity as mystical exaltation, an inner force that supposedly inspired the whole of this art. This opinion was confirmed and expanded by Paul Styger, note 3, who maintained that since these scenes were not confined to funerary monuments (as Joseph Wilpert [*Die Malereinen der Katakomben Roms* (Freiberg im Breisgau: Herder, 1903)] and Le Blant assumed, given the evidence that then existed), they should be taken in their historical sense, as reported in the Old and New Testaments, that is without regard for any symbolic significance or indirect reference to death. See Pierre DuBourquet, *Early Christian Art*, trans. Thomas Burton (London: Weidenfeld and Nicolson, 1972), p. 56.

5   Erich Dinkler, *The Age of Spirituality* (Princeton: Princeton University Press, 1979), pp. 399-401.

6   DuBourquet, p. 56.

7   The Joseph story can be found in the text of Joseph's Testament from *The Testaments of the Twelve Patriarchs*, "I struggled against a shameless woman, urging me to transgress with her, but the God of Israel my Father delivered me from the burning flame." See Gary Vikan, "415. Bowl with Joseph Scene and the Three Hebrews in the Fiery Furnace," *The Age of Spirituality*, p. 465, quoting de Jonge.

8   The only other nude example is a fresco lunette that was found in the catacomb of Vigna Massimi. A liturgical scene of an agape, which may represent the miracle of loaves and fishes, is the subject of the opposite lunette (Princeton Index 31 R76, CyVgM, 25, 2, A, B).

9   The Hebrew word for "angel" means simply messenger or envoy. Angels may appear to men in human form, as related in Gen. 18. It would be in keeping with this tradition that the artist could choose to represent him as another man. In the Eastern Orthodox Church this fourth figure is not an angel and not a man, but rather "Logos" (the Word).

10 Although it could be argued that the four-sided shape of the capital would lend itself to placing one figure at each corner or in the center of each face, in a similar composition on a nearby capital in the Cloister of Moissac, "Le Martyre des Saints Fructueux, Augure et Euloge," all three figures stand amid the consuming flames in an orant position on one face of the capital.

11 This symbolic use of the Dove to represent the Holy Spirit can be found in Matt. 3:16, Mark 1:10, Luke 3:22, and John 1:32 where the Spirit of God is said to have come upon Jesus after his baptism "like a dove." W. S. McCullouch, *Interpreter's Dictionary of the Bible* (Abingdon Press, 1962), 1:867.
The source of this symbolism can only be surmised but probably it lies in Jewish thought, scriptural and otherwise. Thus we have the 'hovering' of the Spirit of God in Gen. 1:2; the role which the dove played in the flood tradition (Gen. 8:8-12); the acceptability of pigeons and doves as bird offerings (Matt. 10:16).

12 St. Jerome stated that the youths were not men but eunuchs (Cabrol, V. 6, p. 2108). He may have been influenced by the charge given to Ashpenaz, the master of the eunuchs by King Nebuchadnezzar, who told him in Daniel 1:3-4, ". . . to take certain of the Israelite exiles, of the blood royal and of the nobility, who were to be young men of good looks and bodily without fault, at home in all branches of knowledge, well-informed, intelligent, and fit for service in the royal court; and he was to instruct them in the literature and language of the Chaldeans." Raymond Hammar, *The Book of Daniel Commentary* (New York: Cambridge University Press, 1976), p. 17.

13 Daniel 1:17, 19; 2:17, 49; 3:28-30.

14 Dr. Marilyn Chiat has suggested that this knob may represent a phylactery.

15 There is still dispute as to the meaning of the various words used here for the clothing. Behrmann suggests that the three articles mentioned were meant to represent the three items that Herodotus says were the characteristic Babylonian garments. It is possible that the three garments were articles of official attire, i.e., they had come to the assembly in court dress. *Sarbal*, the Iranian word in the Aramaic text, can be translated as trousers as well as mantles; tunics also is an Iranian word and also can be translated as turbans as well as trousers. Hats is translated from the Akkadian word *Karbellatu*, meaning helmet or bonnet. Gerald Kennedy, *The Interpreter's Bible* (Nashville: Abingdon Press, 1958), 6:402.

16 Walter Lowrie, *Art in the Early Church* (New York, 1947), p. 82.

17 Lowrie, p. 81:
But there is reason to believe that what attracted the Magi into the cycle of sepulchral art was a more trivial circumstance, namely, a formal likeness to the Three Children in the fiery furnace, which was one of the earliest subjects in the catacombs. The Magi, of course, were Persians; and in representing the Three Children the artists faithfully followed the Biblical description (Dan. 3:21): 'in their mantles, their hosen and their hats, and other garments.' That is to say, they wore the dress which is conventionally attributed to Persians: the Phrygian cap, a short fluttering cape fastened above the right shoulder, a short girdled tunic and tight-fitting pants. With better reason the Magi were dressed in the same way and ulti-

mately their number (which is not indicated in the Bible) was fixed at three, to correspond with Shadrach, Meshach and Abed'nego.

18 Kurt Weitzman, *The Icons: The Monastery of St. Catherine at Mount Sinai*, vol. 1 (Princeton: Princeton University Press, 1976), p. 81.

19 The box-type furnace can be seen in examples found in the Cemetery Pontianus, the Cemetery or Basilla of St. Hermes, the Cemetery of Protus and Hyacinth, and the Cemetery Domitilla, Cubicle II, as well as in many sarcophagi made before the sixth century.

20 Erika Dinker-von Schubert, "383. Wall Painting with the Three Hebrews in the Fiery Furnace," in *The Age of Spirituality*, p. 425.

21 Ernest Rupin, *L'Abbaye et les Cloîtres de Moissac* (1897 reprint ed., Treignac: Edition les Monédières, 1981).

    Face septentrionale . . ANGE(LU)S D(OMI)NI - ABDENAGO
    Face occidentale . . . . MISAELIS - MISAC
    Face méridionale . . . . AZARIAS - SIDRAC
    Face orientale . . . . . . ANANIAS - IGNIS IN FORNACE

22 Hans Swarzenski, "The Song of the Three Worthies," *Museum of Fine Arts Boston Bulletin* 56, no. 303 (1958): 47.

23 The full quotation from the Apocrypha Vulgate text of an addition to the Book of Daniel, coming in between Chapter 3, verses 23 and 24, is called "The Song of the Three" (quoting below verses 26-30) Swarzenski, p. 42:

> But the Angel of the Lord came down into the furnace together with Azarias and his fellows and he smote the flame of the fire out of the furnace, and made the midst of the furnace as it had been a moist whistling wind, so that the fire touched them not at all, neither hurt nor troubled them. Then the three, as out of one mouth, praised and glorified and blessed God in the furnace, saying: Blessed art thou, O Lord, thou God of our fathers, and to be praised and exalted above all forever.

24 Swarzenski, p. 42.

25 Milos M. Velimirovic, "Liturgical Drama in Byzantium and Russia," *Dumbarton Oaks Papers*, no. 16 (Washington, D.C., 1962), p. 352 and Louis Bréhier, *L'Art Chrétien* (Paris: Librairie Renouard, 1928), p. 359.

26 Velimirovic, p. 359.

Pre-Carolingian Concepts of Architectural Planning

W. Eugene Kleinbauer

The Plan of St. Gall in the Library at St. Gall is a unique and major monument of the Carolingian age (Fig. 1). Comprising five separate sheets of vellum sewn together and the whole measuring 30½ by 44 in. (77 by 112 cm.), it presents a design drawn to scale for a single monastery of forty buildings. Each building is drawn in red ink, with brown ink for explanatory titles defining the purpose of all the structures and the nature of their furnishings. The whole scheme was to measure about 213 by 160 m. It dates probably between 816/17 and 823. The fundamental publication of the plan is Walter Horn and Ernest Born's three-volume monograph, a monumental scholarly achievement of over 1,000 pages that is superabundantly illustrated.[1] It clearly informs us of the importance of the Plan in the Carolingian period. In the subtitle of the book we find the answer to its importance: "A Study of the Architecture & Economy of, & Life in a Paradigmatic Carolingian Monastery." "Paradigm," "master plan," and "prototype" are terms constantly repeated. They translate into the central thesis of the monograph: the Plan of St. Gall is a faithful freehand tracing of a plan worked out at the imperial court in connection with two reforming synods convened at Aachen by Louis the Pious in 816 and 817 to serve as a prototypal and authoritative guide for all monastic architecture in the Carolingian empire. The Plan of St. Gall is an official architectural statement that incorporates the official policies of the monastic reformers to standardize monastic life according to the Rule of St. Benedict and the realities of ninth-century Europe.

Space does not permit me to examine the validity of this central thesis. Suffice it to say in passing that I am not convinced by it, because the evidence for it is inconclusive.[2] Rather, I want to raise several important questions intimately related to Horn and Born's central thesis: Does the Plan of St. Gall represent an innovation in architectural practice in terms of providing an exemplar for future uses? Was architectural drawing of this kind original, or rooted in tradition? Is the Plan of St. Gall the first preserved or even recorded use of an accurate scale drawing to convey architectural concepts? And is it the first paradigmatic drawing of a group of buildings, or even of one building?[3] These questions may be posed independent of whether the Plan of St. Gall is an original drawing or a copy that traced a now lost *exemplum*.[4]

From the outset it should be stressed that evidence of architectural drawings in the pre-Carolingian Latin West or the Eastern Mediterranean is scarce. Both the scarcity of parchment in earlier centuries and the losses of original literary sources explain in part this phenomenon. Written sources, including *vitae* and tax records, provide clues but require close investigation for more data about the number and character of the drawings that once existed, and this is a task for future study.

The Plan of St. Gall is one of the earliest, if not the earliest, extant architectural drawings of the Middle Ages. Since it is well known that architectural drawings existed earlier, one question that arises is whether the Plan of St. Gall bears any points of comparison with pre-Carolingian drawings by architects, master builders, or draftsmen.

Architectural drawings are recorded among the Sumerians, Egyptians, Greeks, Romans, Byzantines, and Armenians. Evidence for the Sumerian use of architectural plans is preserved. Two statues of Gudea of Lagash (ca. 2150 B.C.) depict him with a drawing table on his lap, equipped with stylus and ruler, and on one of these tables (in a statue in the Louvre) a ground plan of a temple is engraved.[5] It is uncertain whether this plan is drawn to scale, though the ruler is finely divided accurately as if for precise measurements.[6] And allowance is made for the thickness of walls. From about the same time, clay tablets from Tell Asmar (ancient Eshnunna) in

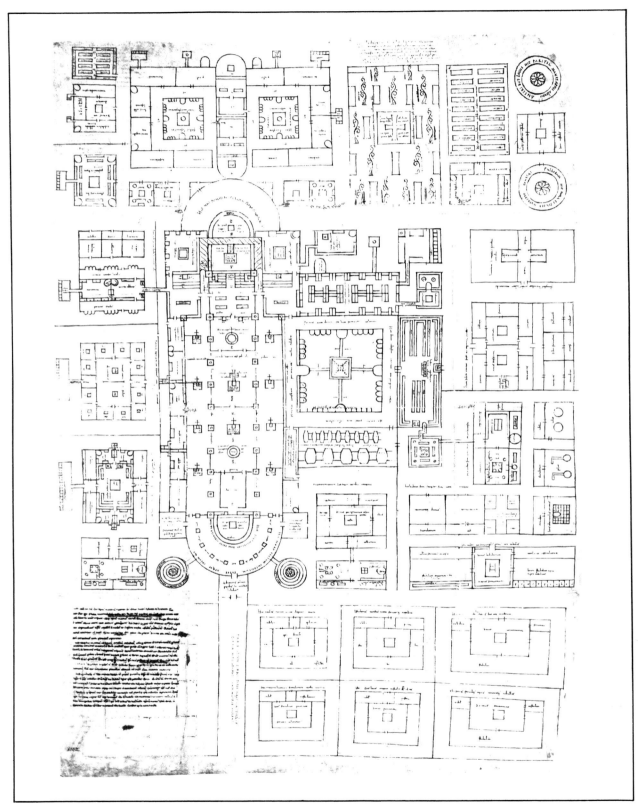

Fig. 1. Plan of St. Gall, Stiftsbibliothek Ms. 1092 (courtesy of University of California Press and Lorna Price, Walter Horn, and Ernest Born).

Iraq preserve ground plans that show the walls in vertical line projection and indicate their thickness as double lines, two features that characterize the church and a few other buildings on the Plan of St. Gall. The buildings on the Sumerian tablets are said to be ideal house plans.[7] If this interpretation is correct, these tablets provide the earliest, and indeed the only pre-Carolingian parallels to the ideal buildings on the Plan of St. Gall. Yet they lack the "blueprint" character of the Carolingian plan.

Ancient Egypt provides far more abundant evidence of architectural ground plans as well as elevations and even bird's-eye views (that is, drawings in which what is behind is shown above).[8] Preserved Egyptian plans are rendered mostly on flat limestone flakes (called *ostraka* in Greek), but a few plans on papyrus as well as on stuccoed tablets and

panels of wood also survive. As early as the Third Dynasty (twenty-sixth century B.C.), diagrammatic methods were used on a flake of limestone to convey building instructions.[9] Since this and other flakes were small, these working drawings never were drawn to scale. Perhaps the oldest preserved Egyptian ground plan on papyrus is the plan in Turin of the tomb of Ramesses IV at Thebes (twelfth century B.C.).[10] Originally measuring about 0.45 by 1.50 m., it was a linear drawing drawn only roughly to scale, made no allowance for the thickness of walls, and, in contrast to known Sumerian ground plans, combines a linear ground plan in vertical line projection and outline elevation in straight-on view. Thus the combination of vertical line projection and straight-on view found on the Plan of St. Gall is a traditional method of drawing. Although the papyrus plan gives

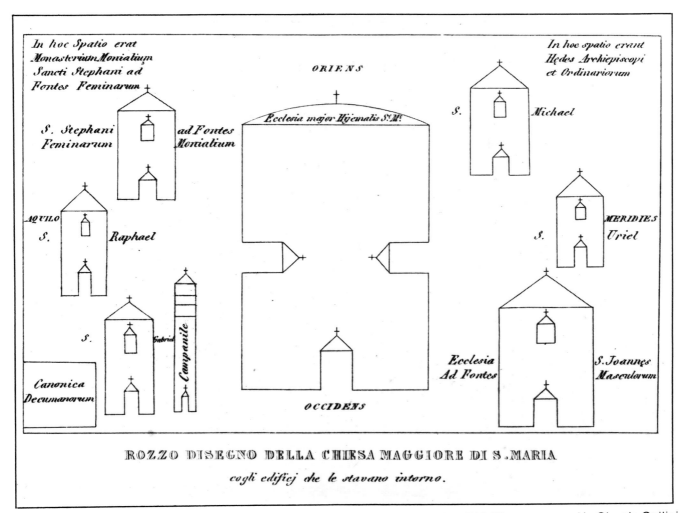

Fig. 2. S. Maria Maggiore, Milan, church compound, plan, originally drawn before 745 (?), as preserved in Giorgio Guilini, *Memorie della città e campagne di Milano ne' secoli bassi*, II, Milan, 1854, 196 b, plate (courtesy of the Biblioteca Ambrosiana, Milan).

measurements to the fraction of a cubit, it is a sketch plan that seems to have been taken from the tomb as constructed and measured, and drawn for some future use, like a modern drawing of record.

Perhaps the most pertinent Egyptian antecedent of the Plan of St. Gall is the red and black ink design on a white stuccoed board (11 by 9 in.) from Thebes, which has been ascribed to the Eighteenth Dynasty.[11] This is an architect's plan probably of a real, or possibly of a projected (rather than imaginary), estate. It is provided with minute measurements but seems not to have been drawn to scale. It shows a broad expanse of water, a park with a double row of trees, a square enclosure occupied by a tank, and some walls.

The Egyptians also prepared drawings only of the elevations of monuments. Elevations, however, were not necessarily a single exterior view from one side but more often than not combined a series of elevations, one for each important section of the plan, flattened out on the ground and not drawn to exact scale. The lack of scale characteristic of all Egyptian plans reflects the Egyptian attitude toward building. Proportions were matters of convention rather than problems of design and aesthetic sensibilities.[12]

The surviving archaeological and literary evidence for architectural drawings and models among the ancient Greeks is more difficult to assess, and hence is more controversial. It cannot be established that the classical Greeks made drawings or models drawn to scale. As Coulton has argued, the rules of proportion (what architects today call formulae) and the fixed conventions of classical Greek buildings made scale drawings unnecessary: "for, used within conventions, the rules not only allow a given effect to be recreated, and provide the architect with an easy means of calculating the required block sizes; they also allow a given effect to be predictably varied by changing the appropriate rule."[13] Thus Coulton deduces that for buildings the classical Greeks developed a system of planning based on calculation rather than on drawing.

No ground plans or elevations of Greek buildings are preserved, and there is no definite mention of them in Greek literature or building inscriptions before the Hellenistic period. Nor have any Greek instruments for technical drawing been found thus far. Moreover, Greek treatises on architecture were always based on actual buildings rather than on ideal plans. It is true that, according to some scholars, Polykleitos composed his workshop treatise known as the Canon (ca. 450 B.C.) before he cast his celebrated Doryphoros that embodies the fifth-century artist's belief in ideal proportions and the principle of symmetria. But this scholarly tradition pertains to the realization of proportions in sculpture and an ideal nature in man, and provides no proof for or intimation of the existence of architectural drawings based on ideal proportions or of ideal building complexes, as in our Carolingian drawing.[14]

Our understanding of ancient Greek architectural practice was furthered by a recent major discovery at the Temple of Apollo at Didyma. In 1979 Lothar Haselberger noticed finely etched lines on some of the podium walls encircling the adytum of the temple that cover an area of approximately 200 sq. m. as well as on the surfaces of the individual layers of the stepped platform of the building.[15] This discovery at a site long known yielded the most extensive and most complete set of plans that have come down to us in all of ancient architecture. The work of practiced draftsmen, including probably the master builder himself, these drawings consist of straight lines up to 20 m. long and circles whose radii extend as far as 4.5 m. Parallel lines, polygons, and subtending angles have been constructed, and distances were accurately subdivided. The drawing surface was originally colored with red chalk to make the drawings stand out. These drawings are plans of individual parts of the temple and its naiskos that were laid down on the wall and floor surfaces in their full dimensions (on a scale of 1:1) with the utmost precision. They are working drawings which were used to elaborate and refine the component parts of the monument in accordance with the master builder's aesthetic sensibilities, and they served as tentative tracings to guide the stonemasons. This theory is confirmed by minor but measurable discrepancies between the drawings of component architectural members and the actual members that were executed.

By the middle of the third century B.C., when the "rough drafts" at Didyma were made, each stage of change and refinement between such working drawings and the final products was aided by stones that were incised and, possibly, drawings on papyrus, parchment, whitewashed wood tablets, or flat stones.[16] It is virtually certain that architectural drawings originated no later than the end of the Hellenistic period, as Vitruvius' adoption of the Greek terms ichnographia, orthographia, and skenographia shows.[17] Vitruvius is here quoting from an unknown Greek source, and thus is not referring to a Roman innovation. But we do not know when or where in the Hellenistic period the Greeks introduced such drawings, or for what purpose. Were they scale drawings, working drawings, or diagrammatic drawings?[18] The discoveries at Didyma and other sites have not answered these questions.

The ability of Greek architects to make detailed scale drawings on papyrus has been questioned on the grounds of the limited size of the drawing area.[19] On a relatively small drawing area, a building of any size could be drawn only at a small scale, and details in plan and elevation could not be shown effectively. The same observation could be made about parchment in the Roman period; besides, parchment was then scarce. But if whitewashed board or large stone blocks were used, a much larger working area would have been available for drawings with far more detail, including dimensions and specifications.

Writing about 25 B.C., Vitruvius provides architectural information on actual buildings.[20] His text was originally illuminated; he refers to ten illustrations but may have included others that go unmentioned. All are lost. Perhaps they were diagrammatic—e.g., one showing how to set out a spiral volute with compasses. For all its technical detail, his account of the famous basilica at Fanum on the Adriatic coast was unillustrated.[21] His rules for temple design could be followed without the use of scale drawings. Yet he declares that an architect should be a skilled draftsman.[22] From his remarks on the nature of architecture in his first book he took architectural drawing for granted. Architectural drawings (ground plans) and drafting tools have survived from the Roman period, so that we can take Vitruvius at his word.[23]

A close pre-Carolingian parallel to the Plan of St. Gall is provided by the Forma Urbis Romae that the emperor Septimius Severus commissioned between 203 and 211.[24] This is an actual detailed survey map of the city of Rome on 151 marble slabs that were affixed as a unit to a wall of one of the halls adjoining the Library of Peace at Rome; originally it measured 42½ by 59 ft. It would have been available to the Carolingians; today it is sadly fragmentary. Unlike the Plan of St. Gall, it shows a group of buildings actually existing rather than paradigmatically conceived, but, exactly as in the Carolingian plan, it depicts them both in remarkably accurate vertical line projection and, in a few instances, in straight-on view. As we have seen, both are age-old methods of architectural drawing.[25] The marble plan also provides an antecedent for a group of buildings of all sorts drawn to scale—in this case, probably at 1:240 or 1:250 (i.e., 1/20th of an inch to a foot, compared with a scale of 1:192, which, according to Horn and Born, characterizes the Plan of St. Gall).[26]

Like most preserved Roman architectural plans, the marble plan is not a working drawing of the architect or draftsman but is a fragment of a cartographic survey of an established locality or monument. Other Roman plans are surveyors' plots.[27] Occasionally fragments of plans of Roman buildings were executed in mosaic or paint, and may originally have been placed in tombs.[28] An interesting example of this phenomenon is a fragmentary Roman bath ground plan in mosaic that is housed in the Musei Capitolini at Rome. This plan renders walls as solid thick lines (in tesserae) and gives the dimensions of the chambers in Roman numerals. Perhaps this mosaic copies an architect's drawing of an actual thermal establishment.[29]

Although the Plan of St. Gall uses single lines to represent most walls, double lines are employed for the walls of the church building and a few of the other major structures. Double lines were sometimes used in Roman plans (the above-mentioned bath plan in mosaic reflects such usage), and they appear in copies of *De locis sanctis*, a late seventh-century manuscript by Adamnan, abbot of Iona, giving an account of a visit by a contemporary bishop from Gaul, Arculf, who went on a pilgrimage to Palestine and a few other sites in the Eastern Mediterranean. The earliest manuscripts of Adamnan are ninth-century Carolingian copies.[30] When describing the Holy Sepulchre at Jerusalem, Adamnan reports the following pertinent observations about Arculf's "drawings": "We have drawn these plans of the four churches after the model which (as already stated) the holy Arculf sketched for me on a wax surface. Not that it is possible to exhibit their likeness in a drawing, but in order that the *monumentum* of the Lord might be shown, placed as it is in the middle of the round church, albeit in a rough sketch, or that it might be made clear which church is situated near or far away from it."[31] Arculf was recalling from memory his visit to the site and made diagrams not drawn to scale or with any dimensions. In one Carolingian copy of Arculf's diagram the monument is shown in vertical line projection, save the tomb of the Lord, which is rendered in straight-on view.[32] Adamnan's work also was copied in the ninth century at the scriptorium on the lake of Reichenau, where the Plan of St. Gall itself was drawn.[33] Whether these Carolingian renditions reproduced Arculf's plans faithfully or altered their character awaits future study. It may be noted, however, that strikingly analogous methods of drawing occur in *agrimensores* illustrations of the sixth century in Italy. In the Codex Arcerianus A at Wolfenbüttel, for example, one finds purely diagrammatic illustrations of solutions to patterns of land division.[34] The buildings represented in this manuscript are rendered in a simple linear manner or with pictorial conventions and are shown in ground plan or in elevation, with walls as simple thin lines or as thick lines to indicate wall thickness. Ground plans of streets, rivers, and geographic areas in outline indicate their relative rather than actual location in the landscape. These illustrations employ chorographic cartography, utilizing topographic vignettes for maplike representations. The linear diagrams call to mind the plans by Arculf.

So far, attention has been focused on preserved plans. What of literary sources mentioning architectural drawings? Do they clarify possible antecedents of the Plan of St. Gall? From the Eastern Mediterranean in the late Roman Empire we possess two pertinent texts describing an ideal church building. The first is the *Apostolic Constitutions*, an early Christian collection of ecclesiastical law *without illustrations*, which is believed to date from about 375 and is based in part on the earlier third-century *Didascalia Apostolorum*, written probably by a physician in north Syria in the third century A.D.[35] Here a church building should be oriented with chambers at the east end, the bishop's throne in the middle. The text even specifies where the presbyters, deacons, and laity should stand or sit, and that the congregation should be divided not only according to sex but also according to age groups. It is believed that this text was written not as an innovative master plan for church buildings to follow but in response to pre-existing architectural and liturgical practice.[36]

The second text is the brief unillustrated treatise *Testamentum Domini nostri Iesu Christi*, which was originally composed in Greek in the fourth/fifth century but which survives only in a Syriac translation made in the seventh century.[37] It was probably a private compilation and hence does not represent the official practice of the Church. This document contains detailed regulations on matters of ecclesiastical order and church building, and a complete liturgy. In a chapter called "How to Build a Church," it too describes the schematic features of an ideal church building. It begins: "I will tell you how a sanctuary ought to be." It goes on to specify that the church building should contain, *inter alia*, a forecourt with a portico running around it, a narthex for the catechumens, and for the exorcists, a *cathedra* at the east end of the nave, which is to be flanked by two aisles, a separate structure to serve as a baptistery, 21 cubits in length and 12

cubits in breadth; and a hostel nearby for the archdeacon to receive strangers, and a house of the bishop near the forecourt; a house for the priests and deacons is also mentioned. As in the *Apostolic Constitutions*, the position of the clergy is even noted. This work, too, is believed to reflect past building experience, rather than to have been composed as a paradigmatic account.[38] What is unclear, however, is whether the *Testamentum Domini* is based on existing church buildings or reflects a single existing source.[39] Inspiration from several sites and from liturgical practice is perhaps likely.

If there were multiple sources, this text provides an interesting parallel to the Plan of St. Gall, which, it has been argued, draws upon architectural features of a number of contemporary or earlier buildings at different sites. For example, the 300 ft. long nave of the main church is found in contemporary church buildings (e.g., at Carolingian Cologne Cathedral),[40] the semicircular atrium at the west end of the main church calls to mind ecclesiastical sites in North Africa (e.g., at Damous el Karita), Greece (e.g., at St. Leonidas at Corinth-Lechaion), and Merovingian villa design in Gaul (e.g., at Montmauran),[41] and the unusual detached round stair turrets may reflect Carolingian St. Riquier at Centula or, possibly, an Anglo-Saxon source.[42] Yet it is significant that all of these distinctive characteristics are not known to have existed at any single site. No evidence to date attests to knowledge of either of these early Christian texts at Aachen, Reichenau, or St. Gall in the ninth century; yet analogous texts may possibly have been available. But no such textual source, with or without illustrations, would have been needed by the creator and transmitter of the Plan of St. Gall, who has been identified as Haito, abbot of nearby Reichenau and bishop of Basel. The discussions about the reforms of monastic customs at the imperial synods at Aachen in 816 and 817 may possibly have provided him with the impetus to formulate and program the Plan of St. Gall. They easily could have set Haito thinking about the new arrangements required by the new decrees.[43]

Having surveyed early Christian texts describing an ideal church building, let us now turn to what is known of architectural drawings and other devices of draftsmen in early Christian and Byzantine times. Plans, sections, and models of buildings must have existed in both the Eastern Mediterranean and the Latin West in these periods. Writing on behalf of the Ostrogothic king Theodoric, in a letter to "Aloisius the Architect" at Ravenna, Cassiodorus provides the formula of what he terms the palace architect, presumably the royal State architect.

Cassiodorus advises the architect to study Euclid—"get his diagrams well into your mind; study Archimedes and Metrobius."[44] He goes on to state that "when we are thinking of rebuilding a city, or of founding a fort, or a general's quarters, we shall rely on you to express our ideas on paper," and that he (Aloisius) should act as director of all the building craftsmen in all trades. The drawings to which Cassiodorus refers are not further identified. What might they have looked like?

In his *De diversis fabricis architectonicae*, Marcus Cetius Faventinus, third or fourth century author of the West, refers to *ichnographia*, the plan; *orthographia*, "the elevation is the setting out of the proposed side walls and height"; and *scenographia*, "the perspective is the display of the façade and the whole building with the help of painting."[45] These terms were clearly inspired by Vitruvius and establish a tradition of Vitruvian compendia.[46]

Perhaps we come close to the diagrammatic character of drawings that have here been postulated for the Vitruvian tradition, at least in the Latin West, by the ninth- or tenth-century copy of the episcopal church of Santa Maria Maggiore at Milan, which was probably drawn before 745, and which survives in a seventeenth-century rendering located in the Ambrosian Library at Milan (Fig. 2).[47] The drawing shows the large episcopal church, which must have been an aisled basilica (though aisles are absent in the drawing) surrounded by two baptisteries, a bell tower, and, at the four cardinal points, four oratories dedicated to archangels. Showing these structures in a combination of vertical line projection and straight-on view, without any indication of dimensions or of wall thicknesses, this rendering may be characteristic of architectural drawings before the creation of the Plan of St. Gall, and stands in complete contradistinction to its detailed "blueprint" character. The Milan plan is generalized at best and unreliable in most details. The intention of its draftsman should, however, be kept in mind. Unlike the programmer of the Plan of St. Gall who intended to provide accurate measurements and specific information on furnishings, gardens with herbs, beer barrels, and the like, the creator of the Milan plan, presumably like nearly all other early medieval draftsmen, wanted to signify only selected salient aspects of a building or building compound. No wonder that when a medieval builder "copied" a prototype, he adapted only one or two of its major formal hallmarks, and usually its dedication.[48]

What of the Eastern Mediterranean? Procopius, the sixth-century biographer-historian of the age of the emperor Justinian, establishes that architects used at least ground plans. Writing in Greek, he refers to *schema*, which could mean a diagram.[49] He also uses *indalmata* and *skiagraphia*, which perhaps refer to nothing more complicated than a diagram or ground plan.[50] A passage in Heron of Alexandria (probably first century A.D.), as reported in the Constantinian period by Pappas of Alexandria, proves that perspectives or projected views of buildings were in use during the late antique period. Heron refers to *skenographikon* as "the suitable method of drawing images (or pictures, *eikones*) of buildings."[51] But these, too, were created for specific monuments. No evidence intimates that ideal plans were formulated. Indeed, no plans of any kind have come down to us. But although we may assume that some plans were drawn to scale (as, perhaps, in the case of the planning by Anthemius of Tralles and Isidorus of Miletus of the Justinianic rebuilding of the cathedral of Saint Sophia at Constantinople), we may doubt that any were intended as exemplars for future use.

The same would seem to be true of the *skariphos* or ground plan on paper of a cross-shaped church building that the fifth-century empress Eudoxia shipped to Gaza for the design of the cathedral to be erected there between 402 and 407 on the site of the recently destroyed Temple of Zeus Marnas.[52] This is reported by Mark the Deacon in his *vita* of Bishop Porphyry of Gaza, who fails to mention where Eudoxia got the plan. The plan had to have been sketchy and rudimentary. I suspect that it was inspired by the layout of the Constantinian Apostolorum at Constantinople, and if I am right, it was not ideal or paradigmatic.

Our knowledge of early Byzantine architectural practice was expanded by a recent discovery in the basilica of the Holy Cross at Resafa in Syria, a church dedicated in 559. A set of concentric lines was found engraved in the pavement of the nave, made on a scale of 1:1 for the construction of arches in the nave arcades of this church.[53] These drawings recall ancient Greek practice and point to a survival of such practice in the early Byzantine period.

In general, early Christian architects and master builders were executors rather than innovators of church plans, and they all seem to have worked on the basis of fairly sketchy drawings.[54] That is to say, the task of these persons was not so much to design and invent as to follow or improvise on the basis of accepted formulas, conventions, and past practice, which, we have seen, also was true of ancient Egyptian and Greek builders. Indeed, this generalization also pertains as a rule to early Christian and Byzantine iconography in the visual arts.

This observation about the tenacity of tradition is borne out by written sources, such as the sixth-century *vitae* of Saint Symeon Stylites the Younger and his mother Martha (died ca. 560), which allege that the plans of their church buildings were traced by an angel or were revealed supernaturally by the deceased saint, respectively.[55] The plan (*skariphos*) of the church of St. Symeon Stylites the Younger was drawn, of course, not by an angel but a person familiar with the church of Saint Symeon Stylites at Kalat Siman, which served as its model, and of which a master builder or draftsman may have made a diagrammatic sketch or two.[56] The *Vita S. Marthae* reports that at first a man called Angoulas had directed Theodore Apothetes, one of the Isaurian builders who had come to the region of Antioch in search of work, to follow his own design for a triconch chapel of the monastic church, but Theodore Apothetes soon thereafter left the scene and was replaced by a certain Paul, an experienced builder from Isauria, who finished the martyrial chapel.[57]

This article has referred to architects' use of architectural models.[58] Models of church buildings in early Christianity are represented in numerous apse mosaics in late antique Rome, Ravenna, and elsewhere, as well as in Byzantine art of the post-Iconoclastic period.[59] In early Christian and medieval Armenia, stone models of church buildings in the round and in relief sculpture were made as early as the sixth or seventh century.[60] Some are held by donors, others served as reliquaries or as *acroteria*, yet others were maquettes created by architects in their designing of actual monuments. The degree to which the model bears resemblance to the corresponding building varies widely; no actual scale model, however, has survived.[61] Nonetheless, the Armenian architect Trdat is said to have prepared a model for his reconstruction of the dome of Saint Sophia at Constantinople in the year 989, but whether it was dimensionally scaled is unmentioned.[62]

Scale models existed in antiquity, though exactly when they came into existence is unclear from the evidence. The Greeks might have used scale models in architecture since they made small models of siege machinery and artillery by about 300 B.C., but it cannot be demonstrated that architectural models made to scale existed before the Hellenistic period.[63] If architectural scale models existed, how were they used by ancient architects? In antiquity, it seems, they were made not in the planning process or as didactic devices for craftsmen to follow but to demonstrate architectural concepts to patrons,

especially in competitions.[64] Although Vitruvius disapproved of them, they were not uncommon in the Roman Empire.[65] Besides their possible use to show to clients, they may have been produced to be placed in an architect's tomb, or in the tomb of a person who had commissioned a temple or some other monument.[66]

Available evidence shows that, quite aside from the central thesis of Horn and Born that the Plan of St. Gall is an exact tracing of an imperial *exemplum*, the Plan of St. Gall provides the first recorded evidence (at least since ancient Sumeria) of an ideal plan by a draftsman for individual buildings as well as for a compound of buildings. Moreover, it is original in that the whole compound was drawn to scale. For the first time in Western or Eastern Mediterranean art, in the second or third decade of the ninth century, a drawing played a large role in conveying one individual's architectural concepts to someone else, in this case, from Haito, abbot of Reichenau and bishop of Basel, to Abbot Gozbert of St. Gall.[67] Ironically, however, Haito, the programmer (but not the draftsman) of the Plan, was not an architect or craftsman, so far as is known, and the Plan was never fully converted to stone at St. Gall.[68] The site of St. Gall accommodated a church not of 300 ft. (as drawn on the Plan) but only of 200 ft. when it was begun in 830. The Plan of St. Gall, in my view, was Haito's own personal guide to actual construction, and an original drawing rather than a copy of a lost imperial exemplar, as Horn and Born argue. It represents one of a number of Carolingian works of significant originality, without known precedent, in Merovingian Gaul itself or in the Eastern Mediterranean. It stands as an innovative Carolingian contribution to the history of Western art.

Notes

1 W. Horn and E. Born, *The Plan of St. Gall: A Study of the Architecture and Economy of, & Life in a Paradigmatic Carolingian Monastery*, 3 vols. (Berkeley, 1979). That the Plan of St. Gall is a drawing for an ideal site is reiterated by K. Hecht, *Der St. Galler Klosterplan* (Sigmaringen, 1983), pp. 304ff. The exact date of the Plan has not been satisfactorily established. Horn and Born, *Plan*, 1, p. 25, date it between 816 and 830, and suggest that the traditional date of ca. 820 might be retained. For the view that the architectural drawing and the accompanying inscriptions were not necessarily accomplished in a single, continuous campaign (as maintained by Horn and Born), see W. Sanderson, "The Plan of St. Gall Reconsidered," *Speculum* 60 (July, 1985): 615-32, especially 619ff.

2 Accepted by Hecht, *Klosterplan*, the paradigmatic theory of Horn and Born has been rejected by P. Meyvaert, review of Horn and Born, *Plan*, in *University Publishing* (Summer, 1980): 18-19 (Horn replied to this review in a letter to *University Publishing* [Winter, 1981]: 25 and 31, and Meyvaert responded in the same number, 31.) Others who rejected the theory are L. Nees, "The Plan of St. Gall and the Theory of the Program of Carolingian Art," *Gesta* 25, 1 (1986): 1-8; and R. E. Sullivan in a review of the Horn and Born monograph that appeared in *Catholic Historical Review* 67 (1981): 421-32, especially 428-29. For Horn's most recent response to his critics, see W. Horn and E. Born, "The Medieval Monastery as a Setting for the Production of Manuscripts," *Journal of the Walters Art Gallery* 44 (1986): 16-47, especially 46-47.

3 These questions have not even been raised in other studies concentrating on the Plan of St. Gall or in those dealing with it peripherally.

4 That the Plan is a copy of an earlier work has been seriously questioned by A. de Vogüé, "Le Plan de Saint-Gall: Copie d'un document officiel?" *Revue Bénédictine* 94 (1984): 295-314; and by N. Stachura, "Der Plan von St. Gallen—ein Original?" *Architectura* 8, 2 (1978): 184-86; idem, "Der Plan von St. Gallen: Der Westabschluss der Klosterkirche und seine Varianten," *Architectura* 10, 1 (1980): 33-37. Stachura's findings have been challenged by G. Noll, "The Original of the so-called Plan of St. Gall," *Journal of Medieval History* 8 (1982): 195. Noll accepts the notion that the Plan of St. Gall is a copy of a lost prototype, and he identifies the author of the prototype as Theodore of Tarsus, who is said to have drawn it in Canterbury (ibid., 236ff.). But Stachura's observations are cogent, and Noll is wrong: cf. F. Bucher, in *Journal of the Society of Architectural His-*

torians 43 (March, 1984): 96-97. An instructive survey of literature on the Plan of St. Gall during the past decade can be found in W. Jacobsen, "Ältere und neuere Forschungen um den St. Galler Klosterplan," *Unsere Kunstdenkmäler* 34, no. 2 (1983): 134-51.

5 J. J. Coulton, *Ancient Greek Architects at Work; Problems of Structure and Design* (Ithaca, N.Y., 1977), p. 52, Plate V, for the example with the engraved ground plan.

6 In this paper the following definitions of architectectural drawings are used: (1) *Scale drawings* are any plan, elevation, or section of a building or of a part that has been scaled and exactly measured so that it can serve as the self-sufficient guide to building. If the scale is 1:1, the drawing can be fully transferred directly from the parchment to the ground. (2) *Working drawings*, preparatory studies (plans, elevations, or sections) are executed during the process of designing a building. Drawn by the architect or master builder, they can control the broad components of a design but are not scaled or exactly measured. (3) *Diagrammatic drawings*, line drawings, including fantasy and paradigmatic sketches, which are schematic (not drawn to scale or measured) and which are devised by the architect or master builder for his personal use or to suggest general ideas to his patron, craftsmen, or the public. Modern architectural graphics are different from those under consideration in this study and include five general categories: (1) schematic drawings (my diagrammatic drawings), (2) working drawings (my scale drawings), (3) presentation drawings for the patron and the wider public, (4) large-scale shop drawings or templates for the execution of details, and (5) the drawing of record, for the finished building. For these modern categories, see R. Sturgis, *A Dictionary of Architecture and Building*, 3 vols. (New York, 1902), cols. 202ff., 207, 412, 1128. On these modern categories and the possible use of such drawings in the late Middle Ages, see F. Toker, "Gothic Architecture by Remote Control: An Illustrated Building Contract of 1340," *Art Bulletin* 67 (March, 1985): 67-95, esp. 70-71 and notes 15-16.

7 S. Kostof, ed., *The Architect; Chapters in the History of the Profession* (New York, 1977), p. 18, Fig. 5.

8 See, in general, A. Badawy, *Le dessin architectural chez les anciens égyptiens* (Cairo, 1948).

9 E. Baldwin Smith, *Egyptian Architecture as Cultural Expression* (New York, 1938), p. 232, who refers to this and other examples of flakes of limestone used in Egyptian architecture. Chap. 10 of this book, "Egyptian Architects and Their Methods," is still useful.

10 H. Carter and A. H. Gardiner, "A Tomb of Ramesses IV and the Turin Plan of a Royal Tomb," *Journal of Egyptian Archaeology* 4 (1917): 130-58, Plate XXIX. For an outline elevation, see a papyrus from Ghorab,

probably Eighteenth Dynasty (sixteenth century B.C.), in the Museo Egiziano at Turin (Kostof, *Architect*, Fig. 1), which shows the front and side elevations for a shrine. Drawn in black ink, these elevations were overlaid with a square grid in red that may have served to control the proportional inner structure of the design. This calls to mind the modular system that Horn and Born have worked out for the Plan of St. Gall, an important question that this paper will not take up. See also the Egyptian drawing of a small shrine, a work of carpentry rather than architecture, which similarly combines front and side elevations (Coulton, *Greek Architects at Work*, pp. 52-53). Bird's-eye views of Egyptian architecture also are recorded but were apparently far rarer than elevations: see N. de G. Davies, *The Rock Tombs of El Amarna* 1 (London, 1903), Plate XXVI; Kostof, *Architect*, p. 9, Fig. 2.

11 N. de G. Davies, "An Architect's Plan from Thebes," *Journal of Egyptian Archaeology* 4 (1917): 194-99, Plate XXXVIII, now apparently in the Metropolitan Museum of Art in New York. Another board surely showing more of the site was once attached to one side of the preserved board.

12 Smith, *Egyptian Architecture*, p. 233.

13 J. J. Coulton, "Greek Architects and the Transmission of Design," in *Architecture et société de l'archaïsme grec à la fin de la République romaine. Actes du Colloque international organisé par le Centre national de la recherche scientifique et l'Ecole française de Rome (Rome 2-4 décembre 1980)*. Collection de l'Ecole Française de Rome, 66 (Paris and Rome, 1983), pp. 453-70, especially 466. Cf. idem, *Greek Architects at Work*, pp. 51ff., 67, *passim*.

14 J. J. Pollitt, *Art and Experience in Classical Greece* (London and New York, 1972), pp. 105-10.

15 Consult the preliminary reports by L. Haselberger, "Werkzeichnungen am Jüngeren Didymeion," *Istanbuler Mitteilungen* 30 (1980): 191-215; idem, "The Construction Plans for the Temple of Apollo at Didyma," *Scientific American* 253 (December, 1985): 126-32. I am grateful to François Bucher and Wolf Rudolph for knowledge of this discovery and its publication.

16 Haselberger, "Construction Plans," p. 132, conjectures that each stage of refinement between the original "rough draft" and the final execution of the parts of the edifice was aided by the use of plans on papyrus, parchment, whitewashed wood tablets, or flat stones. No such plans on paper or wood have been uncovered at Didyma or at other sites, but plans on stones have been discovered—e.g., a scaled-down sketch of the pediment of the Temple of Athena at Priene on a block of stone that was later filled into the monument itself (ibid.).

17 *De architectura libri decem* 1.2, 2 (translation F. Granger, Loeb Classical Library). This is an important but problematical passage.

18 Vitruvius' term for perspective, *skenographia*, first occurs in Aristotle (*Poetics* 1449a18) in the literal sense of scenery painting, but Vitruvius claims elsewhere that some sort of perspective drawings were made as early as the fifth century B.C. For the Roman architect's use of this term, see J. White, *Perspective in Ancient Drawing and Painting*, Society for the Promotion of Hellenic Studies, Supplementary Paper no. 7 (London, 1956), pp. 43ff.; J. J. Pollitt, *The Ancient View of Greek Art: Criticism, History, and Terminology* (New Haven, 1974), pp. 236ff., 240-47, who concludes (p. 242) that Vitruvius took *skenographia* to refer to the representation of spatial perspective in the visual arts. But Vitruvius' words for ground plan and elevation have not survived in earlier Greek (Coulton, *Greek Architects at Work*, pp. 70-71). A. Petronotis, *Zum Problem der Bauzeichnungen bei den Griechen* (Athens, 1972), p. 17, has suggested that treatises written before Vitruvius sometimes included ground plans and elevations of the buildings they treated. For the possible Greek use of architectural models, see p. 70.

19 Coulton, *Greek Architects at Work*, p. 53.

20 E.g., *De architectura*, 5.1, 6.

21 Ibid.

22 Ibid., 1.1, 3. This insistence may go back to the fourth-century Ionian architect Pytheos (Coulton, *Greek Architects at Work*, p. 71).

23 See, e.g., G. Carettoni, A. M. Colini, L. Cozza, and G. Gatti, *La pianta marmorea de Roma antica* (Rome, 1960), pp. 207-10; C. Huelsen, "Piante iconograpfiche incise in marmo," *Römische Mitteilungen* 5 (1890): 46-63, Plate III; a marble votive plaque of the mid-first century in Perugia showing architectural plans, probably of a funerary monument and giving dimensions of the various rooms in figures (Coulton, *Greek Architects at Work*, Plate 6); the fragment of a Roman bath plan (Kostof, *The Architect*, Fig. 8). See also H. W. Dickinson, "A Brief History of Draughtsmen's Instruments," *Transactions of the Newcomen Society* 27 (1949/51): 73-83, Plate XVI. Cf. M. S. Briggs, *The Architect in History* (Oxford, 1927), pp. 42-44.

24 Consult Carettoni et al., *La pianta*, pp. 207-10.

25 See p. 69 above. this observation is also duly noted by Horn and Born, *Plan*, I, pp. 53-63.

26 Ibid., pp. 83ff. For the marble plan J. B. Ward-Perkins suggests a scale of 1:250 (in A. Böethius and J. B. Ward-Perkins, *Etruscan and Roman Architecture* [Harmondsworth, 1970], p. 567, note 6, while G. Gatti has proposed 1:240 in Carettoni et al., *La pianta*, p. 206). It must be stressed that the concept of 1:240 (or 1:192) is not Roman (or Carolingian or even medieval) but modern, meaning that when an architect today lays out a drawing at a scale of, say, 1:240, one unit on his drawing corresponds to 240 identical units on the ground. The base of this ratio is decimal, and the medieval architect could not have

expressed himself in these terms since the two basic units of measurement with which he worked, the foot and the inch, were internally divided not into tenths but into twelfths and sixteenths or into twelfths and twentieths. For this, see W. Horn and E. Born, "The 'Dimensional Inconsistencies' of the Plan of Saint Gall and the Problem of the Scale of the Plan," *Art Bulletin* 48 (September-December, 1966): 285ff., especially 286-87, 300ff.

27   For these, see J. N. Carder, *Art Historical Problems of a Roman Land Surveying Manuscript: The Codex Arcerianus, A, Wolfenbüttel* (New York, 1978), pp. 178ff. These other Roman surveying maps were diagrammatic in type, their squares drawn in grid-plan notwithstanding. Their scale, roughly 1:6,000, is fairly large, and thus all small detail is omitted.

28   Kostof, *Architect*, p. 31.

29   Carettoni et al., *La pianta*, p. 209; Kostof, *Architect*, p. 31 and Fig. 8.

30   For Arculf's description and four rough sketch plans, see Adamnan, *De locis sanctis libri tres*, in P. Geyer, *Itinera Hierosolymitana*, Corpus Scriptorum Ecclesiasticorum Latinorum, vol. 38 (Vienna, 1898); *Adamnan's De Locis Sanctis*, ed. D. Meehan, Scriptores Latini Hiberniae, vol. 3 (Dublin, 1958).

31   Has itaque quaternalium figuras ecclesiarum iuxta exemplar quod mihi, ut superius dictum est, sanctus Arculfus in paginola figurauit cerata depinximus, non quod possit earum similitudo formari in pictura sed ut Dominicum monumentum licit tali uili figuratione in medietate rotundae eclesiae constitutum monstretur aut quae huic propior ecclesia uel quae eminus posita declaretur. (Meehan, ed., *Adamnan's De Locis Sanctis*, pp. 46-47 for the Latin text and English translation.)

32   E.g., the Carolingian copy in Vienna, Nationalbibliothek cod. 458, fol. 4v, attributed by Meehan, *De locis sanctis*, p. 30 (and Plate opposite p. 30) to Salzburg about the middle of the ninth century.

33   Zurich, Zentralbibliothek, Codex Rheinaugiensis 73, redrawn by Walafrid Stabo (died 849). Horn and Born, *Plan*, 1, reproduce the four Arculf plans in the Zurich manuscript: Figs. 41 (fol. 5r), 42 (fol. 9v), 43 (fol. 9r), and 44 (fol. 18v). Horn and Born do not cite the copy of Adamnan in Vienna (see the preceding note), or two other Carolingian copies: Paris, Bibliothèque Nationale, MS lat. 13048, from Corbie), and Brussels, Bibliothèque royale, MS 3921-22, from Stavelot. See further in Meehan, *De locis sanctis*, pp. 30ff.; C. Heitz, *L'architecture religieuse carolingienne* (Paris, 1980), p. 212, Figs. 167-68.

34   See Carder, *Codex Arcerianus*, pp. 36ff., *passim*.

35   F. L. Cross and E. A. Livingstone, eds., *The Oxford Dictionary of the Christian Church*, 2nd ed. (Oxford, 1974), pp. 75-76, with bibliography (the *Apostolic Constitutions*), p. 401, with bibliography (the *Didascalia Apostolorum*). An English translation of sections of the text of the *Apostolic Constitutions* that

deal with the design of church buildings can be found in C. Mango, *The Art of the Byzantine Empire, 312-1453* (Englewood Cliffs, N.J., 1972), p. 24.

36   C. H. Kraeling, ed., *Gerasa; City of the Decapolis* (New Haven, 1938), pp. 175-84.

37   *Oxford Dictionary of the Christian Church*, p. 1353, with bibliography. For an English translation of the pertinent passages, see Mango, *Art*, pp. 25ff.

38   Kraeling, ed., *Gerasa*, pp. 175-84.

39   No preserved church ruin in Syria corresponds in all respects to the descriptions in this text or in the *Apostolic Constitutions*.

40   Horn and Born, *Plan*, 1, pp. 187, 213, Fig. 172; Heitz, *L'architecture*, pp. 87-93, *passim*.

41   Horn and Born, *Plan*, 1, pp. 204-6. These parallels are not exact, as has been pointed out by C. B. McClendon, *The Imperial Abbey of Farfa; Architectural Currents of the Early Middle Ages* (New Haven, 1987), p. 161, note 78.

42   Horn and Born, *Plan*, 1, pp. 206ff., adduce the stair turrets at San Vitale at Ravenna. But an Anglo-Saxon source is suggested by the round tower at Schänis, as proposed by F. Bucher, in *Journal of the Society of Architectural Historians* 43 (March, 1984): 96f. From the outset St. Riquier at Centula featured, presumably, six circular turrets when it was built 790-99, but they were incorporated into the body of the church rather than being detached elements.

43   See Horn and Born, *Plan*, 1, pp. 20ff., for the point of view that the Plan of St. Gall is related to the monastic reform movement. This contention is found in scholarship that is nearly a century old. But it has not met with widespread acceptance. See now E. A. Segal, "The Plan of Saint Gall and the Monastic Reform Councils of 816 and 817," *Cuyahoga Review* 1 (1983): 57-71, who throws this theory into serious doubt. A major source of our knowledge of the synod of 816 is the commentary of the *Statuta Murbacensia*, whose text is now generally attributed to Haito. Segal contends that the opinions in this document are always in accord with the layout of the Plan of St. Gall. He goes on to maintain that the partially traced background of the Plan that Stachura demonstrated (see note 4 supra) is best explained by the supposition that Haito made a prototypical plan and from this exemplar undertook a few modifications for transmission to the abbot of St. Gall in the preserved Plan of St. Gall.

44   Cassiodorus, *Variae*, 7.5 *The Letters of Cassiodorus, being a Condensed Translation of the Variae Epistolae of Magnus Aurelius Cassiodorus Senator*, trans. T. Hodgkin (London, 1886), p. 323. Cf. Briggs, *Architect in History*, pp. 47-50.

45   See H. Plommer, *Vitruvius and Later Roman Building Manuals* (Cambridge, 1973), especially pp. 40-41.

46   For Vitruvius' use of these Greek terms, see Coulton, *Greek Architects at Work*, pp. 68-71. See also p. 70

supra. For the survival of Vitruvius in the later Roman period and the Middle Ages, see H. Koch, *Vom Nachleben des Vitruv,* Deutsche Beiträge zur Altertumswissenschaft, 4 (Baden-Baden, 1951); C. H. Krinsky, "Seventy-eight Vitruvius Manuscripts," *Journal of the Warburg and Courtauld Institutes* 30 (1967): 36-70, for Carolingian copies with illustrations; B. Bischoff, "Die Ueberlieferung der technischen Literatur," in *Artigianato e tecnica nella società dell'alto medioevo occidentale,* Settimane di studio del Centro italiano di studi sull'alto medioevo, 18, part 2 (Spoleto, 1971), pp. 267-96, Plates I-IX; K. J. Conant, "The After-life of Vitruvius in the Middle Ages," *Journal of the Society of Architectural Historians* 27 (1968): 33-38; C. Heitz, "Vitruve et l'architecture du haut moyen-âge," in *La cultura antica nell'Occidente latino dal VII all'XI secolo,* Settimane di studio del Centro italiano di studi sull' alto medioevo, 22 (Spoleto, 1975), pp. 725-57, Plates I-XIV; G. Scaglia, "A Translation of Vitruvius and Copies of Late Antique Drawings in Buonaccorso Ghiberti's Zibaldone," *Transactions of the American Philosophical Society* 69, 1 (1979): 1-30, especially 13ff. for Carolingian copies.

47 P. Verzone, "Les églises du haut moyen-âge et le culte des anges," in P. Francastel, ed., *L'art mosan* (Paris, 1953), pp. 71-80, Plate IX (my Fig. 2). Compare the *Iconographia Rateriana,* a drawing of Verona, probably of the mid-tenth century (now lost but recorded in later copies), which shows a combination of medieval with surviving classical monuments: C. Cipolla, "L'antichissima iconografia di Verona, secondo una copia inedita," *Atti del Academia Lincei, Memorie,* ser. 5, 8 (1903): 49-60; B. Ward-Perkins, *From Classical Antiquity to the Middle Ages: Urban Public Building in Northern and Central Italy A.D. 300-850* (Oxford, 1984), pp. 225-28, Fig. 4.

48 As demonstrated by R. Krautheimer, "An 'Introduction to an Iconography of Medieval Architecture,'" *Journal of the Warburg and Courtauld Institutes* 5 (1942): 1-38. For the problem of the nature of medieval drawings of picture cycles and individual paintings—these seem to have been outline drawings—see E. Kitzinger, "The Role of Miniature Painting in Mural Decoration," in: *The Place of Book Illumination in Byzantine Art* (Princeton, 1975), pp. 99ff., especially 109ff.

49 *De aedificiis,* 1.1, 32, 35. Vitruvius uses *schema* for plan (*De architectura,* 1.6, 12). Cf. Pollitt, *Ancient View of Greek Art,* pp. 258ff., on the Greek and Roman use of this term (a general term for "design" or "format").

50 *De aedificiis,* 1.1, 24 (*indalmata*), 2.3, 13 (*skiagraphia*). Cf. G. Downey, "Byzantine Architects: Their Training and Methods," *Byzantion* 18 (1946-48): 115. Procopius also uses *ektopoma* to mean some kind of representation by means of a drawing or perhaps a model (*De aedificiis,* 2.3-8 and 1.1, 22). Scale models could have existed in the early Byzantine period since they are attested in the Roman period, when they were used by architects to convey their ideas to their patrons: Coulton, *Greek Architects at Work,* p. 72 and note 13 supra. For *skiagraphia* in ancient usage, see Pollitt, *Ancient View of Greek Art,* pp. 248ff. For examples of its usage in the Byzantine world, see Mango, *Art,* pp. 17, 48 note 136, 211.

51 Downey, "Byzantine Architects:" 105ff., 111, and especially 115 ff.; idem, "Pappas of Alexandria on Architectural Studies," *Isis* 38 (1948): 197-200. Constantine of Rhodes in the second quarter of the tenth century uses the term *problema,* which may imply a perspective (Downey, "Byzantine Architects:" 116). For an example of carefully measured drawings of architectural elements such as pendentives, see the codex in Istanbul copied from earlier mathematical manuscripts in the eleventh or twelfth century: E. M. Bruins, *Codex Constantinopolitanus Palatii Veteris no. 1,* 3 vols. (Leiden, 1964), fols. 46r and 51r to 52r, *passim* (reproduced in vol. 2).

52 Mark the Deacon, *Vita Porphyrii,* ed. H. Grégoire and M. A. Kugener (Paris, 1930), chap. 75ff.; English translation in Mango, *Art,* pp. 30-32. The *architekton* Rufinus of Antioch is reported as having marked the outline (*thesis*) of the plan on the ground with chalk (ibid). Cf. p. 70 infra.

53 See I. Bayer, "Architekturzeichnungen auf dem Boden der Basilika," in T. Ulbert, *Die Basilika des Heiligen Kreuzes in Resafa-Sergiupolis,* Deutsches Archäologisches Institut, Resafa II (Mainz am Rhein, 1986), pp. 155-56, Fig. 73, Plate 14, and foldout plan I. I am grateful to Oleg Grabar for bringing this discovery to my attention.

54 Mango, *Byzantine Architecture,* p. 27. For a major exception to the statement about lack of originality in early Christian architecture, see W. Eugene Kleinbauer, "The Double-Shell Tetraconch Building at Perge in Pamphylia and the Origin of the Architectural Genus," *Dumbarton Oaks Papers* 41 (1987): 277-293, where it is held that the double-shell building plan was a Constantinian innovation of great originality. For architects in the pre-Iconoclastic period, see Downey, "Byzantine Architects:" 99-118. For later Byzantine architects, see A. Petronotis, "Der Architekt in Byzanz," in *Bauplanung und Bautheorie der Antike: Diskussionen zur archäologischen Bauforschung* 4 (Berlin, 1984): 329-343. For medieval architects, see Briggs, *Architect in History,* pp. 53ff.; Kostof, *Architect,* pp. 59-95; F. Bucher, "Medieval Architectural Design Methods, 800-1560," *Gesta* 11, 2 (1972): 37ff.

55 Mango interprets these texts in his "Isaurian Builders," in *Polychronion: Festschrift Franz Dölger zum 75. Geburtstag,* ed. P. Wirth (Heidelberg, 1966), pp. 359ff. Cf. idem, *Byzantine Architecture,* pp. 27ff. Compare the account of Procopius, *De aedificiis* 2.3, 2-6, of the Alexandrian master builder Chryses being advised in a dream how to dam up the river in the

gorge at Dara in Mesopotamia before it reached the city.

56 For the excavations at the monastery church of St. Symeon Stylites the Younger, see W. Z. Djobadze, *Archaeological Investigations in the Region West of Antioch-on-the-Orontes*, Forschungen zur Kunstgeschichte und christlichen Archäologie, 13 (Wiesbaden, 1986).

57 *Vita S. Marthae*, as translated by Mango, *Art*, pp. 126ff.

58 Here an architectural model is defined as a reproduction, usually much smaller than the building existing or to be constructed, though its scale can vary. In late antiquity models may have been made of a part of the building but normally, I believe, showed the entire building. And I doubt that architectural models exhibited all the accessories in detail (e.g., doors, windows, and decoration).

59 E.g., the apse mosaic of San Vitale at Ravenna. For this and other examples, consult E. Lipsmeyer, "The Donor and his Church Model in Medieval Art from Early Christian Times to the Late Romanesque Period" (Ph.D. diss., Rutgers University, 1981), pp. 57ff. For the question of the usefulness of the model for the reconstruction of a church building, see W. Eugene Kleinbauer, "Tradition and Innovation in the Design of Zvartnotz," *Proceedings of the Second International Symposium on Armenian Art 2* (Erevan, 1978): 35ff. (also available as a separate reprint, as well as in Russian translation).

60 P. Cuneo, "Les modèles en pierre de l'architecture arméniennes," *Revue des études arméniennes*, n.s. 6 (1969): 210ff.

61 A scale model may be indicated by Gregory of Nyssa in his Easter sermon, *In sanctum Pascha, vulga In Christi resurrectionem oratio III, Gregorii Nysseni opera, Sermones pars I*, ed. W. Jaeger and H. Langerbeck (Leiden, 1967), 9:256.

62 Stephen Asolik, *Histoire universelle (2e partie)*, trans. F. Macler (Paris, 1917), pp. 132ff.

63 Vitruvius, *De architectura* 10.16, 3; Philon of Byzantion, *Belopoeia*, 55.12-56.8, cited by Coulton, *Greek Architects at Work*, p. 72, note 68; cf. ibid., pp. 71-72.

64 So Coulton, *Greek Architects at Work*, p. 72.

65 See O. Benndorf, "Antike Baumodelle," *Jahreshefte des Oesterreichischen archäologischen Institutes in Wien*, 5 (1902): 175ff.

66 So Kostof, *Architect*, p. 31. From the early Middle Ages in the West only one architectural model is attested, a perplexing example recorded for St. Germain at Auxerre: J. von Schlosser, *Schrift-quellen zur Geschichte der karolingischen Kunst* (Vienna, 1892), p. 193, no. 602.

67 Haito had previously been involved in the reconstruction of his cathedral at Basel and of his own monastery at Reichenau: see Heitz, *L'architecture*, pp. 118-23 (for Haito's rebuilding of Reichenau)

and p. 130 (for Haito's cathedral at Basel). See also C. Wilsdorf, "L'évêque Haito reconstructeur de la cathédrale de Bâle (Premier quart du IXe siècle). Deux textes retrouvés," *Bulletin monumentale* 133 (1975): 175-84.

68 For the results of the 1964-67 excavations at St. Gall, revealing parts of Gozbert's constructed church and decoration, see H. R. Sennhauser, "Das Münster des Abtes Gozbert (816-37) und seine Ausmalung unter Hartmut (Proabbas 841, Abt 872-83)," *Unsere Kunstdenkmäler* 34, no. 2 (1983): 152-67.

Iberia and North Africa:
A Comparative View of
Religious Heterodoxy

Clara Estow

The purpose of this paper is to examine the works of three Muslim historians of the late Middle Ages to discover their attitudes toward the Jews. The authors selected, Ibn al-Khaṭīb (d. 1375), Ibn Khaldūn (d. 1406), and Ibn Marzūk (d. 1379), are arguably among the most prominent and respected men of letters of the Western Mediterranean during the late medieval period.[1] Their testimony is of great value in this effort to elucidate comparative responses to religious heterodoxy. Given the paucity of other sources related to this question, the views expressed by these distinguished authors are particularly important. Their accounts will be used, specifically, to shed some light on the subject of Muslim toleration toward Jewish minorities. Their views also will contribute to a comparative perspective, since the experiences of Jewish minorities among Muslims in the Middle Ages differed sharply from the pattern of relations between Jews and Christians in predominantly Christian states during the same period. The works of these historians help us understand some of the reasons for these differences. The history of the Jews in Iberia also will be briefly highlighted. There, Jews coexisted with a dominant Muslim majority in the kingdom of Granada and, for a shorter time, with Christian majorities in the rest of the peninsula, namely in Castile, Aragon, Portugal, and Navarre.

In the three principal Christian Iberian kingdoms—Castile, Aragon, and Portugal—the peaceful coexistence between Jews and Christians began to break down in the late fourteenth century. This was not the case with Granada, nor with Muslim states in North Africa. In these Muslim states during the last medieval centuries, Jews—sometimes persecuted, many times the target of pietistic and literary attacks, and always officially designated second class in the world of dar-al-Islam—were nonetheless spared the harsh treatment their coreligionists received in Christian Spain.

Political and economic factors are not sufficient to explain this difference. Many of the debilitating conditions that plagued the rest of the peninsula affected Granada and the Western Mediterranean with equal intensity, i.e., internecine strife, demographic shock, and international war.[2] Additional aggravating factors also were apparent: by the mid-fourteenth century, for example, Granada had an economy of dependency devoted to the cultivation of luxury products for export and relied on importing the larger part of its food supply. The small kingdom, vulnerable to fluctuations in international affairs, was a frequent pawn in endless rivalries and struggles for power in both Muslim North Africa and Christian Spain. Bad harvests, onerous taxes, frequent shortages, and the high cost of food and housing were commonplace. The Granadines, as vassals to the Castilian Crown, also were obligated to pay a burdensome yearly tribute, further straining their economy and depleting their gold supply.[3] North African states fared no better; tribal and dynastic disputes consumed the attention and resources of much of the region's inhabitants.

Despite the potential for instability inherent in these factors, investigation does not reveal anything approximating the virulent anti-Jewish developments documented in Christian peninsular kingdoms during the second half of the fourteenth century. In contrast, the Muslim populations of the Western Mediterranean and the kingdoms' authorities remained consistently tolerant of the Jews residing in their midst. In fact, Granada, Morocco, and Tunis become havens for Jews escaping Castilian violence during the civil war of the 1360s and the forced conversions of 1391. Jews settled in these lands in considerable numbers, and were able to establish a large, stable, and affluent community in several important cities. Their experience in Tunis stands out as one of the most successful.

The history of the Jews in Christian Spain, in

spite of auspicious beginnings, followed a different trajectory. The fate of the Jews has generated a large volume of comment, from sophisticated scholarship to propaganda. Divergent as these positions often are, they have one thing in common: They agree that the Jewish populations of the Christian kingdoms of the Iberian peninsula during the Middle Ages enjoyed a greater degree of well-being, relative physical safety, and religious autonomy for a longer time than their coreligionists elsewhere in the Christian West.[4] This distinction is not due to the absence of Christian hostility toward Jews in Iberia; rather, it stemmed from a particular and unique environment wherein, in spite of this hostility, cooperation and interaction between Christians and Jews prevailed. A crucial contributor in the creation of this environment was the Crown and its willingness to intervene on a regular basis, to safeguard the status it had conferred on the Jews, that of wards of the king (*homines regis; servi regis*) and part of his personal patrimony.[5]

The *Siete Partidas*, the comprehensive Castilian legal treatise of the late thirteenth century, reflected the often contradictory approach that constituted official policy toward Jews in Christian Spain.[6] The law code attempted to combine ecclesiastically generated objections against Jews with a practical recognition of their positive function in the expanding economy and society of late thirteenth-century Iberia. On the one hand, the *Partidas* defined the Jews as a necessary evil in Christian society. Although the law prescribed formal discrimination at a number of levels, it also guaranteed Jews their right to exist and to practice their religion in safety.[7] The code also assured the Jewish communities a truly extraordinary measure of autonomy and self-government. When these two aspects of the policy were in balance, the result was an atmosphere of tolerant discrimination—tolerance here being the absence of overt persecution. The scales, however, could tip in either direction; Jews could achieve a measure of fame, fortune, and influence impressive enough to become fixtures at court and be ranked among the kingdoms' grandees.[8] At the same time, they could be the victims of violent repression for reasons completely outside their control. The obvious ambiguity inherent in this situation made Jews rather vulnerable and created an atmosphere wherein anti-Jewish outbursts were a permanent possibility.

The conditional toleration of the Jews that the *Partidas* formulates, a balance known in Spanish historiography as *convivencia*, deteriorated during the second half of the fourteenth century into the increasingly open display of popular resentment and mistrust toward the Jews. At the same time, the

Crown neglected its mission to protect its wards, a neglect that was not always intentional yet always disastrous.

Several factors are cited to explain the breakdown of *convivencia*: the psychological and economic aftershocks of the first outbreak of the Black Death; the peninsular wars of the mid-fourteenth century; the hostilities unleashed by the Castilian civil war of the same period; the divisiveness and rivalries within the Jewish community; the divisiveness within the Church; and the rise of popular anti-Jewish preaching.[9] One tragic consequence of this deteriorating climate was the attack by popular mobs on Jewish quarters in several cities of Castile and Aragon in 1391, while civil authorities, powerless, stood by.[10] Growing anti-Jewish sentiment and the unforeseen complications brought on by the mass conversion of Jews to Christianity following the riots eventually crystallized into the conception of the Jews *cum* religious minority as an obstacle for the continued well-being of the state. In 1492 the Catholic monarchs ordered all Jews to abandon Spain. This expulsion decree, which had as its goal a society free of Jews, would appear, given the scenario just outlined, as the logical culmination of a series of historical developments. Given the realities of Christian Spain in the late Middle Ages, Christians and Jews could no longer coexist.

A different situation developed in the Muslim lands of the Western Mediterranean. In al-Andalus, or Muslim Spain, for example, the general course of the Jewish experience is reported to have been fairly smooth; after a long period of fruitful *convivencia* during the caliphal era, Jews continued to enjoy safety and prosperity in the small *taifa* (party) kingdoms that sprang up in the wake of the collapse of centralized rule in the eleventh century. The high degree of social, economic, cultural, and even political integration bordering on assimilation that Jews experienced during this period has been well documented.[11] The twelfth century, however, was not nearly as felicitous; it witnessed the devastation of the Jewish communities by the invading forces of the Almohads, whose religious fundamentalism and violence against nonbelievers were unique in the history of medieval Islam. The damage the Almohads caused prompted one of our contemporaries to comment, not without overstatement, that "Jewish life in the little that was left of Islamic Spain ceased to exist."[12] Many found their way to Christian Spain; others scattered throughout the Mediterranean. Nevertheless, the Jewish presence in Muslim Granada, the sole Muslim state able to survive in Iberia from the thirteenth to the fifteenth centuries, did not disappear. Records show that approximately one thousand Jews lived in the small kingdom by the end of the fifteenth century, most of them in the capital city. This community also had a degree of economic strength that made Jews the target of official greed, and the Jewish community of Granada produced individuals of intellectual stature comparable to the luminaries of the earlier Golden Age.[13]

As Bernard Lewis and others have pointed out,[14] Muslim hostility toward Jews in the Middle Ages was nontheological; the anti-Jewish polemic of the Cordovan theologian Ibn Ḥazm (d. 1064) was the exception, not the rule.[15] Muslim hostility toward Jews was also nonethnic; the world of Islam was, and is, a highly pluralistic one. Jews and Christians, as Peoples of the Book, were accorded a special status based on Mohammed's acknowledgment of the validity of Jewish and Christian revelation. Several passages in the Koran served as the basis for the formulation of a special type of agreement or pact, the dimmah, a permanent, nonrenewable condition by virtue of which Christians and Jews living in Muslim lands were assured their public and private rights. Those encompassed by the covenant, the dimmah, were officially recognized as a protected minority and were able to enjoy a high degree of autonomy in religious and communal matters. They also were able to benefit from an array of private rights, such as the freedom to travel, to engage in a number of professions, to buy, sell, and own property, to marry whom they wished (within the dimmah), to regulate their internal affairs, and to enjoy a variety of other freedoms denied to other groups of nonbelievers.[16]

However, dimmihs were denied political rights and the right to bear arms. This last restriction must have been interpreted rather loosely; we learn of Iberian and North African dimmihs operating military equipment and manning military posts and garrisons, and of Christian soldiers serving as the personal guards of Granadine and Moroccan sovereigns. The dimmihs also were subject to the inescapable yearly gizya or poll tax, an obligatory tribute paid by all adult males. This tax served as a permanent reminder of the intrinsic inferiority of the dimmihs with regard to the true believers. In Muslim Spain, for reasons not entirely clear, the term dimmih was applied exclusively to Jews; Christians were referred to as mū'ahidūn, or those who have sealed the pact.[17] The two terms, however, appear to be synonymous.

At different times and throughout the vast lands that comprised the Islamic world, certain rights and privileges extended to the dimmihs were amended or curtailed. They also were relaxed only to be reapplied with renewed vigor. Common examples of lax enforcement led to such violations as constructing houses taller than those of Muslims; selling wine and pork at Muslim markets; riding saddled horses—sometimes any type of horse as opposed to the more appropriately humble donkey or ass; wearing "nondistinctive" clothing—occasionally applied only to clothing that made dimmihs indistinguishable from the upper classes or, for that matter, from any Muslim when the rule was enforced more strictly.[18]

The three historians selected for analysis in this paper, Ibn al-Khaṭib, Ibn Marzūk, and Ibn Khaldūn, had the opportunity to experience and reflect on the implementation of these restrictions in the Western Mediterranean, and they have left some valuable impressions. Al-Khaṭib was the only European of the three; he was born in Spain, in Muslim Granada, where he spent most of his life, except for two periods of involuntary exile in North Africa. After a career in politics, public service, and writing, he died in Fez in 1375. Many of his longer works, including a history of Granada, are not known to non-Arabic readers, since they have not been translated into other languages. Ibn Marzūk was born in Tlemecen circa 1311 and died in Cairo in 1379. He spent some time in Granada and established numerous political and intellectual contacts there. Ibn Khaldūn was born in Tunis in 1332; he lived and worked throughout the Mediterranean basin, including notable sojourns in Morocco, Granada, and Egypt. The quality of his extensive writings established him as one of the leading lights of Muslim thought, a reputation that he enjoys to this day.

Ibn al-Khaṭib recorded several instances of strict implementation of restrictions against Jews in Granada of the fourteenth century. He reported that around 1320 Abul-Walid Ismāēl I revived sumptuary and other dress practices that had fallen into disuse, ordering all Jews to wear a distinctive symbol to set them apart from the faithful. This injunction appears to have been triggered by the Jews' refusal to pay higher taxes. They eventually paid the stepped-up assessments, a fate they preferred to walking around wearing humiliating garb. Ibn al-Khaṭib remarked that Ismāēl's reign enjoyed high revenues and a healthy treasury, a prosperity that the historian attributed to the financial contributions of the Granadine Jews.[19] Dress restrictions, however, must have remained in effect throughout the century or must have been renewed frequently because reports state that Jews were wearing a yellow emblem some fifty years after Ismāēl's order.[20]

Al-Khaṭib also wrote that at the beginning of the

fourteenth century, Mohammed III (1302-9) financed the building of the mosque and adjoining baths at the Alhambra palace complex in Granada with monies gathered from the *gizya*.[21] These two examples support the above statement that the Jews of Granada were able to reestablish a degree of economic solvency under the Naṣrid dynasty, the rulers of Granada from the thirteenth to the fifteenth centuries. Without some measure of prosperity, it is unlikely that the Jews would have been victims of two involuntary yet successful fundraisers within twenty years.

Al-Khaṭīb's treatment of the episodes where Granadine Jews appear contains neither censure nor surprise. They were recorded because of their newsworthiness. That the victims were Jews a comparable Christian account might have felt the need to justify, but the identity of the victims received no special notice here. The author assumed that the demands placed on them were legitimate, and that it was their duty as *dimmihs* to fulfill them. To Ibn al-Khaṭīb the lowly status of the Jews was a given, to be replaced and accepted without a trace of ambiguity.

The second writer, Ibn Marzūk, betrayed a higher degree of hostility, perhaps because of the openly propagandistic and self-serving purpose of his book. His *Musnad* was written in 1371 as a tribute to the Marinid sultan Abū l-Hasan (1331-51), who had been dead for twenty years, in an effort to secure the patronage of his heirs, the highly cultured rulers of Morocco.[22] The author, after years of political intrigue and failed conspiracies, found himself homeless and without a patron. The avowed aim of the work, however, was to record Abū l-Hasan's numerous acts of courage, wisdom, intellectual merit, piety, and largesse. We learn of his almsgiving; his leadership in the construction of new mosques and the repair and rebuilding of old ones; his founding of schools and academies; his frequent and generous support of pilgrims; his interest in building roads and fortresses; his effective management of affairs of state; his lowering of taxes; and his many other virtuous deeds. One additional virtue was Abū l-Hasan's refusal to employ *dimmihs*, in any capacity, no matter how impressive their credentials or how pressing his need. In fact, the sultan displayed such strength of character in this regard that he becomes even more exemplary.

In one example, Marzūk related how Abū l'Hasan victoriously entered Tlemecen where he learned of the existence of an eminent Jewish physician— who remains nameless. While in Fez, the sultan, in great pain from an inflamed cyst on his right elbow, sent for the Jewish doctor who, after a careful examination, made an excellent diagnosis and prescribed a cure. The sultan and Marzūk the author—who admitted to being well acquainted with the doctor—both felt the urgency to convert the doctor to Islam. Their efforts failed. Abū l-Hasan, Marzūk wrote, had no choice; he had to refuse the treatment indicated by the *dimmih* physician and continued to suffer bravely until Muslim doctors could be summoned.[23]

In a second example, dealing with tax collection, Ibn Marzūk cited the traditional proverb: "Secretaries and courtiers are the banner of the kingdom while its viziers are its crest" to highlight the fact that Abū l-Hasan never employed *dimmihs*, unlike contemporary Oriental rulers and the rulers of al-Andalus and the Maghreb of times past.[24] One of Abū l-Hasan's first official acts after the conquest of Tlemecen was to reduce taxes and remove Jews, Christians, and foreigners as customs duty collectors and inspectors. As a result, the *Musnad* stated, Muslims were no longer victims of the ignominy and ugliness of being searched, in and out, by *dimmihs*.

Marzūk continued the account, quoting a complete version of Abū Ishāq al-Ilbiri's infamous anti-Jewish poem composed in the mid-eleventh century.[25] In it the Jews are portrayed as inferior, undeserving, and inept, able to rise to positions of influence not because of their own ability but because of the wishes of misguided Muslims. Only in Granada of his time—the eleventh century—the poet adds, were Jews somebodies; elsewhere they were what they deserved to be, outcast dogs. Marzūk followed the transcription of the poem with a brief account of how al-Ilbiri's words inflamed anti-Jewish hatred and cost four thousand Granadine Jews their lives in 1066. The chapter concludes as the writer explains that he cited the poem in its entirety because it was reported to have been a favorite of Abū l-Hasan.[26]

Ibn al-Khaṭīb in his *History of Islamic Spain* also devoted a chapter to the aftermath of the anti-Jewish riot in eleventh-century Granada, presumed to have been caused by al-Ilbiri's words. Al-Khaṭīb cited only a fragment of the poem, treating the popular outburst as one unremarkable chapter in the history of Granada under the Zirids.[27]

The last author, Ibn Khaldūn, offered a somewhat more complex approach to the Jews. In his introduction to his universal history, *The Muqaddimah*, he used the story of the Jews to illustrate the view that groups are destined to fail when they are unable to maintain "continuous and firmly established royal authority."[28] To Khaldūn, Jewish history was the history of a people overpowered by a succession of invading nations until, at last, the Romans scattered them forever.[29] With regard to questions of character, Ibn Khaldūn accepted the "typical" view of the Jews as being of bad character and notorious "everywhere" for their insincerity and trickery. For Ibn Khaldūn, however, these qualities were not tribal, religious, or geographic. They were shared by all who had been victimized and had been forced to live under the tyranny of others; students, slaves, and children of overbearing parents also belonged in this category. Like some Arabs, he believed, the Jews often harbored delusions of grandeur, believing themselves to be superior because they once had one of the greatest "houses" in the world. Those days, Khaldūn observed, long had been over; since then, the Jews had suffered humiliation and indigence. For thousands of years they had known only enslavement and unbelief and during this time they lost the right to think themselves superior.[30]

Fischel and others have remarked on Khaldūn's frequent use of episodes from Jewish history and have pointed out that Jews are not singled out for censure, nor are they chided for not reacting to what were, after all, the inexorable and inevitable forces of historical change.[31] This analysis does not imply that Khaldūn concluded that all peoples are alike; the weaknesses of character that he attributed to the Jews would be sufficient reason to justify their inferiority and to confirm their status as *dimmihs*.[32] At the same time, it is clear that Khaldūn would not favor the persecution and oppression of the Jews, unless, of course, they became enemies of the Muslim faith, or behaved in any way detrimental to the true religion.

Khaldūn's *History of the Berber Dynasties* reflects a somewhat different tendency.[33] Unlike *The Muqaddimah,* in which groups were treated as abstract categories, this account deals with very specific individuals and events and offers little generalization. The historian devotes a chapter to recounting, as one would a fable, the rise and fall of a family of court Jews, the Khalīfa Ibn Raqqasa, in fourteenth-century Morocco. The family in question achieved great influence through politics with Khalīfa the Elder who began his career as wine steward to the crown prince. Khalīfa rose quickly and his power was such that the leading chiefs of the tribe, viziers, sharifs, and other dignitaries, courted him and his family. When the prince became sultan as Yusūf b. Ya'qūb (1286-1307), one of his loyal followers, distraught by the influence of this family of court Jews, succeeded in persuading Yusūf to eliminate them. The sultan then ordered the arrest, torture, and mutilation of most of the members of the family. The chapter ends with the following epitaph: "With these executions, the empire was delivered from a stain that tarnished it and a domination that vilified it."[34]

Ibn Khaldūn's hostile words are not merely a literary convention or an example of a formulaic refrain so common in much of Islamic prose of this period (i.e., Ibn al-Khaṭib's diplomatic correspondence[35]). The eminent author includes this condemnation for the benefit and comfort of his readers. Such comments helped explain acts of great violence not easily justified simply by appealing to conventional morality. Khaldūn could use the Jews as scapegoats; resentment toward the Khalīfas gave him the ideal opportunity, both literary and political, to attack Jews in general. Yet he chose not to do so. His attacks were restricted to this particular episode, a striking example of a Jew who forgot his subservient status. Once such an irregularity was exposed, it needed to be corrected. At the same time, Khaldūn's choice of language was quite purposeful. His description assured the reader that the offense had been avenged and the kingdom thoroughly cleansed.

Khaldūn did not relate any violent episodes against Jews in Granada during the same period, although we can assume that in the peninsular kingdom, relations between Muslims and Jews resembled conditions across the Strait.[36] We know that at least one Jew, the court physician Ibn Zarzār, had risen to a visible and important enough position to make him a potential target of resentment in much the same way as the Khalīfa family of Morocco. And, as in North Africa, Ibn Zarzār's prominence did not go unnoticed. One of his Muslim colleagues, the Granadine physician Muhammed al-Lajmī al-Saquīri, irked by Ibn Zarzār's fame, was reported to have written an anti-Jewish treatise, now believed lost.[37] At the same time, Ibn Marzūk pointed out that Jews in Granada of the second half of the fourteenth century no longer performed many of the official duties they had carried out earlier; he referred specifically to tax collectors.[38] There is disagreement as to the position of Jews at this time. To D. Corcos, the use of Jews in official capacities indicates their economic importance.[39] Stillman takes the view that the Jewish public servant is another example of Jewish marginality. They were so vulnerable, he argues, that they offered no threat to established vested interests. This vulnerability made them not only nonthreatening but also dependable, and ultimately discardable.[40]

The authors who are the focus of this paper showed no ambivalence with regard to the proper place for the Jews. At the center of the episodes recounted and the opinions expressed or implied was the necessity to reaffirm the superiority of the true believers over the *dimmihs* and to continue to assert this superiority as a self-evident truth. The relationship between the two groups should never be a relationship between equals. The Koran so prescribes it, and so it should be. The perceived unwillingness on the part of the Jews to comport themselves with the right measure of humility constituted a violation of this principle and, consequently, a just cause for their repression. Punishment, however, only applied to specific cases of offending individuals, and not to the entire group. The faithful Muslim reader was assured of the continued vigilance of responsible authorities who would act with dispatch should the need arise. It was precisely this clear and unambiguous position adopted by Islam, put in motion on several occasions with highly instructive value, that diffused resentment by making the limits well known. In the long run, it was the simplicity and clarity of this position that permitted an atmosphere of coexistence to prevail in Muslim states, long after it had disappeared in Christian Spain.

Notes

1   See p. 82 above.

2   For details of the history of the Islamic states of the Western Mediterranean, see Charles Emmanuel Dufourcq, *L'Espagne catalane et le Maghreb aux XIIIe et XIVe siècles* (Paris, 1966) and his "Les relations de la Péninsule Iberique et de l'Afrique du Nord au XIVe siècle," *Actas del I Simposio de Historia Medieval* (Madrid-Barcelona, 1973), 39-65; Roger Le Tourneau, *Fez in the Age of the Marinides*, trans. B. A. Clement (Norman, Okla., 1961); Georges Marçais, *La Berbérie musulmane et l'Orient au Moyen Age* (Paris, 1946); Jacques Berque, *Maghreb, histoire et sociétés* (Alger, 1974); Mohamed B. A. Benchekroun, *La vie intellectuelle marocaine sur les Mérinides et les Waṭṭāsides* (Rabat, 1974); Robert Brunschvig, *La Berbérie orientale sous les Hafsides des origines à la fin du XVe siècle*, 2 vols. (Paris, 1940-1947); E. García Gómez, *Andalucía contra Berbería* (Barcelona, 1976).

3   For Granada under the Muslims see Miguel Angel Ladero Quesada, *Granada. Historia de un país islámico (1232-1571)* (Madrid, 1969); Cristóbal Torres Delgado, *El antiguo reino nazarí de Granada (1232-1340)* (Granada, 1974); Ahmad Mujtar Al-'Abbadi, *El reino de Granada en la época de Muhammad V* (Madrid,

1973); Pierre Guichard, *Al-Andalus*, trans. Nico Ancochea (Barcelona, 1973); Rachel Arié, *L'Espagne musulmane au temps des Naṣrides (1232-1492)* (Paris, 1973), hereafter cited as *L'Espagne*; a slightly revised version appeared in Spanish as *España musulmana (siglos VIII-XV)* (Barcelona, 1982), hereafter cited as *España*.

4   The best comprehensive treatment of the Jews in medieval Spain is still Yitzhak F. Baer, *A History of the Jews in Christian Spain*, 2 vols. (Philadelphia, 1961), hereafter cited as Baer. In this paper the Spanish translation *Historia de los judíos en la España cristiana*, 2 vols. (Madrid, 1981) is used because it is an updated version of the original Hebrew and subsequent English editions; the Spanish version also contains a complete set of footnotes left out in the English translation.

5   The original formulation of this particular approach to the legal status of Jews in Christian society is attributed to St. Augustine. The earliest mention of it in peninsular sources appears in the 1176 municipal charter of Teruel; see Ramón Gonzálvez, "Las minorías étnico-religiosas en la edad media española," in *Historia de la Iglesia en España*, ed. Ricardo García-Villoslada (Madrid, 1979), vol. II-2, *La Iglesia en la España de los siglos VIII al XIV*, ed. Javier Fernández Conde, p. 519; Baer, 1:7.

6   The section of the *Partidas* devoted to the Jews is Book VII, Title xxiv, Laws 1-11 (7.24.1-11).

7   The most recent commentary on the Jews in the *Partidas* is Dwayne E. Carpenter, *Alfonso X and the Jews* (Berkeley, 1987); see also his "Jewish-Christian Social Relations in Alphonsine Spain: A Commentary on Book VII, Title xxiv, Law 8 of the *Siete Partidas*," in *Florilegium Hispanicum. Medieval and Golden Age Studies Presented to Dorothy Clotelle Clarke*, ed. John S. Geary (Madison, 1983), pp. 61-70.

8   Yusūf of Ecija, for example, figured prominently in several capacities in the financial administration of the kingdom of Castile during the 1320s and 1330s; Samuel Halevi of Toledo (d. circa 1361) was Chief Treasurer of King Pedro I of Castile. In the regions of the Crown of Aragon, Jews did not generally occupy high-ranking posts during the fourteenth century as they had earlier.

9   See Julio Valdeón Baruque, *Los judíos de Castilla y la revolución Trastámara* (Valladolid, 1968).

10 Philippe Wolff, in his study of the anti-Jewish riots of Barcelona suggests that economic and social conditions, not just anti-Semitism, must be taken into account as strong motivating factors in mob violence; see his "The 1391 Pogrom in Spain. Social Crisis or Not?" *Past and Present* 50 (1971): 4-18. Angus Mackay reaches similar conclusions in his analysis of several Castilian uprisings of the fifteenth century: "Popular Movements and Pogroms in Fifteenth-Century Castile," *Past and Present* 55 (1972): 33-67.

11 David Wasserstein, *The Rise and Fall of the Party-Kings. Politics and Society in Islamic Spain 1002-1086* (Princeton, 1985), pp. 190-223.

12 Norman A. Stillman, *The Jews of Arab Lands. A History and Source Book* (Philadelphia, 1979), p. 61.

13 The term Golden Age of Jewish culture in Iberia has been used to refer to the cultural achievement of Jews living under Islam beginning in the eleventh century and coinciding with the establishment of the *taifa* or party kingdoms of the note above; see Bernard Lewis, "The Pro-Islamic Jews," in his *Islam in History: Ideas, Men and Events in the Middle East* (London, 1973), pp. 123-37, 315-17.

14 B. Lewis, *The Jews of Islam* (London, 1984), pp. 3ff.

15 For a complete edition and critique of Ibn Ḥazm's theological work *Fisal*, see Miguel Asín Palacios, *Abenházam de Córdoba y su Historia crítica de las ideas religiosas*, 5 vols. (Madrid, 1927-32). For the polemic against the Jews see 2:210-392.

16 The rights of *dimmihs* are examined in Antoine Fattal, *Le statut légal des non-musulmans en pays d'Islam* (Beirut, 1958), hereafter cited as Fattal.

17 *España*, p. 186; Fattal, p. 73.

18 Fattal, pp. 101ff.

19 *L'Espagne*, p. 215. Fattal states that Ismaël's dress restrictions imposed on the Jews followed the example of his Christian neighbors, p. 108.

20 Fattal, p. 108; *L'Espagne*, p. 330.

21 *España*, p. 75.

22 Ibn Marzūq (Marzuk), *El Musnad: Hechos memorables de Abu L-Hasan, Sultán de los Benimerines*, trans. and ed. Maria J. Viguera (Madrid, 1977), hereafter cited as *Musnad*.

23 *Musnad*, p. 315.

24 *Musnad*, p. 236.

25 An English translation of the poem appears in Stillman, pp. 214-16. For an analysis of this poem and other works on the Jews see Moshe Perlmann, "Eleventh Century Andalusian Authors on the Jews of Granada," in *Medieval Jewish Life*, ed. Robert Chazan (New York, 1976); and his "Polemics between Islam and Judaism," in *Religion in a Religious Age*, ed. S. D. Goitein (Cambridge, Mass., 1974), 103-38.

26 For the complete text of the poem see *Musnad*, pp. 312-14.

27 *Islamische Geschichte Spaniens*, German translations and edition of al-Khaṭīb's *Kitāb A'māl al-A'lām*, trans. Wilhem Hoenerbach (Zurich and Stuttgart, 1970), pp. 419-23.

28 Ibn Khaldūn, *The Muqaddimah. An Introduction to History*, trans. Franz Rosenthal, 2nd ed., 3 vols. (Princeton, 1980), hereafter cited as *Muq*. The bibliography on Ibn Khaldūn is enormous; for a large sample see Aziz Al-Azmeh, *Ibn Khaldūn in Modern Scholarship. A Study in Orientalism* (London, 1981), 231-318. For his role in the development of North African historiography see Maya Shatzmiller, *L'Historiographie Mérinide. Ibn Khaldūn et ses contemporains* (Leiden, 1982).

29 *Muq*. 1:334; 1:473-76.

30 *Muq*. 1:244-45.

31 Walter Fischel, *Ibn Khaldūn in Egypt* (Berkeley, 1967), p. 139. Kalman Bland, "An Islamic Theory of Jewish History: The Case of Ibn Khaldūn," in *Ibn Khaldūn and Islamic Ideology* (Leiden, 1984), pp. 37-45.

32 *Muq*. 3:305-6.

33 Ibn Khadoun (Khaldūn), *Histoire des Berbères et des dynasties musulmanes de l'Afrique Septentrionale*, trans. M. le Baron de Slane, 4 vols. (Alger, 1852-56).

34 Ibid., 4:167-68.

35 Ibn al-Khaṭīb, Lisan al-din, *Correspondencia diplomática entre Granada y Fez (siglo XIV). Extractos de la "Raihana alcuttab" de Lisaneddin abenaljatib el Andalosi*, ed. M. Gaspar Remiro (Granada, 1916).

36 On the Jewish communities of North Africa see H. Z. J. W. Hirschberg, *A History of the Jews in North Africa* (Leiden, 1974); David Corcos, "The Jews of Morocco under the Marinides," *Jewish Quarterly Review*, n.s. 54 (1964): 271-78; 55 (1964-65): 55-81, 137-50.

37 *L'Espagne*, p. 333, and n. 6.

38 *Musnad*, p. 236.

39 See note 36 above, 55 (1964-65): 139-40.

40 Stillman, p. 78; Baer believes that Jews can be truly safe only in their own homeland.

Prostitution of Muslim Women
in the Kingdom of Valencia:
Religious and Sexual Discrimination
in a Medieval Plural Society

Mark D. Meyerson

During the medieval period religiously plural societies were structured in such a way as to maintain the political dominance and reflect the professed theological superiority of the group in power. Religious minorities, therefore, often were deliberately excluded from positions of political power and assigned specific functions in the economy. Minority groups expected as much and desired little more than the right to practice their religion and govern their communities in accordance with their own laws and traditions. However, the minorities' powerlessness sometimes left them vulnerable to forms of exploitation that were far more dehumanizing than the accustomed political and economic subjection. This paper will focus on one such form of exploitation—the prostitution of Muslim women in the Christian kingdom of Valencia during the late fifteenth and early sixteenth centuries. Yet to interpret this state of affairs solely as a result of the policy of the majority is to oversimplify a complex interchange between religious groups and to underestimate the resilience of the minority's distinctive social structures. Through an analysis of the laws found in Valencia's *Furs* and *Aureum opus,* of the ordinances of the king and the royal bailiffs, and of additional archival documentation that sheds considerable light on the internal life of the Muslim minority, I will show that the sexual exploitation of minority women was as much a consequence of their minority culture's having placed them in a vulnerable position as it was the result of the laws and institutions of the ruling majority.

The kingdom of Valencia had a Muslim population, known as the Mudéjars, which ranged in size from eighty percent of the total just after the Christian reconquest of 1238 to thirty percent in

the late fifteenth century.[1] With such a large Muslim population playing a diversified role in the Valencian economy, frequent contact between Muslims and Christians was unavoidable.[2] Although Valencia's kings viewed Muslim-Christian economic interaction favorably, because it redounded to the kingdom's prosperity, they had some misgivings about the social relations between Muslims and Christians who mingled inevitably in the workshop and the marketplace.

Fernando II, whose reign (1479-1516) defines the chronological scope of my research, was not unusual in this respect. He and the ecclesiastical authorities, especially the Inquisitors, were of the opinion that comradeship between Christians and Muslims was a moral evil and led to the corruption of Christians. Consequently, Fernando reiterated the discriminatory legislation of his predecessors, which, for instance, demanded that Muslims wear special blue garb to make them distinguishable from Christians, or required Muslims to lodge in special royal inns (*fonduks*) and drink in royal taverns designed to segregate them.[3] Although such laws were not consistently enforced, and although a substantial portion of the Christian populace did not agree with the king that Muslims should be segregated, royal and ecclesiastical fears were that the social mingling of Muslims and Christians was somehow conducive to the moral debasement of the latter. Such fears were sustained when members of both faiths often were found together partaking in Valencia's riotous tavern life. In the taverns of the kingdom, Muslims and Christians gambled together, drank together, and even slept together.[4] Thus Fernando wanted the Hostal del Palomar in Albayda razed, because ". . . there are committed many evils and damages, since many men of evil life and practices congregate there, and since it is found that Moors sleep with Christian women...."[5]

Indeed, it was the violation of this sexual taboo that was most disturbing for the Christian authorities. In the thirteenth century, laws had been passed expressly forbidding such relations. The laws provided that in the case of a Muslim man sleeping with a Christian woman, both parties were to be burned alive.[6] However, in the case of a Christian man sleeping with a Muslim woman, the man received no punishment at all, while the woman was punished according to Islamic law for fornication or adultery (unless she was a licensed prostitute).[7] As John Boswell has pointedly observed, "... those members of the society with no power, i.e., Muslims and women, were penalized for unions which were permissible for members with power, i.e., Christian men."[8] In this way the Crown protected Christian women, while ensuring the recreation of Christian men.

The severity of the prescribed penalities did not deter Muslims and Christians from such liaisons. Because of the abundance of Christian and Muslim prostitutes in the kingdom, prevention was nearly impossible. In fact, in the large majority of illicit unions between Muslim men and Christian women, the women were prostitutes. The law, however, made no distinctions with respect to the status and profession of the Christian woman, so that Muslims were punished for sexual relations with Christian prostitutes as well as with Christian wives and maidens. Guilty Muslims were only rarely sentenced to the ultimate penalty of being burned; usually they were heavily fined.[9]

Very few instances were recorded of sexual relations between Christian men and Muslim women who were not prostitutes or slaves. Cases like that of the Muslim girl from Liria, who ran off with her Christian lover, Jacob Ricarder, converted to Christianity, and set up house with him, were a rarity.[10] The jealousy with which Mudéjar fathers guarded the chastity of their daughters—against other Muslims and certainly all the more against Christians—precluded such liaisons.

The sexual exploitation of Muslim women by Christian men is most evident, therefore, not in the carrying on of casual or romantic affairs, which almost never occurred, but in the Christian authorities' promotion of Muslim prostitution. The Crown's position on prostitution in general ran somewhat against the grain of its wider program of moral reform, in which laws were issued prohibiting gambling, sorcery, usury, and blasphemy.[11] The royal policy regarding prostitution was to license it, regulate it, and tax it. Also, attempts were made to confine the activities of prostitutes to the brothels, and to clean up the profession by restricting the involvement of unsavory procurers, or pimps, and by prohibiting Christian husbands and parents from prostituting their wives and daughters.[12]

There was, of course, a definite difference between the Crown's view of the prostitution of Christian women—which it tolerated, though for ethical reasons discouraged—and that which it manifested vis-à-vis the prostitution of Muslim women. The latter was more than tolerated; it was encouraged. For why should a Christian king concern himself with the morality of Muslim women, who were, in any event, irredeemable on account of their profession of Islam? Since, according to the contemporary Catholic theological position, all Muslims were damned, the Christian authorities had no qualms about treating Muslim women as essentially soulless and exploitable objects.

It is not surprising that the motives of the Christians involved in the prostitution of Muslim women—the king, the nobility, and the owners of female Muslim slaves—were blatantly economic, inasmuch as all prostitution was subject to taxation. The Crown's legal stance on the question set the tone for related abuses: Muslim women could practice prostitution only with a license purchased from the Crown, and all unlicensed prostitutes were to be penalized with enslavement to the Crown. On a number of occasions, the bailiff general (the superintendent of the royal patrimony) dispatched deputies to arrest all unlicensed prostitutes, who, the bailiff noted, were plying their trade "... in great damage and detriment of the rights and revenues of the lord king." Once arrested, these women were sold into slavery for the profit of the Crown.[13] Although laws prohibited the owners of female slaves from putting out their slaves as prostitutes,[14] many masters did just that with impunity, retaining the earnings of the women.[15] Thus, these enslaved prostitutes were forced to commit for another's profit the same acts for which they had originally incurred punishment.

The realization that revenues were to be had from the promotion and regulation of Muslim prostitution moved Christians to interfere flagrantly in the communal and private lives of the Mudéjars. Royal and seigneurial officials gave considerable attention to what transpired in the kingdom's Islamic courts, hoping to find, among the condemned, new recruits for the brothels. Because the Mudéjar qāḍīs (judges) were not permitted to administer corporal punishment, the penalties to which they had sentenced adulteresses—flogging or death by stoning—were normally commuted to slavery to either the king or a baron.[16] Many of the women thus enslaved probably were sent to work in the royal brothels. If the *aljamas* (Mudéjar communes; from the Arabic for society or corporation, *al-jam'īya*) did not object to Christian interference in this sensitive area, it was because the rigid sexual mores of the Mudéjars relegated adulterers and fornicators to the status of family and social outcasts. The enslavement of these women was, the Mudéjars realized, by no means a merciful act, but a form of execution more gradual than stoning, though no less symbolic of their social death in the eyes of the Muslim community.

By the latter half of Fernando II's reign, the bailiff general was going so far as to order his subordinates to seek out and apprehend Muslim men and women who had committed adultery. Significantly, this order was contained in the same letter that demanded the arrest of all unlicensed prostitutes.[17] Together, the two formed a cruel and relentless strategy in which the sexual exploitation of Mudéjar women for the financial gain of the Christian authorities is patent: all Muslim adulteresses were to be arrested, punished, and reduced to enslaved prostitution, and all prostitutes were to be licensed, regulated, and taxed by the Crown. The case of Axa of Villamarchant, a widow and mother of three, attests graphically to this policy. While in Valencia, Axa met another Muslim, Çale Duraydach. Çale took her to a hostel, and there they slept together. As they lay together, royal officials burst into their room and demanded to know if they had committed "adultery" (as all illicit sex was euphemistically labeled). Axa confessed to her "crime" and so was arraigned before the tribunal of the bailiff general. The bailiff and the *qāḍi* general (the head Muslim judge in the kingdom) sentenced her to death by stoning, and this sentence was of course commuted to enslavement to the Crown.[18] Of Axa we know no more, though an educated guess as to her fate might be posed. It is, in any case, clear that the basis for this systematic and humiliating exploitation of Muslim women was the law that allowed Christian men to enjoy their sexual favors with impunity. By virtue of their political authority and professed religious superiority over the Mudéjars, the Christian governing classes assumed the moral authority to judge Muslim sexual misconduct, using standards far more rigorous than those which they applied to members of their own faith. Ironically, this assumption was associated with an increasing under-

standing of the Mudéjars themselves and of their strict sexual morality; sadly, the motives of the authorities for utilizing this knowledge were not paternalistic but predatory.

More documentation exists regarding the strategy the Crown pursued to staff its brothels than concerning the life of the prostitutes within the brothels. The main center of Muslim prostitution was the capital city, Valencia, which, with its 75,000 inhabitants, housed one quarter of the kingdom's population.[19] The prostitutes were permitted to receive customers only in the Crown brothel located in the *morería* (Muslim quarter) and were prohibited from frequenting other taverns and inns.[20] The task of supervising the brothel and collecting the tax (or *tarquena*) fell to the lessee or *basto* of the *morería*'s tavern and brothel. Thus, when Pedro de Toledo became *basto*,

> he went personally to the bordello of the *morería* and commanded and intimated to the prostitutes that were there that they should hold . . . [him] as the lessee of the *basto* . . . of the said *morería* . . . and that they should render to him the taxes pertaining to the said lessee . . . and they [the prostitutes] answered that they were content with these things. . . .[21]

The *basto* also was responsible for maintaining order in the *morería*, which had gained a reputation as a center for lowlife, disorder, and scandalous behavior.[22]

In the *morerías* of other towns, most prostitution seems to have taken place on the premises of the royal *fonduks*, a combination of tavern, inn, and goods depository intended for non-Christians.[23] The prominence that royal leases give to prostitution as a source of income for the *fonduks*' Christian lessees suggests that most *fonduks* functioned as quasi-brothels.[24] In Játiva, the Crown paid Muslim carpenters repairing the *fonduk* specifically for their work on the prostitutes' rooms.[25] Some Muslim prostitutes seem to have been more itinerant, and with their royal licenses they moved from place to place, plying their trade under the watchful eye of their Muslim procurers.[26]

As for the prostitutes' clientele, the evidence suggests that it would have been mixed, both Muslims and Christians.[27] Some Mudéjar communities appear to have been disturbed by the riffraff that the *fonduks* often attracted. Thus the elders of the *aljama* of Játiva complained that Christian youths were entering the *morería* at night and that the Christian proprietress of the *fonduk* was traipsing about "dishonestly dressed" and scandalizing Muslim youths.[28] Still, such protests were of no avail, for the kingdom's laws sanctioned a situation in which Christian men had easy access to Muslim prostitutes, whereas Muslim men could solicit Christian prostitutes only at considerable risk to themselves.

It has been suggested that a number of Muslim prostitutes did not enter the profession by choice; rather, having been condemned by their own society for the crime of adultery, they then became the slaves of Christian masters who forced them into this lifestyle. However, some women reluctantly opted for a career of prostitution. A discussion of the structure of Mudéjar society and the position of women will enable us to gain a deeper understanding of why some women resorted to prostitution.

Within each Mudéjar village or urban *morería*, the fundamental unit of social organization was the patrilineal family or lineage group, unified by a feeling of solidarity, or *'aṣabīya*, between male kin. This agnatic solidarity both fueled and was necessitated by the extensive feuding between rival families. The pervasiveness of this feuding is evidenced by the 120 truces that the Crown sponsored between Muslim families, not to mention the numerous assaults and homicides often committed by two or more agnates.[29] This feuding was not a social aberration, but a social process, a consequence of the competition for material wealth and local status. Much of the feuding seems to have involved the resolution of questions of honor, which sublimated baser political and material motives. By allocating the commodities of wealth, power, and honor, the Mudéjar feud served to stratify individual communities.[30]

The importance of *'aṣabīya* and family honor in the Mudéjar feuding society to a large degree determined marriage strategies and the position of women. In the local scheme of feuding relations, the woman was valued primarily for her reproductive power. Therefore, Mudéjar families preferred endogamous marriage for their daughters—that is, marriage to the son of the paternal uncle—so that offspring would be retained within the lineage, thereby increasing its economic potential, power, prestige. Endogamy also enhanced the solidarity of the lineage.[31] If exogamous marriage was necessary— and it often was—it was better and more honorable for the lineage to receive than to give a woman in marriage. Because Mudéjar daughters could inherit from their fathers, the lineage sustained an economic loss when the daughter married outside.[32] Moreover, the children from an exogamous marriage remained with the husband's lineage, sometimes even after the husband died and was survived by his wife.[33] If the daughter had to be given away in marriage, she

was wedded to a family with whom alliance would prove most useful.

However, the local political and economic concerns of the lineage did not always correspond to the wishes of prospective brides. In some cases of endogamy, the women were less than enthusiastic about marrying their cousins, and therefore either resisted the forthcoming nuptials in court or later sued for divorce.[34] Other marital problems seem to have been associated with exogamy. The wife, while living with and bearing children for her husband's family, was still closely tied to her father's family by bonds of affection and responsibility. This was in keeping with the solidarity of the patrilineal group. Consequently, the wife sometimes experienced a feeling of divided allegiance that contributed to the instability of some exogamous marriages. When a Mudéjar wife separated from her husband, she usually returned to the home of her father. For example, when Sucey, the wife of Abrahim Çuleyman of Valencia, went to her father's home in Petres to attend her brother's wedding, she never returned, ". . . her father, mother, and brother detaining her and not allowing her to come in the power of her husband."[35] Or, when Ali Mançor changed vassalage from Benimuslem to Castellón de Játiva, his wife refused to accompany him and demanded the payment of her dower.[36] Indeed, that the husband brought the dower to the marriage and was compelled by Islamic law to relinquish it entirely to his wife in the event of their divorce seems to have given some women greater maneuverability and emboldened them, when discontented, to extricate themselves from the bonds of wedlock.[37]

Nevertheless, although the father's household offered a haven to a woman in case of an unhappy marriage, it also harbored the harshest judges of her behavior. Daughters could not bring honor to a family; they could bring only shame through sexual impropriety. An adulterous woman's shameful conduct mainly affected the honor of her father's lineage; that of the husband's remained unstained. Therefore, it was the responsibility of the woman's agnates to see that she was punished to erase their own shame. In some traditional Arabo-Berber societies, the agnates took the law into their own hands and executed the offending woman themselves.[38] However, in Valencia, Mudéjar males went through the appropriate legal channels and prosecuted their wayward daughters and sisters in the qāḍi's court. The sensitivity of the Mudéjars in this regard is reflected in the documentation, where royal officials recorded a large number of cases of adultery, in which the *Sharī'a* penalty was commuted by Christian magistrates to servitude.[39]

The passive role of women in the maintenance or loss of family honor, which was linked to the economic and local political considerations underlying much of Mudéjar feuding, is evinced not only in the emphasis placed on their reproductive role and sexual propriety in marriage, but also in the anxiety of Mudéjar fathers to defend the chastity of their unmarried daughters. The violation of a daughter's chastity, committed with the consent of the daughter or not, constituted an assault on the family's honor; it was, as well, a blow to its economic status, since the daughter's marriage prospects were thereby negated or seriously diminished. Thus, Aragonese Mudéjars conducting business in Zaragoza brought their daughters with them and kept them secluded in the *fonduk,* so that they would not be "maltreated" or spoiled for marriage.[40] The taking of such precautions by Mudéjar fathers may be explained by a phenomenon encountered in Mudéjar society, namely, the abduction of women. By abducting the daughter of a rival family, which implied sexual violation, the men of a family hoped to dishonor their enemies. Such an insult was likely the intention of Mahomat and Omeymet Maixquarn of Valldigna, who paid a fine of 340s to the bailiff of Játiva ". . . for having kidnapped Çayma, Mooress, daughter of the *amīn* [Mudéjar official] of the place of Manuel."[41]

Thus, it may be concluded that the position of the woman in Mudéjar society was to a large degree determined by the strength of her ties to her father's lineage and by the great emphasis placed on her sexual honor. The court confessions of four Muslim prostitutes reveal that these determinants were crucial in moving some women to choose a life of prostitution. Fotayma was an orphan who lacked the essential family support; she lived as the maidservant of a Muslim shoemaker who allegedly mistreated her. Finally, Fotayma ran off with a male servant, Yuçef, and became a prostitute, with Yuçef acting as her procurer.[42]

Nuzeya, originally from Oliva, was married, but soon separated from her husband with whom she had had a son. Because her parents were dead, she had no one to whom to turn, so she journeyed to Valencia with a man who became her lover. There she sold herself in the royal tavern to survive.[43]

Xuxa from Villamarchant was married to a farmer, who was perhaps her cousin, for she lived with him in her father's house. Azmet b. Maymon Berandi from Manises arrived on the scene and convinced her to leave her husband. Clearly, once

she had left her husband and committed adultery with Azmet, Xuxa, thus shamed, could not return to her family. Consequently, she too took up the oldest profession, and moved from town to town with her procurer Azmet.[44]

Mariem from Alasquer had also separated from her husband, though apparently with her family's disapproval, for Mariem testified that her mother was forcing her to return to her husband. She then departed from Alasquer with a certain Cutaydal, who promised to marry her. Cutaydal, however, had deceived her, and he sold her as a slave to a Christian lord who placed her in Valencia's brothel. Mariem further testified that she was to give everything she earned to the lord until she paid off her ransom.[45]

Of these four women, three had separated from their husbands and through their sexual improprieties had shamed themselves and their families. Two of these women had no family at all to aid them, while the other two had incurred the condemnation of their families. The Mudéjar women who became prostitutes had been marginalized by their own society and were destitute social outcasts. The murky underworld of the brothel and tavern was in a sense a fitting place for such women who had lost all meaningful social status.

The attitudes of Mudéjar men regarding the prostitution of Muslim women varied considerably. Certainly, some Mudéjar males made use of these prostitutes, for in their eyes such women, who had essentially effaced their social identities through their previous conduct, merited no consideration. Others were more crudely exploitative, either acting as procurers for the prostitutes or, even worse, selling these women into a servitude of the worst kind.[46]

Yet some Mudéjar men apparently could not bear the thought of Muslim women, however dishonorable, prostituting themselves for the benefit of Christian men, and therefore attempted to help them. Despite their propensity for feuding among themselves, the Mudéjars were united by a religio-cultural and political identity and by a profound sense of belonging to an international Islamic community (*umma*), which enabled them to overcome internal divisiveness and cooperate in the face of Christian oppression.[47] During Fernando's reign, the Mudéjars' Islamic solidarity manifested itself in a number of ways, but perhaps most dramatically in the activities of Mudéjar *aljamas* in ransoming Muslim slaves, both Valencian and foreign, and abetting runaway slaves in their flight to freedom.[48] Hence, it is not surprising that the prostitution of Muslim women would have elicited resentment and determined action from Mudéjar men. Mudéjar efforts on the prostitutes' behalf took two forms. The one, legal, involved ransoming the enslaved prostitutes from their Christian masters. For example, Ali Chanchan of Benimamet and Yuçef Zignell of Valencia pooled their resources and obliged themselves to pay the ransom of the prostitute Nuzeya Zarqua, the slave of Don Johan de Centelles. Nuzeya, however, was not without responsibility in this arrangement, for, until she attained freedom, her daily earnings were to go toward her ransom.[49] The other form of action taken by Mudéjar men was precipitate and illegal: They kidnapped enslaved prostitutes from the royal brothels with the probable intention of freeing them.[50] Although certainly more dangerous, such drastic measures at least quickly terminated the suffering of Mudéjar prostitutes.

In conclusion, the prostitution of Mudéjar women involved a two-tiered social and legal process. First, because of the importance of family ties and the rigidity of sexual mores in the Mudéjar's feuding society, women who lacked family support or violated the sexual ethic, or both, were forced to live on the margins of that society. Second, because of the kingdom's institutional and juridical structures, which allowed Christian men to exploit Muslim women sexually, the Christian authorities were able to staff the royal brothels from the preexisting pool of marginalized Mudéjar women.

Notes

1   For thirteenth-century conditions, see Robert I. Burns, *Islam under the Crusaders: Colonial Survival in the Thirteenth-Century Kingdom of Valencia* (Princeton: Princeton University Press, 1973). Maria del Carmen Barcelo Torres, *Minorías islámicas en el pais valenciano: historia y dialecto* (Valencia: Instituto Hispano-Arabe de Cultura, 1984), pp. 64-70, provides a useful summary on Mudéjar and sixteenth-century Morisco demography, though I find her estimates for the late fifteenth century to be a bit low. My conclusions may be found in Mark D. Meyerson, "Between *Convivencia* and Crusade: the Muslim Minority of the Kingdom of Valencia during the Reign of Fernando 'el Católico,'" (Ph.D. diss., University of Toronto, 1987), pp. 26, 107, note 7.

2   On the economic relations between Muslims and Christians, see Meyerson, "Between *Convivencia* and Crusade," chap. 3, *passim*.

3   Archivo de la Corona de Aragón (hereafter ACA): Cancillería Real (hereafter C): 3605: 149v (22 May 1482): the king commands his officials in the kingdom of Aragon to see to it that "los dichos moros traygan aquellos senyales"; Archivo del Reino de Valencia (hereafter ARV): Maestre Racional (hereafter MR): 92: 321r (23 January 1482): a royal proclamation is made in the city of Valencia regarding "los senyals que los juheus e moros deuen portar"; and ACA: C 3665: 20v-21r (5 December 1486): Fernando expresses concern that Muslims are still dressing like Christians, despite the orders of his father, Juan II, to the contrary, with the result that the Moors are able to kidnap Christians and sleep with Christian women. John Boswell, *The Royal Treasure: Muslim Communities under the Crown of Aragon in the Fourteenth Century* (New Haven: Yale University Press, 1977), pp. 330-32, discusses the legislation of Spanish monarchs on the minorities' dress from Lateran IV (1215) until the mid-fourteenth century. ARV: Bailiá General (hereafter B): 123: 108r-109v: "Lo dit batle general . . . mana que no sia moro algu ni juheu . . . que gosen ni estar, habitar, menjar ni dormir en algun ostal de la present ciutat de Valencia ni ravals de aquella ni en nenguna casa de la dita ciutat sino en lo dit alfondech del dit molt alt Senyor Rey"; and B 123: 142r-v (1493): Muslims are restricted to drinking in the "Taverna Reyal" after the bailiff general is informed that "molts e diversos moros sen vagen a beure e tenir solacos en diverses tavernes."

4   ARV: B 1156: 511v-512r (23 July 1479): Muslims are fined for gambling with Christians in the hostel of Enova, near Játiva. See below, for Muslim-Christian sexual relations.

5   ARV: C 310: 167v (23 January 1498): "Per humil exposicio a nostra Majestat feta per lo spectable comte d'Albayda havem entes que ell te hun hostal en la dita vila de Albayda vulgariment apellat lo Hostal del Palomar, en lo qual se fan molts mals e dans axi per congregatsi alli molts homens de mala vida e pratiques com encara perque s'es trobat que moros se jahen ab crestianes. . . ."

6   *Furs e ordinations fetes per los gloriosos reys de Aragó als regnicols del regne de Valencia*, Lambert Palmart, ed. (Valencia, 1482), Llibre 9. Rubrica 2. 8-9: "Si juheu o serrahi sera trobat que iaga ab crestiana, sien abduy cremats ell e ella."

7   *Aureum opus regalium privilegiorum civitatis et regni Valentie* (1515), fol. 236r: "Sarracenis dicti regni concedimus cum presenti quod si aliqua saracena habens coniugem seu maritum cum aliquo christiano sive judio crimen adulterii commiserit puniatur iuxta eorum çunam [*Sunna*]. . . ." For example, ARV: MR 4276: 1r (1494): Mahomat Bayrini pays a fine of 100s to the bailiff of Onda "per sa filla Mariem perque fonch trobada en una cambra ab un crestia de la dita vila e fonch jutgada per lo alcadi de Vila Reyal ab licencia del alcadi de Bellvis a XXV asots de castich e vista la gran pobresa del dit Bayrini fonch remesa dels dits açots a composada per los dits C sols. . . ."

8   Boswell, *Royal Treasure*, p. 344.

9   ARV: MR 102: 174r (1491): Abrahim Murci is fined 400s because "era anat a una crestiana [prostitute?] a james ab aquella"; and Azmet Mufferix is fined 1000s "perque's era jagut ab una dona crestiana del bordell en lo grau de la mar." ARV:B 1433: 119r-23v (1 February 1501): numerous Muslims are sentenced *in absentia* to death by burning for having had sexual relations with a Christian prostitute, Angela de Vanya; the severity of the penalty may be attributed to Angela's accusations that the Muslims had forced her to sleep with them. ARV: C 126: 40v-41v (1 September 1479) concerns the more unusual case of an adulterous love affair between Caterina, the wife of Christofol Pujol, and a Muslim, Ayet Capo.

10 ACA: C 3653: 157r-v (23 March 1498).

11 *Aureum opus*, fols. 230r-32r (Fernando II): "Contra jugadors e tenints tarfureria e prestants diners en joch. Item contra juradors e blasfemadors. Contra reccorents a adeuins... Item contra usurers e corredors de usura."

12 *Aurem opus*, fols. 216r-v (Fernando II): "Quod mulieres de turpi questu viventes non possint permanere nec habitare per aliqua loca civitatis nisi tam in luppanari"; and fols. 230r-32r: "... contra alcavots. Contra hostalers qui en lurs hostals tenen dones de guany. Contra pare, mare o marit qui liure lur filla o muller per diners...."

13 ARV: B 1161: 452r-v (16 September 1497): "... accedeixcan personalment a tots qualsevol ciutats viles e lochs del present Regne de Valencia... diligentament cerquen totes e qualsevol çabies [Muslim prostitutes] que atrobaren e aquelles que atrobaren en abit de çabies e que usen del offici de çabies sens licencia del dit noble batle general o nostra pendren a mans vostras e de nostra cort...." It is also noted that all unlicensed çabies are practicing their trade "en gran dan e menyspreu dels drets e regalies del dit molt alt Senyor [Rey]" and are, therefore, "caygudes en pena de catius." ARV: B 1162: 98r (22 October 1500) is another order of the same tenor.

14 *Furs de València*, 4 vol., Germá Colon and Aracadi Garcia, eds. (Barcelona: Editorial Barcino, 1970-83), Llibre 1. Rubrica 9.3 (vol. 2, 85): "... que negu qui haura sarrahina no la tingue per putana sabuda ne'n prengue soldada...."

15 ARV: B 1162: 7v (21 January 1500) discusses "dos mores catives," one owned by the Infant Enrique and the other by knight Francesch Aguilo, who were placed under the supervision of the bailiff (or *basto*) of Valencia's *moreria*, who supervised the prostitutes of the royal brothel; and ARV: B 1433: 57v (23 June 1491): Mariem, a prostitute from Alasquer, testifies that she was sold to Don Altobello de Centelles, who then sent her to work as a prostitute in the royal brothel.

16 ARV: C 129: 1v-2r (23 January 1481): Mariem of Beniarjo is made a slave and sold by her lord as a punishment for adultery; and ARV: C 132: 108r-v (3 August 1484): Mahomat Vaquer and Mariem Tagarinia of Gilet are convicted of adultery and made slaves. ARV: MR 942: 1v (1480): a Muslim woman is made a slave "per esser sen anada de poder de son marit e esser stada atrobada en adulteri"; and similar cases from Alcira: MR 950: 4r (1493), MR 958: 4r (1501), and MR 959: 4v (1502); and from Játiva: MR 3054: 7r (1494), MR 3062: 15r-v (1502). Also, Vicente Pons Alos, *El Fondo Crespí de Valldaura en el Archivo Condal de Orgaz (1249-1548)* (Valencia: Universidad de Valencia, 1982), pp. 198, 219-21, lists instances in which the lord of Sumacarcer accepts as slaves adulterous Muslim vassals who had been condemned to death by stoning by the *qāḍī* of Játiva.

17 ARV: B 1162: 409v-410r (11 February 1503): "... com son ... çabies qui viven del quest o guany desonest sens dita licencia e encara aquells moros e mores qui cometen adulteri en les ciutats e viles reyals e de la esglesia.... E molts moros e mores axi vassalls de la reyal Magestat com de la esglesia ... cometen crim de adulteri, los quals son encorreguts en pena de mort segons çuna e xara [*Sunna* and *Shari'a*], los quals dits casos que fins al present dia de huy seran seguits e dels que de açi avant se seguiran...."

18 ARV: B 1433: 321r-25v (31 May 1502).

19 Ricardo García Cárcel, "El censo de 1510 y la población valenciana de la primera mitad del siglo XVI," *Saitabi* 26 (1976): 171-88.

20 ARV: B 123: 30r-v (1488): "Item que alguna çabia mora stranya ni privada no gos posar ni tenir solaz de beure de dia ni de nit dins la dita ciutat en algun ostal o taverna ni en altra casa alguna ni fer algun adulteri sino en aquella casa o taverna que per lo dit arrendador [*basto*] los sera assignada dins la moreria."

21 ARV: B 123: 132r-v (21 May 1493): "... lo dit arrendador ana personalment al bordell de la moreria e mana e intima a les çabies que alli eren que tinguessen per arrendador del basto ... de la dita moreria ... e que li responguessen dels drets al dit arrendador pertanyents ... e respongueren que eren contentes de les quals coses...."

22 Boswell, *Royal Treasure*, pp. 70-72, shows that the *moreria* had this reputation since at least the mid-fourteenth century. ARV: B 123: 31r-v (1488) discusses the "molts escandels e bregues desordens que seguexen de cascun jorn en la moreria de la present ciutat"; and B 123: 30r-v lists the duties of the *basto*, which include seeing to it that Muslims do not bear arms in the *moreria*, travel at night without a lamp, gamble, drink wine outside of the royal tavern, or dress in excessive finery, all infractions being punishable by a fine.

23 On the institution of the *fonduk* in the kingdom of Valencia, see Robert I. Burns, *Medieval Colonialism: Postcrusade Exploitation of Islamic Valencia* (Princeton: Princeton University Press, 1975), 64.

24 For example, ACA: C 3654: 89v-90v, regarding the *fonduk* of Zaragoza; and ACA: C 3636: 201v-3v, regarding the *fonduk* of Castellón de Játiva.

25 ARV: MR 3056: 16v (1496): "cambres per star les çabies."

26 ARV: B 1433: 545r-v (6 May 1504): Xuxa, a prostitute from Villamarchant, testifies that she practiced her trade in Játiva, Castelló de Rugat, Ribarroja, Benaguasil, Manises, Mislata, Alaquas, etc., and that she was traveling with her procurer ("amo") Azmet ben Maymon.

27 ARV: B 1431: 55v (28 June 1491): Fotayma, a prostitute, testifies that she had many Muslims of Gilet as customers. Presumably, the royal brothels staffed with Muslim prostitutes were intended for both Muslim and Christian clients.

28 ARV: MR 3055: 5v (1495).

29 Pierre Guichard, *Structures sociales "orientales" et "occidentales" dans l'Espagne musulmane* (Paris: Mouton & Co. and Ecole de Hautes Etudes en Sciences Sociales, 1977), analyzes the social structure of the Arabs and Berbers in Islamic Spain. Julio Caro Baroja, *Los Moriscos del Reino de Granada* (Madrid: Ediciones Istmo, 1976), pp. 65-80; and Bernard Vincent, "Les éléments de solidarité au sein de la minorité morisque," in *Le concepte de classe dans l'analyse des sociétés méditerranéennes XVIe-XXe siècles* (Nice: Université de Nice, 1978), 91-100, note that agnatic solidarity remained a potent social force among the Muslims of Granada after the conquest (1492). There is, of course, a difference between this situation and that of Valencia's Mudéjars who had been living under Christian rule for some 250 years. The truces between feuding Mudéjar families are located in the registers ARV: B 217-221 (1479-1500). In contrast to the 120 truces between Muslims, only 21 were concluded between Muslims and Christians. The registers of the royal chancery, bailiff general, and Maestre Racional record numerous incidents of feuding violence. For example, ARV: C 132: 194r-v (18 January 1485): the two Araye brothers kill Azmet Thorruc because Azmet and Ali Thorruc killed their brother Azmet Araye; ARV: B 1431: 64v-99v (3 June 1491): the trial of Açen Muça, who stabbed Abdalla Çentido to death in revenge for Abdalla's murder of his half-brother; or ARV: MR 957: 6r (1500): Mahomat and Abdalla Giber of Valldigna are fined for having wounded another Muslim from the same valley.

30 The work of the social anthropologist Jacob Black-Michaud, *Feuding Societies* (Oxford: Basil Blackwell, 1975), is especially suggestive in this regard. He goes so far as to say that "feud can be regarded as a social system per se" (p. 171). In a number of the official truces, both of the parties subscribing were practitioners of the same craft, which suggests that economic competition was at the root of some feuds. ARV: B 1158: 403r-v (19 April 1487), 413r-v (5 May),

414r-v (9 May), and 415r-v (12 May) concern a feud between two factions struggling for political power in the *morería* of Castellón de la Plana. Some sense of the Mudéjars' punctilious concern for honor can be gleaned from ARV: B 1433: 394r-426v (16 June 1503): the trial of Azmet Torralbi, in which it is clear, from the testimonies of Ysabel Sanchiz (406v-407v) and Franceseh Centelles (415v-416v), that Azmet attacked Abrahim Murci because the latter had publicly insulted him; and B 1431: 64v-99v (3 June 1491): the trial of Açen Muça, in which it is clear that the timing of Açen's vengeance (see note 29) had much to do with Abdalla's attempt to shame him publicly (88v-89r). Also, see Guichard, *Structures*, 37-41, 91-96, 154-59; Black-Michaud, *Feuding Societies*, 175-84; and the essays collected in J. G. Peristiany, ed., *Honour and Shame: the Values of Mediterranean Society* (London: Weidenfeld and Nicolson, 1965).

31 Guichard, *Structures*, p. 27-36, 59-64; Robert F. Murphy and Leonard Kasdan, "The Structure of Parallel Cousin Marriage," *American Anthropologist* 61 (1959): 17-29; and Reuben Levy, *The Social Structure of Islam* (Cambridge: Cambridge University Press, 1957), p. 102. In 1526 the newly converted Moriscos requested that Carlos V not invalidate their endogamous marriages; see Pascual Boronat y Barrachina, *Los moriscos españoles y su expulsión* (Valencia: F. Vives y Mora, 1901), 1:423-24, document no. 5. An example of a Mudéjar endogamous marriage is ARV: B 1157: 94r (22 August 1481): ". . . Fotoix mora, filla de Mahomat Xativi, esposada qui's diu de Ali, fill de Abrahim Xativi, vassalls de la morería de la vila de Algezira. . . ."

32 Guichard, *Structures*, 41-45; and Murphy and Kasdan, "Marriage," 24-28. An example of an exogamous marriage is ARV: C 131: 61v (18 April 1483): ". . . scivit dictum Jocessum Alcamba et Mahomam Belvis esse coniunctos quadam affinitate, quod filius dicti alcadi Belvis nupserat nepoti sive nebota predicti Juceffi Alcamba filie Yahe Alcamba eius fratris. . . ." Concerning the right of Mudéjar daughters to inherit, ARV: B 1156: 856v (14 September 1480): Two Muslim daughters inherit a carob orchard from their father. In contrast, Levy, *Social Structure*, 245-46, notes that in many Islamic societies women did not inherit.

33 For example, ARV: C 126: 120r-121r (23 February 1480): Fotayma resides in Sot with her new husband while her daughter Axa lives with two guardians in Quart, the home of her (Fotayma's) first husband, now deceased.

34 ACA: C 3648: 219r-v (15 October 1491) concerns the litigation between a reluctant bride, Fatima bint Mahomat Margnan of Huesca, and her cousin Ybraym ibn Mofferiz Margnan; and ACA: C 3647: 60v-61r (15 February 1490): Fatima bint Jayel de Gali of Zaragoza sues for divorce from her cousin Faraig ibn Juce de Gali, on the grounds that Faraig

maltreated her.

35 ARV: B 1162: 497r-v (30 December 1503): "Com siam estas informats que Sucey mora filla de Cacho moro del loch de Petres muller de Abrahim Culey-men moro vassall de la maiestat del Senyor Rey de la moreria de Valencia sia anada ensemps ab Yuçeff Cacho germa de aquella al dit loch de Petres a les bodes del dit son germa prometant tornar aquella en poder del dit son marit pasada la dita boda, la qual fins ahuy no es tornada ni lo dit son germa no la ha tornada en poder del dit son marit detenint aquella lo pare e mare e germa de aquella no lexant venir aquella en poder del dit son marit. . . ."

36 ARV: B 1160: 780r-781r (4 December 1493). Another example is ARV: C 148: 125v (17 December 1492): Çoltana departs with her father from the seigneury of Castell de Castells, even though her husband is still living there.

37 On the dower (*mahr* or *sadāq*) and the woman's right to it in the event of divorce, see F. H. Ruxton, ed. and trans., *Māliki Law, being a summary from the French translations of the "Mukhtasar" of Sīdī Khalīl* (1916, reprint ed., Westport, Conn.: Hyperion Press, 1980), pp. 91-92, 97, 105-8; and John L. Esposito, *Women in Muslim Family Law* (Syracuse: Syracuse University Press, 1982), pp. 24-26. Regarding the woman's control over her dower during her marriage, the opinions of Māliki jurists varied. One view was that the woman had no proprietary rights over her dower at all; another view was that the conclusion of the marriage contract involved the immediate delivery of half the dower to the wife (*Māliki Law*, Ruxton, ed., 111). Mudéjar *qādīs* seem to have held the latter opinion, for in ARV: B 1220 VI: 35r (19 May 1487) the *qādī* general ruled in favor of Axa, the wife of Mahomat ben Yunis, who was suing to receive from her husband half of her dower, lest it all be lost to her husband's creditors. There is no evidence of Mudéjar women having dowries, nor is there evidence as to the extent of control they exercised over their own inheritances.

38 A.M. Abou-Zeid, "Honour and Shame among the Bedouins of Egypt," in *Honour and Shame*, Peristiany, ed., pp. 256-57.

39 See note 16.

40 ACA: C 3567: 150v (8 February 1496): "A nos ha sido recorrido por parte de la aljama de moros de essa ciudat con humil e querellosa exposicion, diziendo como en sua alfondiga ellos suelen e acostumbran tener algunas moras apartido, las quales trahen y tienen en custodia los moros que de otras morerias han conduzido aquellas affin que no sean maltractadas ni echen a perder lo que ganan como de aquello se hayan a mantener e casar segun sus costumbres."

41 On the abduction of women, see Abou-Zeid, "Bedouins," pp. 253-54; and Guichard, *Structures*, pp. 41, 51, 107, 109. ARV: MR 3056: 6v (1496) concerns the punishment of the Maixquarns "per haver furtat a

Çayma mora, filla del alami del loch de Manuel." Another example comes from Alcira—MR 944: 8r (1488)—where the Capo family pays a 240s fine on behalf of Azmet Capo, who "era estat condemnat per haver sen portat fugitivament la filla de Chanchan moro de la dita moreria."

42 ARV: B 1431: 55r-56v (28 June 1491).

43 ARV: B 1431: 391r-93r (3 April 1494).

44 ARV: B 1433: 545r-v (6 May 1504).

45 ARV: B 1431: 57r-61v (23 June 1491).

46 See the above cases of Fotayma, Xuxa, and Mariem.

47 I have described aspects of the Mudéjars' Islamic solidarity elsewhere, in "The War Against Islam and the Muslims at Home: the Mudéjar Predicament in the Kingdom of Valencia during the Reign of Fernando 'el Católico,'" *Sharq al-Andalus: Estudios Árabes* 3 (1986): 103-13; and "The Survival of a Muslim Minority in the Christian Kingdom of Valencia (15th-16th Centuries)," in *Indigenous Christian Communities in Medieval Islamic Lands: Conversion and Continuity* (forthcoming).

48 Meyerson, "The War Against Islam," 109-10. I am currently preparing a detailed study of the situation of Muslim slaves in the kingdom of Valencia.

49 ARV: B 1222 VI: 4r-v (20 June 1499): "Ali Chanchan moro de Benimamet e Yuçef Zignell fill de Yaye Signell moro vassall del Senyor Rey de la moreria de Valencia e Nuzeya Zarqua mora çabia tots ensemps e cascun per si e per lo tot . . . prometeren e voluntariment se obligaren en poder del noble batle general e cort sua en donar e pagar al noble don Johan Centelles . . . sis lliures dos solidos dos diners restants de major quantitat de rescat de la dita Zarqua cativa. . . . E per attendre e complir les dites coses obligaren ses persones e bens. . . . E encara la dita Zarqua sots virtut de jurament per aquella prestat promes de no exir de la ciutat de Valencia fins que primerament lo dit don Johan sia pagat de la damunt dita quantitat o ab licencia del dit noble don Johan Centelles. E que tot lo que guanyara cascun dia que portara al dit don Johan Centelles prenent aquell compte de son deute. . . ."

50 For example, ARV: B 1160: 17v (25 January 1491): "Dos moros la hun del loch de Mizlata l'altre de la ciutat de Xativa sen hagen portat huna sclaua mora çabia del dit Don Altobello Centelles, la qual sen han portat del bordell de la moreria de la dita ciutat. . . ."

Arabic Books in Jewish Libraries:
The Evidence of Genizah Booklists

Moshe Sokolow

The medieval Jewish fondness for books was expressed eloquently by Judah Ibn Tibbon—of twelfth-century Spain and Provence—progenitor of four generations of authors and translators from Arabic to Hebrew, who wrote in a letter to his son, Samuel: "I have honored thee by providing an extensive library for thy use, and have thus relieved thee of the necessity to borrow books. Most students must bustle about to seek books, often without finding them. But thou, thanks be to God, lendest—and borrowest not."[1]

"Booklists" are lists of titles of books that were prepared and kept by a variety of individuals and institutions for any of several purposes (which will be detailed below). Sometimes the titles accompany such ancillary information as the names of their copyists, owners, or purchasers, as well as their physical appearance or condition—particularly if that information affected their price or value. Most often, however, the lists contain titles exclusively.

The project in which I am currently involved[2] was initiated by the late Professor Nechemiah Allony,[3] and consists of a catalog of the more than 4,500 entries, comprising over 2,500 individual works named in the 120 published booklists from the Cairo Genizah.[4] The catalog is expected to be of interest to intellectual, social, and even economic historians (not to mention bibliophiles), by providing the raw data regarding the discovery of previously unknown works by noted authors; the diffusion of significant works by previously unknown authors; their purchasers or users; and even the prices paid for their purchase at different places and at different times.

Booklists "are our key to opening doors into the hidden recesses of Jewish communal life in the late Middle Ages. They show us the Jew in his private life, ungoverned by others; in a place where he was free to devote himself to his own interests and to engage in the grand questions of human life and existence. We learn to recognize the spirituality of the Jewish scholar, the degree of his spiritual interests, and their essence."[5] Via booklists we enter into the private, and a very few public libraries, of these medieval Jews. Although some collectors were thoroughly Jewish, others are remarkable for the degree to which non-Jewish wisdom—principally medicine and philosophy[6]—is represented among the books they owned, bought, sold, loaned, or borrowed.[7]

The 120 published booklists[8] cover a broad chronological and geographical spectrum. They range in time from the tenth through the fifteenth centuries: Sixty-two originate in the twelfth century, twenty-seven in the thirteenth, and nineteen in the eleventh.[9] Consistent with the overall complexion of the Cairo Genizah, the lists derive preponderantly from North Africa and the Middle East. Seventy percent were written in the formal, semisquare script known popularly as *Rashi* script,[10] ten percent in oriental square script, and fifteen percent (including all twenty lists kept by Rabbi Yosef "Rosh haSeder") in cursive. Some of these Judeo-Arabic lists also contain entries in the Arabic (*naskhi*) script.

One hundred and nineteen of the published lists were written on paper, whereas a single list (dating from the tenth century) was written on parchment.[11] Ninety-three of the lists contain fewer than fifty entries and eight have over one hundred. The shortest list contains but one title and the longest enumerates more than two hundred.

The lists were kept by a wide variety of people, who represent a cross section of social strata and professions. They include:

Owners of private libraries. Enlightened and creative scholars, the private collectors constitute the majority of listers. Paramount among them was Rabbi Yosef Rosh haSeder (1150-1220), a rabbinical scholar of Baghdad and Fustat, who accounts, individually, for twenty of the published lists.[12]

Booksellers. The book trade was conducted by professional traders as well as teachers, copyists, and authors. In some cases, the listers even recorded the prices they charged for their books. In a few noteworthy instances, these prices are noted in Coptic numerals, a method of encoding not unknown to contemporary dealers. Otherwise the prices are either spelled out or recorded according to standard Hebrew alphanumerics, known as *Gematria.*

Bankers and moneylenders would itemize books that they received as collateral for outstanding loans.

Copyists and Copy-contractors. Many Jews in the Middle Ages regularly copied for themselves the books they needed on a daily basis, such as the *Siddur* and the *Machzor*, the daily and holiday prayerbooks, and the *Chumash* and *Haftarot*, the weekly Torah and accompanying Prophetic readings. Also, professional copyists earned their livings from copying books, and contractors accepted orders for books to be copied and distributed the work among several copyists.[13]

Heirs. When a collection of books was included in an inheritance, the heirs would list them, or scribes or dealers would copy them on their behalf.

Courts. Legally executed bills of sale for property included books.

Two thousand of the 4,500 entries (comprising about forty-five percent) come from the very traditional Jewish realms of *Halakha* (law) and *Midrash* (hermeneutics and homiletics), while 1,150 (twenty-five percent) deal with the Bible and Biblical commentaries, including about one hundred works of exegesis originating with the Karaites, Jewish sectarians, who tended to interpret the Bible more literally than their orthodox (Rabbanite) brethren.[14] The balance is distributed amongst religion and philosophy (150/3 percent), poetry and *Piyyut* (liturgical poetry; 430/9 percent), medicine and science (350/8 percent), grammar and linguistics (270/6 percent), history (90/2 percent), and miscellaneous (90/2 percent).[15]

The two specific subjects, then, that characterize Genizah booklists (as opposed to lists from, for example, Europe) are grammar and poetry, and medicine; these subjects correspond to the outstanding characteristics of the Arabic enlightenment, namely rhetorical and poetic eloquence and general knowledge of the sciences.

Jews, like many ethnic and religious minorities in the Muslim world, adopted Arabic for nearly all their secular and religious literary needs, Jewish

liturgical poetry (*piyyut*) remaining the universal exception. Unlike other cultures, however, the Jews by and large shunned the Arabic *naskhi* script and wrote their original Arabic compositions in the Hebrew alphabet.

Of the total of 2,516 individual titles appearing in the booklists, 1,392 (fifty-six percent) are in Hebrew, and 1,124, fully forty-four percent, are in Arabic. The Arabic titles are further subdivisible into three classifications:

Judeo-Arabic—original Jewish works composed in Arabic written in the Hebrew alphabet, which constitute the great majority of the Arabic titles (928/36 percent of the combined total);[16]

Classica-Arabica—works of Classic Greek literature in Arabic translation, which number fifty-six (two percent of the combined total);

Islamica-Arabica—works of original Arabic literature, which number 140 titles (six percent of the combined total).

Although Judeo-Arabic literature is a significant cultural phenomenon by itself,[17] we shall deal here with the last two categories only, since they constitute the evidence we seek of direct cross-cultural contact between the Jews and their Muslim neighbors.

Forty of the Classic[18] works are in medicine and ten are in philosophy.

The booklists record twenty-five works of Galen and seven of Hippocrates. Galen's works include:[19]

ٱلْأَغْذِيَة (nutrition), ٱلْأَدْوِيَة (medications), ٱلْبُحْرَان (crisis in illness), ٱلذُّبُول (deterioration), مَنَافِعُ ٱلْأَعْضَا (the usefulness of limbs), ٱلْمَعْجُونَات (ointments), ٱلنَّبْض (pulse), ٱلْعِلَلُ وَٱلْأَعْرَاف (illnesses and their symptoms), قَطَا غُنُوس (*katagenos*; medicaments), قُولَنْج (colic), and عَمَلُ ٱلتِّرْيَاق (the preparation of antidotes).[20]

Hippocrates is represented by ٱلْأُسْطُقُسَات (the elements), عَهْد بُقْرَاط (the Hippocratic oath), and ٱلْمَوْلُودِينَ لِثَمَانِيَة أَشْهَار (premature births).[21]

The representation from Classic philosophy is somewhat more eclectic. The booklists cite Socrates' ٱلْأَبْدَاع (creation),[22] Pythagorus' "golden maxims" (إِيثَاغُورَس), Euclid's مُصَادَرَات (axioms), Plato's "Phaedon" (قَابِن),[23] and a work of anonymous Sophists (تَفْسِيرْ سُوفِس). Only Aristotle merits two titles: بَارَامِيْنِيَاس (*peri hermeneius*) and ٱلْكَوْن وَٱلْفَسَاد (De Generatione et Corruptione).[24]

The balance includes Diocrides' "Botany" (أَلْحَشَائِش),[25] and Aristotle's "Politics" (سِيَاسَةُ ٱلْمُدُنِ), "Zoology" (نُعُتُ ٱلْحَيَوَانِ), and "Ethics" (تَدْبِيرُ ٱلرَّجُلِ لِمَنْزِلِهِ).[26]

The breakdown of the Islamic Arabic works is medicine, fifty-five; philosophy thirty-five; astrology, ten; and literature, fifteen.

Works on medicine are:

Ibn Sina: أَلشِّفَاء (convalescence), ٱلْأَمْرَاضُ وَٱلْأَغْذِيَة (illness and nutrition), ٱلْحُمِّيَات (fevers), and ٱلْأُمُورُ ٱلْكُلِّيَّة (nephrology? or: general practice).[27]

al-Kindi: ٱلْمَدُّ وَٱلْجَزْرُ (dilation and contraction).[28]

al-Razi: ٱلْمَنْصُورِي فِي طِبٍّ, a work on medicine dedicated to the Samanid prince Mansur Ibn Ishaq, and مَنْ لَا يَحْضُرُهُ طَبِيبٌ (when no doctor is present).[29]

Ibn 'Adwan: دَفْعُ مَضَارِّ ٱلْأَبْدَانِ بِأَرْضِ مِصْرَ (preventing bodily injury in Egypt), a treatise on the climate of Cairo.[30]

Ibn Rushd: كُلِّيَاتٌ فِي طِبٍّ (general medicine).[31]

And, finally, two treatises by Costa bin Lucca: عِلَّةُ ٱلْمَوْتِ فُجَاءَةً (the cause of sudden death) and عِلَّةُ نَبَاتِ ٱلشَّعْرِ (the cause of hair growth);[32] and an anonymous work entitled

أَنَّ ٱلطَّبِيبَ يَجِبُ أَنْ يَكُونَ فَيْلَسُوفًا

(that the physician must be a philosopher).[33]

In philosophy, Ibn Sina is represented by four works, including the قَانُون (Canon), and by حَيُّ بْنُ يَقْظَانَ (living man, son of the vigilant), whose hero—born on a deserted island and raised by a gazelle—reaches the highest degree of philosophical knowledge solely by introspection and meditation.[34]

Other philosophers are al-Razi: ٱلْكَافِي (Summa), and كَلَامٌ (aphorisms); al-Farabi: مَجْمُوعٌ (Compendium); al-Kindi: كَلَامٌ (aphorisms), and رِسَالَة (essays); and al-Jahiz: عَنَاصِرُ (elements).[35]

Given the marked preference shown by the earliest medieval Jewish philosophers in the Muslim world (such as Sa'adiah Gaon) for the Kalam in general and the Mu'tazila in specific,[36] we note the ٱلْمُغْنِي (Summa) and the أُصُولُ ٱلْخَمْسِ (the five principles) of 'Abd al-Jabbar,[37] and a wide assortment of titles (of undetermined authorship) that reflect that same orientation, such as أُصُولُ ٱلْكَلَامِ (Kalam principles), مَسَائِلُ كَلَامِيَّة (issues in Kalam), عِلْمُ ٱلْكَلَامِ (the science of Kalam), and مَصْدَرُ تَوْحِيدٍ (the inception of unity).

Missing, for perhaps the same reason, are any of the philosophical works of the anti-Mutakallimun Ibn Rushd, although one work appears that reflects that tension: جَدَلُ ٱلْفَلَاسِفَةِ وَٱلْمُتَكَلِّمِينَ (the debate between the philosophers and the Mutakallimun).[38]

The ten astrological works bear the usual titles such as ٱلْهَلِيلَجُ (the ellipse) and ضَرْبُ ٱلرَّمْلِ (geomancy).[39]

In literature we note the كِتَابُ ٱلْأَغَانِي of Al-Isfahani,[40] two anonymous collections: أَشْعَار عَرَبِي (Arabic poetry) and أَقَاوِيلُ لِأَهْلِ ٱلْأَنْدَلُسِ (Spanish works), and the earliest extant reference—by its full title—to أَلْفُ لَيْلَةٍ وَلَيْلَةٍ (the thousand and one nights).[41]

Among the miscellaneous Arabic works we recognize, first of all, a kindred spirit in the فِهْرِسْت of al-Nadim, entitled كُتُبُ ٱلْحُكَمَاءِ (books of the sages).[42] There is also a work on music (أَلْمُوسِيقَى), probably by al-Farabi,[43] one on engineering (أَلْهَنْدَسَة), a treatise on statecraft entitled فَصْلٌ لِتَدْبِيرِ مَدِينَةِ هَارُونَ ٱلرَّشِيدِ for the ruler of the city of Harun al-Rashid, i.e., Baghdad, and another with the fanciful title of مَعْرِفَة مُلُوكُ ٱلْجِنِّ (lore concerning the kings of the spirits). There is a possibly Shi'ite work with the title أَلْهَوْدَى, and, in conclusion, my own personal favorite:

كَشْفٌ كَيْفَ صَارَ مُنْتَحِلِي ٱلْبَحْثِ إِلَى ٱلْبُهُتِ (the disclosure of how those who aspired to scientific exploration were bewildered), cautionary words that all scholars would do well to observe.

When Muhammad referred to the Jews as "the People of the Book" (Koran 3:110 et al.), he could scarcely have known how accurate that sobriquet would become before the Middle Ages was over. We are indebted both to the original compilers of the booklists and then to the scholars who labored to make cultural, intellectual, and even economic sense of their work.

In the final analysis, however, the possession of books was often a very personal, almost aesthetic experience, best left to the bibliophiles themselves to describe. As Judah Ibn Tibbon wrote in the same letter with which we began: "Make thy books thy companions. Let thy cases and thy shelves be thy pleasure grounds and gardens. Bask in their paradise, gather their fruit, pluck their roses, take their spices and their myrrh. If thy soul be satiate and weary, change from garden to garden, from furrow to furrow, from prospect to prospect. Then will thy desire renew itself, and thy soul be filled with delight."[44]

Notes

1 Israel Abrahams, *Hebrew Ethical Wills* (Philadelphia, 1926), p. 57.

2 The project is being undertaken on behalf of the Ben Zvi Institute for the Study of Oriental Jewish Communities (Jerusalem), with the additional sponsorship of the Israel Academy of Sciences and Humanities.

3 I am indebted to Mrs. Idit Allony whose unflagging devotion to her late husband's scholarship has supported the completion of his catalog.

4 It is well beyond the scope of this paper to attempt even a brief description of the Cairo Genizah. For an overview, cf. Paul Kahle, *The Cairo Genizah* (Oxford, 1960); S. D. Goitein, *A Mediterranean Society* (Los Angeles, 1967), 1:1-28.

5 Eliyahu Ashtor, *History of the Jews in Egypt and Syria* (Jerusalem, 1951), p. 359.

6 Ibn Tibbon, for example, writes to his son (cf. note 1): "Seeing that thy Creator had graced thee with a wise and understanding heart, I journeyed to the ends of the earth and fetched for thee a teacher in secular sciences (*chokhmot chitzonot*)." Abrahams, ibid.

7 Cf. the citation from Ibn Tibbon with which we began the paper. A contemporary source, the German-Jewish "Book of the Pious," gives similar advice: "If A has two sons, one of whom is adverse to lending his books and the other does so willingly, the father should have no doubt in leaving all his library to the second son, even if he be the younger" (*Sefer Chassidim*, section 875). For additional information on the medieval Jewish attitude towards books and the care thereof, cf. Israel Abrahams, *Jewish Life in the Middle Ages* (Philadelphia, 1958), pp. 352ff.

8 The earliest publication of a booklist was by Simcha Pinsker, *Liqqutei Qadmoniyot* (Vienna, 1860), pp. 191-92, and the first Genizah booklist by Solomon Schechter, *Saadyana* (Cambridge, 1903), pp. 78-79. The complete list of scholars and bibliophiles reads like a who's who of modern Jewish scholarship, and includes, apart from Allony himself: Jacob Mann,

Samuel Poznanski, Simcha Assaf, Ze'ev (Wilhelm) Bacher, Alexander Scheiber, Eliyahu Ashtor, D. Z. Baneth, and Shraga Abramson.

9 Only thirteen of the lists bear actual dates. The remainder are dated, generally, on the basis of the latest books they cite, with a generation or two added to their composition to give them time to circulate. The virtual absence of lists before the tenth century does not dictate that such lists were not yet kept, but only that they were not yet preserved in the Genizah. The twelfth century, which alone accounts for more than fifty percent of all the booklists, was a particularly prosperous period, both culturally and economically, for Egyptian Jewry.

10 The name *Rashi* script derives from the type used to set the first editions of the commentary of the premier Jewish Bible exegete, Rabbi Shelomo ben Yitzchaq (RASHI; 1040-1105).

11 The basic text on writing materials is A. Grohmann, *Allegemeine Einleitung in die arabische Papyri* (Vienna, 1924), pp. 21-64. The manufacture of paper in the Muslim world began, under the influence of the Chinese, in the eighth century; cf. J. Karabacek, *Neue quellen zur Papiergeschichte* (Vienna, 1888). On the subject of writing materials and Jewish manuscripts, in general, cf. Malachi Beit Arie, *Hebrew Codicology* (Jerusalem, 1981), 20ff. The manufacture of Jewish books, centered in Israel, is described in detail by Nechemiah Allony, "Books and their Manufacture in Medieval Israel," *Shalem* 4 (1984): 1-25.

12 Rabbi Yosef, whose title indicates a position of responsibility within a religious academy (*yeshiva*), made his living as a scribe and copyist providing books for other scholars of both religious and secular disciplines. His disproportionate representation among Genizah booklists (20 out of 120) has made him the subject of numerous and intensive investigations, among which we should note those of S. Abramson, "Rabbi Yosef Rosh haSeder," *Qiryat Sefer* 26 (1950): 72-90, and N. Allony, "Two Autographic Booklists of Rav Yosef Rosh haSeder," *Qiryat Sefer* 38 (1963): 531-57.

13 Cf. Allony, "Books," p. 7.

14 For a general description of Karaite literature and representative selections, cf. Leon Nemoy, *Karaite Anthology* (New Haven, 1952).

15 For descriptions and discussions of philosophy, cf. Isaac Husik, *A History of Medieval Jewish Philosophy* (1916); of poetry, H. Schirmann, *Hebrew Poetry in the Middle Ages*, 4 vols. (Jerusalem, 1955); of grammar and lexicography, H. Hirschfeld, *A Literary History of Hebrew Grammarians and Lexicographers* (London, 1926), and Nahum Sarna, "Hebrew and Bible Studies in Medieval Spain," in R. Barnett, *The Sephardic Heritage* (London, 1971).

16 A comprehensive survey of Judeo-Arabic literature

is provided by A. S. Halkin in L. Finkelstein, ed., *The Jews; Their Religion and Culture* (New York, 1971), pp. 121-54, and a very detailed study is Moritz Steinschneider's *Die arabische Literatur der Juden* (Frankfort, 1902).

17 Most works in these two categories are listed in Carl Brockelmann, *Geschichter der arabischen Literatur* (Leiden, 1937-42), henceforth *GAL* and *GALS* (Supplement), and all citations are from there unless noted otherwise.

18 The translation of classical works into Arabic is discussed by Ignaz Goldziher, *A Short History of Classical Arabic Literature* (Hildesheim, 1966), pp. 91-94, and by Bernard Lewis, *The Muslim Discovery of Europe* (New York, 1982), pp. 71-88, who observes that "the basic criterion of choice was usefulness . . . [which] applied to philosophy no less than to science" (p. 74).

19 Most of the works of Galen were translated into Arabic by the noted tenth-century Jewish physician Hunein Ibn Ishaq. Cf. G. Bergstrasser, *Honein Ibn Ishaq ueber die syrischen und arabischen Galen Uebersetzungen* (Leipzig, 1925).

20 "Nutrition" (appears four times in the lists); cf. *GALS* 1:486/13, 890/17. This translation was itself translated into Hebrew by Ibn Zahr Abu Merwan 'Abd al-Malik of Seville. Cf. M. Steinschneider, *Hebraische Uebersetzungen des Mittelalters* (Berlin, 1893), p. 749/2; "Medications," Bergstrasser, *Honein,* p. 53; "Crisis," Bergstrasser, *Neue Materialen zu Honein Ibn Ishaq's Galen Bibliographie* (Leipzig, 1932), p. 18; "Deterioration," Bergstrasser, *Neue Materialen,* p. 72; "Usefulness" (four times), *GALS* 1:369; "Ointments" (three times), *GALS* 1:595; "Illnesses" (five times), Bergstrasser, *Neue Materialen,* p. 14. "Pulse" is a chapter in this larger work; "Katagenos" (three times), *GAL* 1:205-7, *GALS* 1:366; "Colic" (three times), *GAL* 1:270/15; "Antidotes," Bergstrasser, *Neue Materialen,* pp. 82-83.

21 "Elements" (four times), *GAL* 1:226/11, 369; "Births," *GAL* 1:223/13d; Bergstrasser, *Honein,* pp. 7-8.

22 Socrates, cf. M. Steinschneider, *Hebraische Uebersetzungen,* p. 275.

23 "Phaedon," M. Steinschneider, *Beiheft zum Centralblatt fuer Bibliothekwessen* 13, pp. 21-27.

24 Aristotle's "Generatione," incidentally, was translated from Arabic into Hebrew in the thirteenth century, by Moses ben Samuel ben Judah Ibn Tibbon (the grandson of the author of the letter with which this essay opened). Cf. Steinschneider, *Hebraische Uebersetzungen,* p. 130/16.

25 "Botany," *GAL* 1:227, 229.

26 "Politics," *GAL* 1:594/40; "Ethics," *GAL* 1:573.

27 "Illnesses," *GAL* 1:452 (being parts 3-4 of the "Canon").

28 "Dilation," *GALS* 1:373. (There is a work of Hunein by the same title.)

29 "Mansuri" (fifteen times, making it the most frequently cited of all the Islamic books); Goldziher, *A Short History,* p. 105; "No Doctor," *GALS* 2:947. (There is a work by Orebius by the same title.)

30 *GALS* 1:886/21.

31 Steinschneider, *Hebraische Uebersetzungen,* p. 672.

32 "Sudden Death," *GAL* 1:222; "Hair," *GAL* 1:222/4.

33 "Doctor/Philosopher" (three times).

34 "Canon" (nine times); "Living Man," *GAL* 1:602-3; *GALS* 1:831; Goldziher, *A Short History,* pp. 98-99. (A work by Ibn Tufayl bears the same name.)

35 Al-Razi: "Summa," *GAL* 1:267/9, 269/8; "Aphorisms," *GAL* 1:267; Al-Kindi: "Aphorisms," *GAL* 1:230; "Essays" (three times), *GAL* 1:230-31; Al-Jahiz: "Elements," *GALS* 1:246/IX.

36 Cf., in particular, Harry Austryn Wolfson, *Repercussions of the Kalam in Jewish Philosophy* (Cambridge, 1979).

37 "Summa," George Hourani, *The Ethics of Abd al-Jabbar* (Oxford, 1971); "Five," *GALS* 1:344/7.

38 "Debate," *GAL* 1:209.

39 "Geomancy," *GALS* 1:855.

40 "al-Aghani," *GAL* 1:142-43; *GALS* 1:43, 225.

41 S. D. Goitein, *J.A.O.S.* 78 (1951): 301-2.

42 "Fihrist," *GAL* 1:147, 152; *GALS* 1:226-27; Bayard Dodge, *The Fihrist of al-Nadim,* 2 vols. (New York, 1970).

43 "Music," *GAL* 1:212/8c; *GALS* 1:907.

44 Abrahams, p. 63.

Coptic Alchemy and Craft Technology in Islamic Egypt: The Papyrological Evidence

Leslie S. B. MacCoull

The documents I shall be describing in this paper embody a three-way cultural interaction: the carrying over into medieval times of an ancient Greek tradition of speculative thought and Egyptian practical craft, from Greek into Coptic, and the taking over of words and terms from the language of the Arab conquerors of Egypt into Coptic, as the latter gradually ceased to be the everyday language spoken by Egypt's Christians. These interactions took place in the practical context of the textile industry and in the area of that experimental search for first principles and how they work that became known as alchemy, "the Egyptian art." As will be seen, much of what was disguised with occult-sounding language as "alchemy" was in fact simple craft technology—trade secrets.

The odd amalgam of hermetic-religious doctrine, magic, natural-philosophy speculation, and craft technology that has long gone under the name of alchemy is deeply rooted in the Egyptian cultural background. The recent work of R. Halleux[1] and M. Mertens[2] on the Greek alchemical papyri and manuscripts has done much to sort out the mass of material that has survived to the present day and to begin to understand it in its social and historical setting. Most of the written material of ancient and early medieval alchemy is, however, in Greek; very little has come down to us in Coptic, the other principal language of late antique Egypt. Other than some leaves of a thirteenth-century parchment codex published in 1885,[3] few alchemical texts in the Coptic language are known.

All the more valuable, then, are the two long papyrus rolls numbered A(2)P and A(3)P in the collection of the Bodleian Library at Oxford (Department of Oriental Books and Manuscripts).[4] They contain recipes for various metallurgical and dyeing operations, mostly preparations of metals for making mordants for use in the dye trade.[5] The Coptic texts are written *transversa charta*, across the long direction of the fibers and parallel to the short edge of the roll.[6] The Bodleian Library card index assigns no specific provenance to the papyri; but apparently W. E. Crum, the polymathic Coptic scholar, who cited some words form the texts in his *Coptic Dictionary* (Oxford, 1939), was of the opinion that they, like the medical papyrus mentioned above, now at the French Institute in Cairo, were found at el-Meshaikh (Lepidotonpolis) near Girga,[7] across the Nile just south of Akhmim. A Panopolite/Akhmimic origin for these texts would make sense, considering the importance of Akhmim for both the textile industry and Hermetic arcane philosophy in Byzantine and Islamic times.[8]

From burials at Akhmim, the ancient Panopolis, have come a great many of what art historians generically term Coptic textiles.[9] Both Greek and Arabic papyri attest to the presence of weaving and dyeing facilities in the city and its surrounding area.[10] And Panopolis, the "city of Pan," whose old Egyptian tutelary deity had been that Min (Bes) whose images were smashed by the abbot Shenoute in the fifth century, was the city of Zosimus the alchemist.[11] Panopolis had gained the reputation of a continuing center of "arcane philosophy," i.e., craft technology, which combined with surviving Christianity and a memory of Hellenistic philosophy. Panopolis also had been the city of the poet Nonnus and the home of pagan poets and diplomats.[12] Moreover, the cultural force of the famous monastery of Shenoute at Atripe (Sohag), just across the river from Akhmim,[13] as a Christian pilgrimage center in Islamic times was considerable. It was a thriving monastic site complete with library, scriptorium, and tradespeople, as evidenced by the many manuscripts produced in it, the extent of its fortifications, and the pilgrims' graffiti on its walls.[14] Early Islamic Akhmim was a region of Christian survival and of the textile industry and a heritage of alchemical thought.

The Bodleian texts are in the Sahidic dialect of Coptic, but forms like ΜΑΧΑΝΕ recall the ⲁ-vocalization so characteristic of the Akhmimic dialect in earlier centuries. I should like to postulate that these papyri were written in the area of Akhmim; and, by comparison of the hands with those of the Apa Apollos papyri in the British Library (Bodleian Library Manuscript Or. 6204 and related texts), possibly in the ninth century A.D.[15]

The first text of the two contains over nine separate recipes, in seventy-two lines (much of the beginning is damaged by abrasion). Three of them end with the approving remark ΟⲨⲆⲰΚΙΜΟΝ ⲠΕ ("It is a tested recipe," i.e., "tried and works"). Some ingredients used are: bronze, copper, the potassium hydroxide found in ashes of saltwort, uterine and bladder tissue, *mahaleb* plant, lettuce, metallic sulfur, salt, alum, white vinegar, arsenic?, borax, milk, mercury, and pigeon dung (a widely used fertilizer for which pigeons have long been raised in Egypt, presumably for the nitrates). Among the *Decknamen* or code names for substances we find (line 28) ΜΟΟⲨ ΝΚΗΜΜΕ, which can be either "black water" or "water of Egypt." The writer does not specify most of the purposes or products for which the recipes are designed, but in one case we seem to find ourselves in the realm of what sounds like traditional alchemy. Lines 32ff. state, "If you wish gold, take two portions of *al-boraq* (ⲀⲖⲠⲰⲨⲢⲀΚ) with water, one portion of soda-ash ... put in a good vessel of bronze or silver. It is a rigid body." But in the context of most of the other recipes, which seem to have to do with metallic preparations to be used on fabrics (such as lines 63ff., flax and mercury to be put into an *ampulla* with pigeon dung), we might rather think that what the crafter wants to produce is an inexpensive golden-colored pigment to be used on fabric for decoration.[16]

Indeed, one of the principal searches in ancient and medieval dyeing technology was for cheaper substitutes for the prized murex purple, in Byzantine times a closely guarded imperial monopoly. Less expensive substitutes for actual gold for textile additives such as gold-leaf-wrapped thread for embroideries, or gold foil for stamped ornaments, also were sought for by craftsmen working for the less wealthy market.[17] Also cheaper yellow dyes were desirable, in place of the expensive saffron gathered in Islamic times from crocus.

The second Bodleian text uses a characteristic phrase to introduce its fifteen or so recipes: "The master (ⲠⲤⲀϩ) says" or "The master told me" (sc. "as follows"). Sometimes it is "the wise master" (ⲠⲤⲀϩ ΝⲤⲟⲫⲟⲤ): lines 27ff. give "The wise master says, Rinse out your cup seven times and another three times, until it is properly clean and well prepared (for use) in dyeing a white garment. And find a good measure of the substance [literally "drug"] to be used on the garment." This text is clearly a collection of master-craftsman's technological how-tos for use by Coptic-speaking craft workers being trained in the textile and dyeing industry. Sample processes include: (lines 33ff.) "Take the white garment which you wish to dye. Spread it out in a thin sheet. Put a human bone on it [!] [perhaps this is where the less practical aspect comes in] and add salt. . . . Then take a measure of silver filings, a measure of vinegar, mercury, verdigris and water. . . ." One process uses a substance referred to unfortunately only as "the wise man's dye" or "the philosopher's dye" (ⲠⲤⲰⲠ ΝⲤⲟⲫⲟⲤ). One is to dissolve a half-portion of this wonderful substance in water for seven days, then gradually add more water and put on an old garment one wishes to recondition. "For white garments, they become a fine golden color" (line 61). The papyrus ends with allusions to ⲦΜⲀΧⲀΝΗ ΝⲤⲟⲫⲟⲤ, "the wise man's (or "philosopher's") apparatus," which appears to be not so much a search for the universal solvent ("to undo— ⲂⲰⲖ ΕⲂ ⲟⲖ —any body or ⲤⲰΜⲀ," line 73) as a way of getting usable salts of iron for use as mordants (cf. line 67).

As can be seen, these texts are filled with names of substances that are Arabic loanwords, simply Arabic words transcribed into Coptic letters. Most have been taken over complete with the Arabic definite article *al-*, to which the Coptic article is then prefixed. Of the over twenty of these terms so far seen in the texts, not all have been securely identified. ⲀⲖΜⲀⲢΚⲀϣΙⲐΕ, according to Ullmann,[18] is metallic sulfur; ⲀⲦΙΝⲀΧⲀⲢ is borax; ⲀⲖΜⲟⲨⲠⲟⲨⲖΕ is a chamber pot or urinal (a glass chamber pot is specified for one reaction); ⲀⲖΜΕⲐΕΝΕ is a bladder (a goat's bladder is used for another reaction of which the context is far from clear). Other as yet unsolved Arabic puzzles are probably *Decknamen*, such as ⲀⲖΚⲀⲖⲀΚⲀΝ, "the restless one," i.e., quicksilver? The papyri—both of which are in the same hand—use the well-known visual symbols for gold and silver, ⟨symbol⟩ and ⟨symbol⟩ . There are four instances of cryptographic writing in number A(3)P.[19]

I am far from having established a complete, definitive, annotated text of these two papyri, but I think enough has come out of them to start considering their historical and social background. They are on papyrus, not parchment; and most important, they are in the Coptic language, at a

time when presumably the pressure of the use of Arabic as the *lingua franca* of the public and governmental sphere was beginning to weigh on the use of Coptic as the language of daily life and private correspondence among the Christians (who were by any reckoning still a majority in the country). The story of the replacement of Coptic by Arabic in the record-keeping and speech of Egypt's Christians is an extremely complicated one, which has not yet been written;[20] it certainly did not happen by decree or all at once. But numbers of Panopolite (Akhmimic, not in the narrow dialect sense) Coptic papyri do survive from that region,[21] attesting to the strength and self-consciousness of the local Christians. Even if later, by the tenth to eleventh century, Copts had to speak Arabic in the workplace, they still kept some records in Coptic.[22] The Coptic master craftsperson who put together these texts, obviously thoroughly familiar with the Arabic names for technical matters in the trade, used good Sahidic to record what amounts to trade secrets, the empirical arcana of his craft technology. We can assume that the craftsperson intended them to be intelligible to other Coptic-speakers, initiates versed in the craft.

We have already considered the locality of Akhmim for its importance in the textile industry in late Byzantine and Islamic Egypt, especially for decorative textiles that made use of many dyes and technological processes: many remains of these products are extant, though unfortunately none come from a controlled archaeological context. From recent research in Arabic papyrology we are coming to know more about the role of the indigenous Christians in the textile trade in early Islamic Egypt,[23] especially in centers such as Akhmim (the old Panopolite nome) where Coptic Christianity and the Coptic language persisted in predominance and strength (judging from the remains of documentary papyri) longer than in some other areas of Egypt. Documentary compendia like the Bodleian papyri were well characterized by Pfister as collections of research hints,[24] of pointers towards further work on technological processes and "tricks of the trade" to be worked on by trained craftspeople. We may surmise that the papyri I have described in this paper were written in ninth-century Akhmim, the textile center that also preserved its earlier reputation for arcane philosophy, as collections of research hints by and for Coptic Christian professionals in the fabric trade. These were people who, while they had learned the language of their political masters, carefully preserved their own ancient language, the language of liturgy and the Fathers, as a vehicle of identity and of professional pride.

Notes

*I should like to thank the authorities of the Bodleian Library, Oxford; Dr. Marlia Mundell Mango for checking information in Oxford; Dr. J. Malek of the Griffith Institute, Oxford; Professor Sidney Griffith for help with Arabic; and, as always, looking forward to a new life, Mirrit Boutros Ghali (Ezekiel 32:15).

1 R. Halleux, *Les alchimistes grecs* (Paris, 1981); idem., *Indices chemicorum graecorum* 1 (Rome, 1983).

2 M. Mertens, *Traité gréco-égyptien d'alchimie: la lettre d'Isis à Horus* (Diss. Liège, 1986). I am grateful to Dr. Mertens for illuminating discussions on alchemy.

3 Published by L. Stern in *Zeitschrift für Ägyptische Sprache und Altertumskunde* 23 (1885): 102-19. The content, dealing largely with dyes, is not dissimilar to that of the Bodleian papyri.

4 Dimensions of Manuscript A(2)P: 64.1 x 24.8 cm. Dimensions of Manuscript A(3)P are being checked in Oxford. I thank the Griffith Institute and Dr. Marlia Mundell Mango for access to Crum's transcriptions of these papyri. The Arabic texts on the versos are being gone over by Professor Sidney Griffith of Catholic University (to whom my thanks) in search of further information on provenance and date. According to Professor Griffith, the Arabic texts appear to have been written first: the Coptic writer turned the rolls over to inscribe his Coptic alchemical texts on the other sides.

5 Cf. R. Pfister, "Teinture et alchimie dans l'Orient hellénistique," *Seminarium Kondakovianum* 7 (Prague, 1935): 1-59. The Leiden and Stockholm Greek papyri also contain dyers' recipes.

6 It is interesting that these texts, like the Coptic medical papyrus published by E. Chassinat in Cairo in 1921, are in roll, not codex, form. Perhaps this form of information storage was thought more secure by Coptic craftsmen and professionals practicing their trade under Islamic rule.

7 See E. Chassinat, *Le MS. magique copte 42573* (Cairo, 1955).

8 See G. Frantz-Murphy, "A new interpretation of the economic history of medieval Egypt: the role of the textile industry, 254-567/868-1171," *J. Econ. Soc. Hist. Orient* 24 (1981): 274-97; C. H. Becker, "Akhmim," *Encyclopaedia of Islam* 1, 1 (1913): 234; G. Weit, "Akhmim," *Encyclopaedia of Islam* 2 (1960): 330.

9 See the publications of R. Forrer, e.g., *Die Gräber und Textilfunde von Achmim-Panopolis* (Berlin, 1891). It is hoped that Professor Sheila McNally's excavations at Akhmim will establish good stratigraphy

and proper archaeological contexts for the Akhmim textiles.

10 For documentation see A. Calderini and S. Daris, *Dizionario dei nomi geografici e topografici dell' Egitto greco-romano* 4.1 (Milan, 1983), p. 43, s.v. *Panos polis*, citing *P. Beatty Panop.*, pp. 1-2 (T. C. Skeat, *Papyri from Panopolis in the Chester Beatty Library* [Dublin, 1964]) and P. Berol. 16365+P. Gen.inv. 108 (Z. Borkowski, *Une description topographique des immeubles à Panopolis* [Warsaw, 1975]). For Arabic see C. H. Becker, *P. Schott-Reinhardt I* (=*P. Heidelberg 3*; Heidelberg, 1906): A. Grohmann, *Arabische Papyruskunde* (Leiden, 1966), p. 58 and *Einführung und Chrestomathie zur arabischen Papyruskunde* (Prague, 1955), p. 24. Further Heidelberg Arabic papyri are being published by R.-G. Khoury, and items from Akhmim may be among them.

11 See H. M. Jackson, *Zosimos of Panopolis: On the letter omega* (Missoula, 1978). See also the remarks of M. Plessner on Akhmim the city of adepts of arcana in his *Vorsokratische Philosophie und griechische Alchemie in arabisch-lateinischer Überlieferung: Studien zu Text und Inhalt der Turba Philosophorum* (Wiesbaden, 1975), pp. 130-31 with p. 131, note 322.

12 Triphiodorus; the bishop Cyrus; Harpocration, on whom see G. M. Browne, "Harpocratian panegyrista," *Ill. Class. Stud.* 2 (1977): 184-96.

13 For the medieval period see B. T. A. Evetts, *The Churches and Monasteries of Egypt . . . attributed to Abu Salih the Armenian* (Oxford, 1895), pp. 235-40; A. Mallon, "Copte: épigraphie," *Dictionnaire d'archéologie chrétienne et de liturgie* 3.2 2870-72 for inscriptions (including those from Akhmim itself).

14 For Nachleben see S. Timm, *Das christlich-koptische Ägypten in arabischer Zeit* (Weisbaden, 1984), s.v. "ad-Der al-Abyad," 2:601-34, esp. 610-15 on the monastery's superiors and scriptorium, 616-24 on its survival in the Arab period. On the patronal feast, a great occasion, see H. Quecke, *Untersuchungen zum koptischen Stundengebet* (Louvain, 1970), pp. 488-505, the Paris Manuscript B.N. Copte 68.

15 Cf. also *BKU* 3.436 (P.Berol. 22178).

16 Compare the inexpensive pigments in P.Berol. 8316: A. Erman, *Aus den Papyri der königlichen Museen* (Berlin, 1899), pp. 255-56. This sort of thing is found in the second papyrus also.

17 As in notes 3, 5, and 16 above. Even a late Arabic "alchemical" test like the *Turba Philosophorum* (above, note 11), probably from the tenth-century Akhmim, deals with inexpensive purple and gold dyes. See the English translation (from the Latin) by A. E. Waite, *The Turba Philosophorum* (London, 1876): reprint ed., New York, 1976).

18 M. Ullmann, *Katalog der arabischen alchimistischen HSS. der Chester Beatty Library II: Wörterverzeichnis* (Wiesbaden, 1976).

19 See F. Wisse in *Enchoria* 9 (1979): 101-20 for Coptic cryptograms. Unfortunately, working from the known systems of substitution in these examples, I have not been able to solve the cryptograms in the Bodleian papyri. Four lines from the bottom of papyrus A(2)P appears an Arabic term written in Arabic letters, of uncertain transcriptions ($\bar{a}$-q-h-$\bar{a}$-n-k-eh). It seems to be the name of an apparatus or device (*wusūl*). The lexicon of A. Siggel, *Arabisch-deutsches Wörterbuch der Stoffe . . . in arabischen alchemistischen HSS. vorkommen* (Berlin, 1950) is useful in these puzzles. Perhaps in some cases Arabic itself was used as a kind of code (when not transcribed).

20 See L. S. B. MacCoull, "Three cultures under Arab rule: the fate of Coptic," *Bulletin de la Société d'Archéologie Copte* 27 (1985): 61-70; idem., "The strange death of Coptic culture," *Proceedings of the London Colloquium on Late Antiquity and Early Islam* (June 1986; to appear).

21 For documentation see S. Timm, *Christlich-koptische Ägypten* (above note 14) 1 (Wiesbaden, 1984), 1:80-96, esp. 84-90.

22 The Teshlot papyri from the Hermopolite are an example; see L. S. B. MacCoull, "The Teshlot papyri and the survival of documentary Sahidic in the eleventh century," to appear in *Orientalia Christiana Periodica*.

23 See Y. Ragib, *Marchands d'étoffes du Fayyoum au IIIe/IXe siècle*, 1-2 (Cairo, 1982-85); review (of 1) by G. Frantz-Murphy in *J. Econ. Soc. Hist. Orient* 27 (1984): 219-23.

24 Pfister, "Teinture et alchimie" (above note 5), p. 59.

Technology Transfer Between Byzantium and Eastern Europe: A Case Study of the Glass Industry in Early Russia

Thomas S. Noonan

Most studies of Byzantine relations with medieval Russia or Rus' have focused on political, religious, and commercial issues. Thus, it is often forgotten that Rus' borrowed and adapted Byzantine technology and that this transfer of technology played an important role in helping pre-Mongol Rus' achieve an advanced level of material culture. This study will attempt to illuminate the process of technology transfer between Byzantium and Rus' by examining how and why a glass industry first appeared in early Russia. Although no model of technology transfer involving the medieval Mediterranean can be generalized from this study, it is hoped that this effort will stimulate other works so that the patterns common to many industries in the various areas connected with the medieval Mediterranean might be identified. Such patterns should, in turn, shed further light upon this particular case study.

It is generally agreed that glass was first made in the Rus' capital of Kiev, located along the middle Dnepr River, during the late tenth century. In fact, the origins of a Rus' glass industry are linked with the passage in the *Russian Primary Chronicle* which, under the year 989, states that Grand Prince Vladimir "imported artisans from Greece" to build the Church of the Blessed Virgin, more popularly known as the Church of the Tithe.[1] Apparently, the glazed tiles and mosaics made for the Church of the Tithe by these Greek artisans marked the beginning of a glass industry in Rus'. The leading Soviet specialist on medieval Rus' glass, Iu. L. Shchapova, has thus concluded, along with others, that Rus' glassmaking derived from Byzantium.[2]

In examining the issue of technology transfer,

our first question must address the origins of glassmaking in Kiev. Why was the technology of glassmaking transferred to Kiev around the year 1000 and not earlier, or later, or never? This key problem, to the best of my knowledge, has not received much attention in Soviet studies, which usually seem to discuss the "preconditions" for the Kievan glass industry very briefly and generally. These studies do mention Grand Prince Vladimir's invitation to the Greek masters to help build and decorate his Church of the Tithe. But, beyond this record, there does not appear to be much inclination to examine the various factors that lay behind the highly successful transfer of glassmaking technology from Byzantium to Russia at the very start of the second millennium A.D.

A few glass workshops existed along the northern coasts of the Black Sea during the second to fifth centuries A.D. One workshop, which functioned for about a decade ca. 275 A.D., has even been uncovered at Komarovo along the middle-upper Dnestr.[3] At the same time, some Roman and provincial Roman glass was imported into various sites in the Ukraine and even central Russia.[4] However, the Hunnic invasion and subsequent disruptions seem to have put an end to local glassmaking as well as to the import of glass from Mediterranean centers.[5] Thus, unlike Cherniakhovo sites of the second through fourth centuries A.D., which had some glass along with a variety of other imports from the Mediterranean world, early East Slavic sites of the sixth through ninth centuries are characterized by very basic finds and the almost complete absence of Mediterranean imports.[6] What finds exist of Mediterranean goods and treasures from this time come almost entirely from the graves of non-Slavic nomadic peoples located in the steppe and wooded steppe zones of southern Russia. Thus, any examination of the origins of glassmaking in Kiev must take into account the demise of glass production in southern Russia by the fifth century and the disruption of relations between Byzantium and the East Slavs for several centuries after that time. The Rus' of the late tenth century in Kiev had no early medieval tradition to draw on when it came to glassmaking.

By the early tenth century, at the latest, Kiev had emerged as the center of the new Rus' state, and the rulers of this state had established economic and political relations with Byzantium. During the tenth century, the Rus' state expanded from its center in the middle Dnepr River while trade with Byzantium flourished. Constantine Porphyrogenitus, to cite just one source, described in some detail the annual trade caravans that sailed from Kiev to Constantinople each spring, loaded with slaves, wax, furs, and honey. Constantine also mentioned how the Rus' "mafioso" (that is, the princes and their retainers) spent the winter touring the lands of their East Slavic tributaries, extorting these goods from them.[7]

The development of active trade ties between Kiev and Constantinople in the tenth century brought about some of the preconditions for the successful transfer of glassmaking technology to Rus' from Byzantium. The rulers of Rus' came to be extremely familiar with Constantinople and its wealth and wares. Trade with Byzantium also created great wealth among the Rus' rulers, providing them with the means to acquire and appreciate those Byzantine goods not made in Eastern Europe. Various Byzantine products, including glass beads, glass bracelets, and glazed ceramics began to appear in the Rus' lands during the tenth century.[8]

However, the establishment of a successful glass industry in Kiev depended on more than just the creation of trade ties with Byzantium and the growth of an indigenous ruling class with a taste for conspicuous consumption. The tenth century also witnessed the growth of handicraft production in Kiev. Archaeological excavations in Kiev have uncovered evidence of tenth-century workshops for baking special building blocks, producing pottery, stone-carving, casting decorative plaques, and blacksmithing.[9] In other words, tenth-century Kiev was slowly but surely creating a class of artisans capable of making a wide variety of goods.

Among these tenth-century workshops, particular attention must be paid to the remains of a jewelry workshop uncovered in 1975 along Ulitsa Verkhnii Val in the Podol' section of Kiev. Four slate molds used for casting decorative belt plaques were found in the workshop. An Arabic inscription in the Kufic script of the ninth and tenth centuries had been inscribed into one of these molds. Plaques such as those made from these molds were used widely on belts and bridles in the western Eurasian steppe and usually were imports from the East. But the molds from the workshop in the Podol' suggest that by the tenth century foreign jewelers had settled in Kiev, where they had begun to supply the local demand for belt and bridle plaques.[10] Thus, glass was not the first case of technology transfer involving the growing number of craft workshops centered in Kiev. Already in the tenth century, one or more Eastern masters had introduced the production of cast belt and bridle plaques into the city. Long before Byzantine glassmakers ever appeared in Kiev, the city's artisans had begun to acquire a variety of new skills from abroad while Kiev's ruling class had demonstrated its receptivity to importing foreign craftspeople capable of supplying their needs.

Consequently, several long-term preconditions made technology transfer between Byzantium and Rus' possible. These included the emergence of an affluent local ruling class closely tied with Byzantium and its markets, the development of skilled artisans in Kiev, and at least one case of successful technology transfer of a less complex process. We can summarize these preconditions as (1) *wealth* or the means to acquire goods, (2) *familiarity* with foreign goods, (3) growing *expertise* in craft production, and (4) some *experience* in borrowing more advanced technology.

The wealth, familiarity, expertise, and experience that formed the preconditions for the transfer of glass production from Byzantium were all acquired in Rus' during the course of the tenth century. In other words, it took the Rus' about one century starting from scratch to develop all the ingredients necessary to introduce a technologically advanced industry into Kiev successfully.

In addition to the above preconditions, it also was essential to have particular circumstances in Kiev that would foster technology transfer. Without these immediate circumstances, the long-term preconditions might only have strengthened trade ties. A particular conjunction of events had to make it appropriate to import craftspeople rather than more goods.

The first of these immediate circumstances was,

quite clearly, the conversion of the Rus' to Christianity ca. 988. Having initiated the conversion of his subjects, Grand Prince Vladimir needed to have a major church or cathedral for his capital. Although one or more small wooden Christian churches had existed in Kiev prior to 988, Vladimir quickly realized that a large stone church decorated in a fashion suitable for a Grand Prince of Rus' required Byzantine crafters. After all, this was to be the first stone church in Kiev, and it was to be embellished with glazed tiles on the floors, frescoes on the walls, mosaics, and marble capitals.[11] Vladimir's desire for a great stone church that would make a political and religious statement about the grandeur of the Grand Prince and his city required the importation of Byzantine craftspeople, among whom were specialists who knew how to make glass. To build a proper cathedral in the Byzantine fashion necessitated Byzantine masters.

Once Byzantine masters arrived in Kiev, they found that a second circumstance of that era acted to provide them with continued employment. The Church of the Tithe was completed in 996, and it was not until the 1040s that another great stone cathedral adorned with glazed tiles and mosaics was built in Kiev (St. Sophia). Adorning Rus' churches, especially in the early eleventh century, did not provide regular work for foreign masters or their native apprentices. Under these circumstances, the Greeks might well have returned home and the Rus' sought other, more steady employment. The Byzantine masters and their Rus' pupils might have left no permanent mark on Rus' craft production.

However, starting in the late tenth century, some members of the Rus' ruling class were appointed as local governors, with responsibility for collecting the local tribute. As a result, the Grand Prince, other princes, and their retainers no longer had to spend the winter traveling throughout the Rus' lands collecting this tribute themselves. In addition, the rapid expansion of Kievan power and territory that had taken place during the tenth century now slowed down considerably. The Rus' rulers did not have to spend all their time away from Kiev on expeditions. Large numbers of the ruling class thus could remain in Kiev for most of the year, serving the Grand Prince and pursuing their own interests. Closely connected with the Byzantine trade and strong supporters of Kiev's new state religion, they constituted a good and steady market for luxury goods such as those made of glass. Thus, although the need to build a new stone church initially brought Greek glassmakers to Kiev, it was the "secular"

market of the city's wealthy inhabitants that kept some craftspeople, along with their Rus' pupils, in the city permanently.

The establishment of a glassmaking industry in Kiev by Greek and Rus' masters was the product of both long-term preconditions and favorable immediate circumstances. Without both of these developments there would have been no glassmaking industry in Kiev.

Our next question concerns the process by which the technology of making glass was transferred from Greek to Rus' masters. In this connection, it is pertinent to note that it was the possessors of the technology who were invited to the recipient country. No evidence exists that able Rus' craftspeople were sent to Constantinople to learn how to make glass. Some might suggest that Byzantium consciously sought to prevent others from learning the technology of glassmaking and therefore would not have welcomed Rus' apprentices. If this were the case, however, how do we explain the appearance of Greek glassmakers in Kiev? Certainly, the Byzantine authorities were very much aware that Greek glassmakers working in the Rus' capital for the Rus' Grand Prince greatly facilitated any Rus' efforts to discover the secrets of glassmaking. If the Byzantines had a policy of preventing technology transfer, then this policy was subordinated to the necessity of helping Vladimir spread the new Christian faith and of keeping Rus' in the Byzantine orbit. The politics of conversion apparently put at risk the politics of averting the transfer of key technologies. Some light may be shed on this issue by answering whether Byzantium did indeed have a policy of preventing technology transfer, that is, were Byzantine masters in key industries able to work abroad of their own volition?

The actual transmission of glassmaking technology from Byzantium to Rus' has become a very complex discussion, owing to the analysis of Iu. L. Shchapova, the leading Soviet expert on medieval Rus' glass. Shchapova contends that Rus' glassmakers did not adopt the traditional recipe employed by the Greek glassmakers. Instead of the ancient NaCaSi (sodium-calcium-silicon) recipe, the Rus' allegedly used the non-Byzantine PbSi (lead-silicon) and KPbSi (potassium-lead-silicon) recipes. The earliest Rus' glassmakers therefore seem to have learned how to make glass from the Byzantines, even though they did not borrow the traditional Byzantine recipe for glass. As a result, Rus' glassmakers supposedly produced primarily leaded glass whereas Byzantine glassmakers working in Rus' made a sodium-calcium glass almost exclusively.[12]

Shchapova also claimed that the Rus' failure to take over the NaCaSi recipe was the result of some Byzantine conspiracy to deny the Rus' the knowledge of the ancient recipe. As she has stated: "The conservation of the secret of glass was the principal trait of the policy of the Byzantines with regard to their colleagues in Kiev."[13] Thus, any examination of Byzantine technology transfer to Rus' in glassmaking must deal with Shchapova's fairly rigid ethnic taxonomy for glass production and the "mysterious" apparition of the recipe for lead silicate glass among the novice Rus' glassmakers. In sum, Shchapova's analysis has made it very difficult, if not impossible, to reconstruct the specific process of technology transfer that led to the development of a flourishing glass industry in Kiev.

Shchapova's conclusions regarding the transfer of glassmaking technology from Byzantium to Rus' led me to undertake a fairly lengthy and technical examination of this process. And, my conclusions, although still working hypotheses, are quite different from those of Shchapova. Unfortunately, the critical analysis of Shchapova's two key points cannot be presented in the limited space available for this study. In addition, this analysis clearly shifts our focus from technology transfer to the intricacies of early medieval glassmaking in Europe. I shall only summarize my conclusions here and ask that the interested reader await the full publication of my analysis elsewhere.

Let us turn to Shchapova's two main conclusions regarding the origins of glassmaking in early Rus'. First, no apparent basis exists for her strict ethnic taxonomy, according to which a small group of Greeks in Kiev employed a variant of the classical recipe for over two hundred years while a much larger group of Rus' made lead silicate glasses. Instead of a few Greek masters furtively hiding their secrets and working separately from their Rus' colleagues, it seems far more probable, using the approach of the well-known Soviet art historian, Viktor Lazarev, that Greeks and Rus' worked together from the start in the same workshops, using a variety of glass recipes. In addition, it appears that relatively few Greek masters ever came to Kiev in the first place, and no evidence shows that more than a handful ever stayed.[14] Thus, the rigid ethnic taxonomy of early Rus' glass production should be replaced by an approach that has a few Greek masters working with and teaching a much larger number of Rus' apprentices while both employed a variety of glass recipes. As time went on, the number of Greeks in the Rus' glassmaking industry apparently declined, and they even may have disappeared.

But the techniques and methods they brought to Rus', including the ancient recipe, were preserved by their Rus' pupils and used when appropriate. In short, the terms Rus' glass and Rus' glassmakers really refer to the many Rus' and few Greeks who worked together using a number of different glass recipes.

Second, the mysterious appearance of lead silicate glass among the Rus' turns out not to be so mysterious after all. Lead silicate glass recipes coming from Byzantium found their way into the repertoire of Rus' glassmakers by two main channels. Lead glazes initially were brought to Rus' by the Byzantine specialists invited to prepare glazed tiles for the Church of the Tithe. Very quickly, these lead glazes were applied to pottery and became the basis for a new industry. Thus, a lead silicate glass formula existed in the glazing industry.[15] At the same time, Greek and Rus' mosaicists employed a PbSi recipe to create certain colored tesserae used in decorating the earliest Rus' cathedrals.[16] It was this PbSi smalt that was seemingly utilized to make the first glass beads in Rus'. Lead silicate glass came to Rus' from Byzantium and was employed by Greek and Rus' masters for very good economic, technical, and aesthetic reasons.

Our analysis also suggests that the process that brought glassmaking and glazed pottery to Rus' from Byzantium was not part of a well-conceived, deliberate plan. Rather, glassmaking and glazed pottery arose somewhat accidentally as by-products of employing the decorative glass arts in the earliest Rus' cathedrals. Once Greek specialists in lead glazing and mosaics had completed their tasks in the Rus' churches, they and their Rus' apprentices needed new work. Some, if not most, Greek masters apparently returned home. But those who remained started to work with the newly trained Rus' masters to produce glazed pottery and various glass goods. Happily, the infant Rus' glass industry enjoyed a reasonably strong local market for its Byzantine-type luxury goods among the increasingly sedentarized Rus' ruling classes. It seems doubtful that Grand Prince Vladimir or his advisors ever thought of creating a Rus' glass industry when they invited in the Greek masters to embellish the new Church of the Tithe in the Byzantine fashion. Technology transfer in this case was unplanned and unexpected.

Given the widespread and long-standing prejudice in favor of the state sector as the best agency for economic development, the circumstances surrounding the appearance of a flourishing glass industry in Kiev are worthy of attention. Glassmaking arose as an accidental spin-off from the state's edifice to the initiative and actions of those in the private sector including the church. In his posthumous work on the eighteenth-century Russian economy, Arcadius Kahan noted the dynamism of the private sector and the limitations of the state sector in promoting economic growth. Since the Russian state of that time tended more and more to supervise but not compete with the more efficient private sector, Kahan viewed the "process of market formation during the eighteenth century as much more advanced than official Soviet historical documents would allow."[17] Taking Kahan's approach a step further, it might be argued that Kiev's pre-Mongol glass industry developed so quickly and so successfully precisely because it was not the subject of a state effort to promote economic growth but, rather, a product of market forces operating in the private sector to meet popular demands.

Within a quarter century of the first glass production in Rus', that is, by ca. 1025, Rus' glassmakers also had developed the more versatile KPbSi recipe. Using this recipe, the Rus' glassmakers could produce every major type of glass object that the Byzantine masters made from their ancient recipe. And, the Rus' could produce a sufficient quantity of reasonably well-made glass goods so that they came to dominate the Rus' market. While Byzantine and Near Eastern glass was imported into Kievan Rus' in modest amounts up to the time of the Mongol conquest, Rus' masters manufactured massive quantities of glass goods for a large and growing market. In other words, there was no reason why the Rus' had to borrow the ancient recipe if their lead silicate recipes gave them overwhelming market dominance and relegated Byzantine glass made in Byzantium to a small specialty market. If the Rus' could, for all practical purposes, capture the Rus' market using a KPbSi recipe, why should they adopt the Byzantine recipe? The Rus' glassmakers very quickly learned how to make the type of glass needed to satisfy the demands of the Rus' market.

An examination of early Rus' glassmaking suggests that investigators need not think in terms of Greeks who withheld vital technical information from their Rus' apprentices. Rather, specialists need to explore how it was that the Rus' craftspeople learned so rapidly to use a KPbSi recipe that enabled them to compete successfully with Byzantine glassmakers. As with other Rus' borrowings from Byzantium, Byzantine models were not copied uncritically. In architecture, art, and law, for example, Byzantine forms were given a Rus' content. Something similar seems to have taken place in the glass industry. The Rus' clearly learned how to make glass from Greek masters and many aspects of Rus' glassmaking came from Byzantium; however, the Rus' did not blindly follow the Byzantine process of glass production. They were able to adapt the Byzantine lead silicate recipe by adding potash, developing a recipe that allowed them to dominate the Rus' market.

Just as Greek masters helped to establish a glass industry in Kiev, so masters from Kiev helped to establish a glass industry in other towns of pre-Mongol Russia. In the case of PbSi bracelets, this transfer of Byzantine-derived technology *within* Rus' came very quickly when it finally began. Soon after such bracelets were first made in Kiev, ca. 1130s, they were also made in Liubech. The transfer of glassmaking technology to Liubech proved to be short-lived. However, within a quarter century or so, ca. 1150, the ability to make PbSi bracelets was transplanted successfully into several other Rus' cities. This process of the diffusion of a Byzantine technology within Rus' raises several important issues that so far seem to have been neglected. Why, for instance, did glassmaking die out in Liubech so quickly, while it became self-sustaining in a city like Novgorod? Was glassmaking in Liubech the result of one or two masters temporarily working for a rich patron? What kind of an internal market or patronage network enabled Novgorod to sustain a glass industry over a long time? In some ways, the study of the diffusion of glassmaking within Rus' has just begun.

It is also necessary to ask why three-quarters of a century or so passed by before glassmakers using a KPbSi recipe for bracelets appeared in other Rus' towns, ca. 1200. Was the KPbSi recipe so much more complex than the PbSi recipe, or did Kiev consciously seek to maintain its monopoly over the production of KPbSi glass? Unfortunately, the intriguing questions about technology transfer within Rus' take us beyond our main theme, the cross-cultural contacts of the medieval Mediterranean. Hopefully, some of our Soviet colleagues will begin to address these issues.

In conclusion, I should like to offer a few observations regarding technology transfer between Byzantium and Rus' as seen in this case study of glassmaking.

1. When discussing the cross-cultural contacts of the Mediterranean, it is sometimes forgotten that these contacts went beyond such well-known areas as art, architecture, literature, music, and religion. The ability to make a variety of goods was the source of much interest in and contact with the Mediterranean world.

2. Technology transfer was an important part of the contacts between Byzantium and Rus'. Mediterranean technology, in its Byzantine variant, was successfully transmitted into Eastern Europe.

3. This process of technology transfer, thanks to the studies of Soviet scholars such as Shchapova, can be examined in some detail in the case of glassmaking in pre-Mongol Rus'.

4. Glassmaking was transmitted from Byzantium to Kiev around the year 1000 as the result of both long-term developments (a century of Rus'-Byzantine relations, growing technical skills amongst Kiev's craftspeople, and some successful experience in borrowing less complex foreign technology) and immediate circumstances (the conversion of the Rus' leaders to Orthodoxy that led to the construction of a great stone cathedral by the Grand Prince, and the sedentarization of the Rus' princes and their retinues which created a number of wealthy patrons—a market—in Kiev).

5. The transfer of glassmaking technology was initiated when Byzantine masters went to Kiev. No evidence exists that Rus' apprentices were sent to learn glassmaking in Byzantium.

6. The appearance of these Greek masters in Kiev suggests that Byzantium had no policy preventing the transmission of glassmaking skills abroad. Alternatively, such a policy was ignored when political and religious considerations dictated; or the Byzantines, like the Rus' rulers, had no idea that specialists in lead glazing and mosaics would be instrumental in the establishment of a glass industry in Kiev.

7. The Greek masters who first came to Kiev were specialists in the decorative glass arts of glazing and mosaics. They worked with Rus' apprentices and showed them how to employ a variety of recipes in making glass.

8. Among the recipes used in the early Greek-Rus' workshops were those for lead silicate glass. Lead silicate glasses were used to make glazed decorative tiles as well as certain colored mosaic tesserae.

9. When the earliest Rus' cathedrals were completed, most Greek masters returned home. But some remained in Kiev where they and the newly trained Rus' masters in the decorative glass arts started to make a living by turning out glazed ceramics and glass goods for the Rus' upper classes.

10. The Greeks and Rus' worked together both in the mosaic workshops and in the production of glass goods. Furthermore, they both used and experimented with a variety of glass recipes. There was no distinctly Rus' or Greek glass recipe.

11. It is not yet clear why the Rus'-Greek masters chose a PbSi glass when they made the first glass beads in Kiev ca. 1000. Some technical and/or aesthetic reason may be behind this choice.

12. There is no reason to believe that the use of the KPbSi recipe by Rus' glassmakers came about because the Greek masters kept their ancient recipe a secret. Rather, Rus' and Greek glassmakers in Kiev found that the addition of potash to the PbSi recipe enabled them to produce a glass that could compete successfully with their competitors in Byzantium and the Near East. Glass made in Rus' very quickly dominated the Rus' market and kept Byzantine and Near Eastern glass imports to a minimum.

13. Although it took one hundred years to create all the preconditions necessary to transplant a glass industry into Kiev, this industry matured very rapidly. The transition from PbSi glass to KPbSi glass took only twenty-five years.

14. The development of the PbSi and KPbSi recipes indicates that technology transfer in our case study was not a mechanical imitation of the Greek glassmaking process. The Rus' modified the Byzantine process and adapted it to local conditions and raw materials. It is to be hoped that our Soviet colleagues will be able to determine precisely why and how the modifications were made.

15. Just as Kiev's glassmaking industry was transferred from Byzantium, other Rus' towns borrowed Kiev's technology (lured away some of its glassmakers) and began to develop local glass industries. However, the transfer of glass technology within Rus' required some 125 to 150 years from the time glass was first produced in Kiev by Rus' and Greek masters.

To understand better how a Mediterranean craft like glassmaking took root in Kiev along the middle Dnepr, a comparative study needs to be done on the origins of glassmaking in the entire Orthodox Slavic world and in Christian Caucasia. An examination of glassmaking in these regions, where Byzantine influence was very strong, might well shed light on the Kievan experience. In particular, such a study might help us to decide if the Kievan case was unique or whether it followed a general "Byzantine" pattern of technology transfer. In this connection, it is pertinent to note that the earliest glass workshops in medieval Bulgaria apparently dated to the decades immediately following Bulgaria's conversion to Orthodoxy via Byzantium, ca. 865.[18] It thus might prove fruitful to explore the role of conversion to Orthodoxy in the development of glassmaking among the East and South Slavs. It would also be instructive to examine the spread of the glass industry in medieval western Europe and in medieval Islam.

The kind of cooperative efforts in comparative glass study that are being suggested here clearly run counter to much of the existing structure of medieval studies. Those of us interested in medieval Russia will have to broaden our visions beyond the East Slavic milieu while many self-identified "medievalists" have finally to accept the fact that life worthy of study existed to the east of medieval Germany. Only by breaking down the artificial barriers that separate us can we truly understand such questions as technology transfer and cross-cultural contacts in the medieval Mediterranean.

Notes

1 S. H. Cross and O. P. Sherbowitz-Wetzor, eds. and trans., *The Russian Primary Chronicle: Laurentian Text* (Cambridge, Mass., 1953), s.a. 989, p. 119.

2 Iu. L. Shchapova, *Ocherki istorii drevnego steklodeliia* (*po materialam doliny Nila, Blizhnego Vostoka i Evropy* [Moscow, 1983]), p. 183.

3 Ibid., Fig. 36, p. 136; Idem., "Masterskaia po prozvodstvu stekla u s. Komarovo (III-IV vv.)," *Sovetskaia arkheologiia*, no. 3 (1978), pp. 230-42.

4 V. V. Kropotkin, *Ekonomicheskie sviazi Vostochnoi Evropy v I tysiacheletii nashei ery* (Moscow, 1967), pp. 83-91.

5 Shchapova, *Ocherki*, p. 173; Kropotkin, *Ekonomicheskie*, p. 117.

6 Marija Gimbutas, *The Slavs* (London, 1971), pp. 80-98; I. I. Liapushkin, *Slaviane Vostochnoi Evropy nakanune obrazovaniia Drevnerusskogo gosudarstva*, Materialy i issledovaniia po arkheologii SSSR, No. 152 (Leningrad, 1968), pp. 125-54.

7 Constantine Porphyrogenitus, *De Administrando Imperio*, ed. Gy. Moravcsik, trans. R. J. H. Jenkins (Budapest, 1949), chap. 9, pp. 56-63.

8 Shchapova, *Ocherki*, p. 175; N. A. Shkol'nikova, "Stekliannye ukrasheniia kontsa I tysiacheletiia n.e. na territorii Podneprov'ia," *Sovetskaia arkheologiia*, no. 1 (1978), pp. 97-104.

9 P. P. Tolochko, *Drevnii Kiev* (Kiev, 1983), p. 139.

10 *Novoe v arkheologii Kieva* (Kiev, 1981), p. 302-8.

11 For a discussion of the Church of the Tithe, which was destroyed by the Mongols in 1240, see S. R. Kilievich, *Detinets Kieva IX-pervoi poloviny XIII vekov: Po materialam arkheologicheskikh issledovanii* (Kiev, 1982), pp. 57-69.

12 Shchapova has published her analyses of early Rus' glass and the conclusions to be drawn from this evidence in a number of works, most notably Iu. L. Shchapova, *Steklo Kievskoi Rusi* (Moscow, 1972). She has conveniently summarized her major findings in Julie Ščapova, "A propos de l'histoire du verre de la Russie ancienne," *Annales du 5e Congrès de l'Association Internationale pour l'Histoire du Verre* (Liège, 1972), pp. 89-97; Julia Léonidovna Ščapova, "Apparition de la verrerie chez les Slaves Orientaux," *Rapports du IIIe Congrès International d'Archéologie Slave 2* (Bratislava, 1980): 385-91.

13 Scapova, "Apparition de la verrerie," p. 390.

14 Viktor Lazarev, *Old Russian Murals and Mosaics* (London, 1966), pp. 13-14.

15 See T. I. Makarova, *Polivnaia posuda: Iz istorii keramicheskogo importa i proizvodstva Drevnei Rusi*, Arkheologiia SSSR: Svod arkheologicheskikh istochnikov, El-38 (Moscow, 1967), pp. 36-41; Idem., *Polivnaia kermika v Drevnei Rusi* (Moscow, 1972), pp. 9, 61, 70.

16 See, in particular, the valuable article of V. I. Levitskaia, "Materialy issledovaniia palitry mozaik Sofii Kievskoi," *Vizantiiskii Vremennik* 23 (1963): 105-57, especially 138-54.

17 Arcadius Kahan, with the editorial assistance of Richard Hellie, *The Plow, the Hammer, and the Knout. An Economic History of Eighteenth-Century Russia* (Chicago, 1985), p. 274. This aspect of Kahan's work was emphasized by Jeffrey Brooks in his review in *Eighteenth-Century Studies* 20 (1987): 497-99.

18 Georgi Djingov, "Sur l'Origine de la Verrerie en Bulgarie au Moyen Age," in *Verre Médiéval aux Balkans (Ve-XVe s.) Sredn'ovekovno staklo na Balkanu (V-XV vek)* (Belgrade, 1975), p. 112.

Black and White: Contact with the Mediterranean World in Medieval German Narrative

Stephanie Cain Van D'Elden

The great queen's eyes caused her grievious pain when they beheld the Angevin, who, being of Love's color, unlocked her heart whether she wished it or not.[1] [And what color is love's color?—white presumably.] If there is anything brighter than daylight—the queen in no way resembled it. A woman's manner she did have, and was on other counts worthy of a knight, but she was unlike a dewy rose; her complexion was black of hue.[2] In due time this lady was delivered of a son who was of two colors and in whom God had wrought a marvel, for he was both black and white. *Immediately the queen kissed him over and over again on his white spots, and on her little child the mother bestowed the name of Feirefiz Angevin.[3]*

(The black and white in the title of this essay comes from the story of *Parzival* by Wolfram von Eschenbach. In it Gahmuret, a typical adventuresome knight, a younger son of the Angevin family, wins the hand in marriage of Belacane, a black Saracen queen.)

In the twelfth and thirteenth centuries it was fashionable for German poets to situate their stories, which could just as well have taken place in the northern European forests, in the Mediterranean, even though the setting had no influence whatsoever on the story line. For some, the Mediterranean world provided an exotic, pagan backdrop for a fantastic tale that stretched the boundaries of their artistic imaginations. These stories are replete with lengthy and detailed descriptions of the lavish ambiance of this faraway place. In addition, fashion dictated that poets be up-to-date on current events, and thus many attempted to include aspects of the Crusades in their works even though they were not especially well informed, and few had any personal first-hand contact with Crusaders or the Holy Land. Although German poets were dependent on their French models for plot and atmosphere, they clearly asserted their individual creativity in such works as the *Rolandslied* and *Willehalm*.

The study by scholars in medieval German literature of contacts between blacks and whites, "heathens" and Christians, in the Mediterranean world began in 1925 with an article by Hans Naumann entitled "Der wilde und der edle Heide." Naumann examined almost all Middle High German narratives looking for "wild" and "noble" "heathens." The subtitle to his article "Versuch über die höfische Toleranz" (investigation of courtly tolerance) indicates his overall bias. He was looking for noble "heathens"—used much in the same fashion as "noble savage" was used to describe the American Indian, and with a similar lack of knowledge.[4] Naumann concluded that the older literature displayed an intolerant, strict, church-oriented attitude towards non-Christians: Non-Christians were automatically bad and must be either converted or killed—helped along their inevitable way to hell. With the popularity of chivalry, courtliness, and well-developed institutionalized knighthood came a milder, more tolerant way of looking at non-Christians. They, too, were creatures of God and worth baptizing.[5] This simple, simplistic dichotomy has been attacked and expanded upon by many scholars since 1925.[6] In his zeal for listing examples, Naumann does not notice that in many works both "wild" and "noble" "heathens" exist side by side. Nor is Naumann particularly interested in the contact between Christians and non-Christians, how they affect each other, or the consequences of cross-cultural contact.[7]

Scholars since Naumann, especially Siegfried Stein, have attempted to explain the development in attitudes towards non-Christians that they saw as an evolutionary progression from a mentality that totally rejected the world to a freer perception of the world.[8] In the earlier literature, views towards non-Christians were purely theoretical, not derived from personal contact or from any concept of imminent threat to Christendom.[9] However, with the advent of the Crusades and with German participation, came direct contact with Muslims and a concomitant change in attitude towards non-Christians. Marianne Plocher[10] and Stephen J. Kaplowitt[11] investigated whether the change in attitude hypothesized by Naumann was a reflection of the historical "facts." Kaplowitt, in a very exhaustive examination, looked first at the varying attitudes towards non-Christians in literary works in conjunction with the Crusades, and then he examined whether characters and events portrayed in medieval German literature were based on actual personalities and historical evidence. He was surprised and disappointed to find that what "had been considered reflections of Crusade history could not be shown convincingly to be anything more than the results of coincidence, or turned out to be reflections of general situations rather than specific events."[12] A fictional description of a battle or a siege might seem similar to a historical one until one examined the details closely; similarly, fictional characters could have been based on real persons, but the details never completely matched.

Dieter Haacke[13] rejected the notion of "wild" and "noble" "heathens," asserting that the attitude toward non-Christians reflects the individual poet's perspective of the world. Some works, such as Pfaffe Konrad's *Rolandslied* (the German version of the French *Chanson de Roland*, song of Roland), Otte's *Eraculius*, and Reinbot's *St. Georg* contain what Haacke calls a tendency or movement hostile to the world (*eine weltfeindliche Strömung*), a denial of the world in favor of God that dictates a negative response towards non-Christians. *Graf Rudolf* and *Floyris* manifest an abundance of joy of life (*Lebensfreude*) rather than hostility towards the world (*Weltfeindlichkeit*), no dichotomy between God and the world, and thus no "heathen problem" occurs. It was the great genius of Wolfram von Eschenbach in his *Parzival* and *Willehalm* that reconciled God and the world; Wolfram believed that an exemplary knight, whether Christian or non-Christian, could please both God and the world. Although both were qualified to become members of King Arthur's Round Table, only the baptized knight, of course, could reach the highest pinnacle of the Grail.[14]

Thus we find in Middle High German literature a great range of attitudes toward non-Christians: from the passionate anti-Muslim sentiment of the *Rolandslied* that calls for the complete annihilation of Islam and the merciless slaughter of all who refuse to embrace Christianity, to the epics of Wolfram von Eschenbach, *Parzival* and *Willehalm*, in which both Christians and non-Christians are tolerantly portrayed as members of an "international nobility."

In their search for "wild" and "noble" "heathens," for a chronological development based on attitudes toward God and the world, or for parallel historical events in the Mediterranean world, scholars generally have disregarded certain details of the texts where we find "wild" and "noble" "heathens" side by side, bits and pieces of historical facts indiscriminately scattered about, and usually an uninformed and naive concept of both "heathens" and the Mediterranean world.[15] Evidence is clear of an appalling lack of knowledge about Islam on the part of German poets, who tend to view all nonbelievers as idolaters and to condemn their gods as idols and instruments of the devil. Some Christian leaders fostered this erroneous concept; it was to their advantage to present the Muslim enemy as worshipping many gods rather than as believing in the God of Abraham and recognizing the prophet Jesus Christ.

The erroneous notion of many gods of Islam is expressed by the anonymous author of the *Gesta Francorum*, one of the most important accounts of the First Crusade. He quotes the Muslim general, Kerbogha, in an imaginary letter as saying: "Moreover, I swear to you by Mohammed and by all the names of our gods."[16] Fulcher of Chartres, who took part in the First Crusade and even remained in the Holy Land some twenty years afterward, and who should have known better, wrote: "The Saracens had practiced their rule of idolatry there with superstitious rite. . . ."[17]

In medieval literature we find masses of non-Christian enemies, unbaptized and thus reprehensible according to the Church, pitted against masses of Christian knights. Although the non-Christians are generally painted in the vilest of terms, often the poets become so caught up in their descriptions of the battle, that they forget that the enemy is not Christian; sometimes the poets require a worthy opponent (as they would in a courtly romance) for their masses of Christian knights and thus commend the military prowess of the non-Christian enemy. The same applies even more to the single heroes of the narratives. Individual non-Christian leaders are portrayed in glowing terms as worthy adversaries for their Christian counterparts—often to the detriment of the Christians. A brief examination of some of the major Middle High German works of this period will illustrate these points.

An early and especially rich narrative is the *Kaiserchronik*, completed in Regensburg about 1155, in which the history of the German emperors is told beginning with the time of Romulus down to the present day (*unz ûf den hiutegen tac*),[18] that is to 1147, when Conrad III departed on the Second Crusade. The author avails himself of every opportunity to point out the impotence of the "heathen" religion and the employment by the devil of gods as tools to lead unbelievers astray; however, pagans as people receive less harsh treatment, since even St. Augustine recognized that there could be good "heathens."[19] For example, the account of Emperor Heraclius' expedition to regain the Holy Cross stolen by the infidels expresses strong hostility towards the non-Christians, who have desecrated the sacred places of the Holy Land, resulting in a bloody war in which the non-Christians are ultimately cut down like dogs. Although the enemy is described as fierce and terrible and the events as bloody and awful, they are presented as factual observations and no editorialized verbal abuse is directed toward specific persons or activities.[20] Persons and events are described in a matter-of-fact fashion.[21]

In the *Kaiserchronik* we find two distinctly different attitudes toward non-Christians: a negative one that embraced church-fostered abhorrence of the pagan deities and also antagonism towards those non-Christian emperors who were obstructing the true religion,[22] and a positive attitude of tolerance towards certain individual non-Christian emperors who were deemed good.[23] The author took it for granted that the Christians were to fight against the infidels, but he does not suggest, with the possible exception of the fragmentary account of the Second Crusade, that he was really stirred by the anti-Muslim propaganda of the early Crusades.

Many consider the *Rolandslied* to be more inspired by the spirit of the Crusades and more filled with the crusading fervor of the age than any other Middle High German narrative,[24] even though the action takes place in Spain in Carolingian times. Here we find evidence of violent anti-Muslim sentiment directed against both the infidels and their religion. Charlemagne, the Christian warrior, and his knights have as their goal the aggrandizement of Christianity by either converting or destroying their non-Christian enemy (*Taufe oder Tod*, baptism or death). Although many of the non-Christians could be easily swayed and quickly converted, others were stubborn and had to be slaughtered like animals and sent to hell.[25] Ironically, Genelun, a Christian, was traitor and villain, not the Muslim King Marsilie.

Even in the *Rolandslied* individual non-Christians often acquire positive traits. The Muslim King Amarezur is described as having been born more exalted than all the kings of the earth,[26] and his troops are portrayed as *chûne helde* (brave heroes)[27] whose service would have been a credit to even the noblest king, if they had been fighting for a just cause.[28] Their defeat comes, not through lack of military prowess, but because they are led astray by Lucifer and their own arrogance.[29] Paligan, Marsilie's suzerain, is characterized as an outstanding warrior and a man of honor whose *gebarde were riterlich* (bearing was knightly).[30] In the final battle between him and Charlemagne, it is clear that Charlemagne is saved from disaster only by divine intervention. The non-Christian King Cernubiles, described as black, strong, cursed, and a miscreant, is contrasted with the chivalrous Margariz von Sibilie, also a non-Christian knight, who is described as distinguished, lovable, beautiful, delightful, and a courtly lover.[31]

Thus while the *Rolandslied* may stand on the intolerant end of the wild/noble scale, we observe that masses of non-Christian enemies may be wild but nevertheless admirable fighters and worthy opponents; individual non-Christians often are described in courtly terms and might even be considered noble, if not good. Similarly, at the other end of the scale, in the works of Wolfram von Eschenbach, we also find masses of wild and evil non-Christian enemy in addition to admirable individual non-Christians displaying noble characteristics that make them equal to, if not better than, the Christians.

Gahmuret the Angevin, mentioned above as a great adventurer,[32] wins a second wife, Herzeloyde, the Queen of Waleis. Herzeloyde, referring to Gahmuret's first wife Belacane, maintains: "You should renounce the Moorish woman for my love's sake. The sacrament of baptism has superior power. Therefore give up your heathenry and love me by our religion's law, because I yearn for your love."[33] Even though Belacane had professed her willingness to be baptized, Gahmuret was easily persuaded to accept Herzeloyde. Certainly, Wolfram's audience would readily accede to the notion that marriage between a Christian and a Muslim had little validity.[34]

When the half-brothers, Parzival (son of Herzeloyde) and Feirefiz (son of Belacane), meet for the first time, they are armored and do not recognize each other. In the ensuing duel, it is obvious that Feirefiz is the better warrior, but the duel is interrupted. In this short scene Feirefiz acts much more chivalrous and gracious than does Parzival, who is somewhat petulant and surly. Wolfram obviously has had little experience with the progeny of whites and blacks: Feirefiz is described as black and white like the writing on parchment or the feathers of a magpie. "The rich Feirefiz was black and white all over his skin, except that half of his lips showed red."[35] "They carried Loherangrin to his uncle Feirefiz, but since he was so black-and-white-speckled, the boy would not kiss him. Noble children feel fear even today. The heathen laughed at this."[36] Feirefiz was immediately recognized as a great and rich knight, the epitome of courtly chivalry and was admitted to King Arthur's Round Table. However, the unbaptized Muslim was not permitted to marry the bearer of the grail, Repanse de Schoye; nor was he able to see the grail. Parzival says: "If you wish to have my aunt, you must renounce all your gods for her sake, and ever avenge gladly any insubordination to the Highest God, and with steadfastness keep His commandment."[37] "Whatever I have to do to have the girl," said the heathen, "that I will do, and faithfully."[38] Feirefiz is baptized in order to marry Repanse de Schoye; as an extra reward he is now able to see the grail—which does not interest him at all. Kaplowitt reminds us:

> We cannot, however, assume that, merely because Feirefiz could not care less about converting to Christianity, Wolfram feels the same way. Despite his liberal views towards the heathens, Wolfram still recognizes the acceptance of Christ as the sole means to salvation. Even though Wolfram presents Feirefiz's initial confrontation with Christianity in a humorous light, we must remember that Feirefiz is to function later as a Christian missionary in India.[39]

Wolfram's *Willehalm*, based on the French cycle of William of Orange, takes place in the epic Carolingian world similar in atmosphere to the *Rolandslied*. The Christians and Saracens are engaged in violent hostilities that presuppose considerable animosity. However, remarkably few derogatory statements are made about non-Christians. Willehalm reminds his men that they are fighting "for the twofold love, for the reward of ladies here on earth and for the song of the angels in heaven." He exhorts them: "You should be mindful and not let the heathens revile our faith, for they would rob us of our baptism if they could. . . . Now defend your honour and your land, so that Apolle and Tervigant and the deceitful Mahmete do not trample your baptism underfoot."[40] Although the necessity of fighting against the infidels is never questioned, Gyburg, Willehalm's wife, reminds the Christians that Christ himself forgave those who killed him, and therefore the Christians should be merciful to their defeated Muslim enemies. After the defeat of the Saracens,

Wolfram asks: "Is it a sin to slaughter like cattle those who have never received baptism? I say it is a great sin, for they are all the creatures of God's Hand, and He maintains them."[41] Even though the non-Christians have been deceived by the devil regarding the true nature of God and salvation, they are nevertheless human beings, worthy of equal treatment as such. The idea of mercy is put into practice after the battle when Willehalm frees a noble Muslim prisoner, King Matribleiz, not for ransom, but out of respect for him as a person and a kinsman of his wife. As in the *Rolandslied*, individual non-Christians are praised as persons and warriors.[42] Kaplowitt suggests that Wolfram may have felt poignant in the face of inevitable discord.[43]

Graf Rudolf,[44] mentioned above, fits Haacke's designation of a work so full of joy of life (*Lebensfreude*) that there is no place for hostility towards the world (*Weltfeindlichkeit*) and thus no room for anti-Muslim sentiments. The Christian Rudolf appears at the beginning as a military commander, fighting against the Saracens in the service of a Christian king of Jerusalem. For reasons not specified, he quarrels with this king and deserts to the Muslim, who is clearly a worthier person.[45] Initially Rudolf is imbued with typical Crusader enthusiasm. During the siege of Ascalon, non-Christian women and children are slaughtered like cattle, and no mercy is shown to the captured Saracens who are strung up before the walls in plain view of their compatriots. However, this harshness does not stem from enmity toward non-Christians in general but rather toward a specific enemy who is challenging the Christians' possession of the land.[46] The second half of the story is a love story, in which the Christian Rudolf marries the Muslim princess whom he has wooed in typical courtly manner. Although she voluntarily requests baptism, and proudly adopts the Christian name of Irmengard, this act does not seem to make much difference to Rudolf, although undoubtedly it will simplify their future life together in Flanders.

Here again we have an example of non-Christians in masses treated as the enemy, often with respect for their military prowess, while individual non-Christians are portrayed realistically and favorably. In *Graf Rudolf* there is no suggestion of converting the non-Christian prisoners; the prisoners will be released if they agree to evacuate the country. The Saracen king Halap and his chief adviser, the Saracen knight Girabobe, are characterized by approving epithets. Maurice Walshe calls this a propaganda novel, but the propaganda is not in favor of the crusading ideal; rather it supports the new courtly view of life:

> It reflects the new 'courtly' tolerance of the infidel as human beings and as knights, the crusaders' recognition of the high standard of culture, and the very similar institutions, of their Moslem opponents. The only concession the hero makes to his fellow-Christians in combat is that he strikes them with the flat of his sword instead of the edge.[47]

The noticeable difference in attitudes towards non-Christians in Konrad's *Rolandslied* and *Graf Rudolf* does not represent a chronological development, for both narratives were composed in the early 1170s. As Kaplowitt has observed:

> The contemporaneousness of these divergent viewpoints does not seem strange if we remember that Konrad, a clergyman imbued with a religious fanaticism which clearly derives from the crusade spirit aroused by the preaching of the early crusades, viewed the crusading idea from the idealistic vantage point of a Westerner who had not been to the Latin kingdom of Jerusalem, while the author of *Graf Rudolf*, aware of the political and social considerations influencing the relations between Christians and Moslems in the Holy Land, gave a more or less authentic picture of the situation prevailing at the time he was at work.[48]

In conclusion, there does not appear to be a chronological development in attitude toward non-Christians on the part of Middle High German poets, nor a change based entirely on the courtly atmosphere of "international nobility"; nor did specific events or persons have as much direct influence as we might expect. This tendency to pick and choose fragments from the great array of historical personages and events of the time may seem capricious to us today. However, the German poets were interested in telling a good story and not concerned with propagandizing the cause of Christianity vis-à-vis the non-Christian world, and thus little of the didacticism and moralizing appears regarding Christian/non-Christian topics typical of much of medieval literature. I suggest that the reasons for differences in attitudes towards non-Christians in Middle High German narrative are personal and individual. I have tried to show that within a single work the poets were often inconsistent and thus unable, even in the most anti-Muslim settings, to maintain a totally black and white dichotomy. In telling a good story they needed worthy opponents for their heroes; death for a noble cause was much more honorable than death for an ignominious one. Depth of feeling, too, is very much dependent on the individual poets. Some were imbued with a blind adherence to the teachings of the Church in their condemnation of all non-Christians; others appear to be indifferent

to religion. Some were persuaded that people are human beings, capable of both good and evil, whether they are black or white. Contact with the Mediterranean world did indeed contribute a new dimension to medieval German narrative, albeit a confused one.

Notes

1   *Wolfram von Eschenbach. Parzival*, trans. Helen M. Mustard and Charles E. Passage (New York: Random House, 1961); *Wolfram von Eschenbach. Parzival*, ed. Karl Lachmann (Berlin & Leipzig: Walter de Gruyter, 1926). Page numbers indicate English version, line numbers German edition, p. 14; lines 23: 22-27.

2   *Parzival*, p. 14; lines 24: 7-11.

3   *Parzival*, pp. 32-33; lines 57:15-22.

4   Historically the terms "heathen" and "pagan" appear to come from dwellers of the heath or country, rustics. Later they were expanded to describe nonbelievers, and today they are used (albeit infrequently) to refer to those who hold religious beliefs that are not Christian, Jewish, or Muslim. An "infidel" is one who does not believe in (what the speaker holds to be) the true religion, an "unbeliever." The term "Saracen" generally means an Arab or Muslim, but, according to the *OED*, it can also mean a non-Christian, heathen, pagan, or infidel. In this essay I endeavor to use the term "non-Christian," but in some cases the older terms of "heathen" and "pagan" occur interchangeably with "non-Christian" and reflect the nature of my sources.

5   Hans Naumann, "Der wilde und der edle Heide. (Versuch über die höfische Toleranz.)," in *Vom Werden des deutschen Geistes. Festgabe Gustav Ehrismann zum 8. Oktober 1925*, eds. Paul Merker and Wolfgang Stammler (Berlin & Leipzig: Walter de Gruyter, 1925), pp. 80-101, esp. 85, 88.

6   Dieter Haacke, "Weltfeindliche Strömungen und die Heidenfrage in der deutschen Literatur von 1170-1230 (Rolandslied—Graf Rudolf—Trierer Floyris—Eraclius—Wolframs Willehalm—Reinbots Heiliger Georg)" (diss. Freie Universität Berlin, 1951), p. 1: "Aber die von Naumann eingeführten Begriffe des wilden und des edlen Heiden vereinfachen und verzerren das Problem in unzulässiger Weise."

7   Ludwig Denecke, "Ritterdichter und Heidengötter (1150-1220)," *Form und Geist* 13 (1930): 56-57, maintains that the picture of heathendom comes from the

Crusaders and their perceptions of the enemy, and this picture is quite similar to what the Church preached. The term "wild" appears interchangeably with *grimmic, wuotic, arg,* and *freislich.* It can also appear in the connotation of strange and wonderous; they look strange, have strange habits, and when present in large numbers frequently appear indistinguishable among each other.

8 Siegfried Stein, *Die Ungläubigen in der mittelhoch-deutschen Literatur von 1050 bis 1250* (diss. Heidelberg, 1932; reprint Darmstadt: Wissenschaftliche Buchgesellschaft, 1963), p. 36. Stein attributes this mentality to the Cluniac reform movement; however, he does not take into account other Cluniac teachings pertaining to non-Christians or the Mediterranean world.

9 Stein, pp. 11-17. St. Bernhard in his "De laude novae militiae ad milites templi" (ca. 1136) wrote: "In morte pagani christianus gloriatur, quia Christus glorifica-tur," Jacque Paul Migne, ed. *Patrologiae cursus completus. Series Latina* (Paris: Garnier Fratres, 1879), 182:924. He contended that if the Christians did not destroy the "pagans," then the "pagans" would destroy them.

10 Marianne Plocher, "Studien zum Kreuzzugsge-danken im 12. und 13. Jahrhundert" (diss. Albrecht Ludwig Universität zu Freiburg im Breisgau, 1950).

11 Stephen J. Kaplowitt, "Influences and Reflections of the Crusades in Medieval German Epics" (diss. University of Pennsylvania, 1962), following in the footsteps of Friedrich-Wilhelm Wentzlaff-Eggebert, *Kreuzzugsdichtung des Mittelalters. Studien zu ihrer geschichtlichen und dichterischen Wirklichkeit* (Berlin: Walter de Gruyter, 1960), examined "a wider range of literary works for the purpose of assessing the extent and determining the nature of the connections between the crusades and the literature of the cru-sading era," p. xxiii. Both Kaplowitt and Wentzlaff-Eggebert limited their investigations to the Crusades, ignoring other contacts with the Mediterranean world.

12 Kaplowitt, p. 513.

13 Haacke, p. 302: "Es gibt nicht den 'wilden' und den 'edlen' Heiden, sondern den von weltfeindlichem und ritterlichem Aspekt gesehenen Heiden. Beide begegnen uns aber auch in dieser Form nicht; viel-mehr wirken beide Auffassungen bei jedem Dichter, je nach der Grundhaltung, von der er ausgeht, anders."

14 The dating of these Middle High German works is in some cases highly controversial; they were composed between 1130 and 1230: *Rolandslied* 1130-70; *Eracu-lius* 1210; *St. Georg* 1230; *Graf Rudolf* 1170; *Floyris* 1160; *Parzival* 1210; *Willehalm* 1220.

15 Naumann, p. 83, points out that the distinctions among ancient pagans, Jews, and Muslims are often blurred as were the names of the various gods: Apollo, Ercules, Pallas, Jupiter or Jovinus, Juno, Venus, Mars, and Saturn are placed alongside the gods Machmet, Machazen, Kahun, Bakun, and Tervigant. *Das Rolandslied des Pfaffen Konrad,* ed. Carl Wesle (ATB 69, Tübingen: Max Niemeyer, 1967), lines 3490-96, claims that there are seven hundred gods, the most important of whom is Machmet. Denecke, pp. 59, 78-83, contends that in the *Rolandslied* the three most important gods are Machmet (forty-three times), Apollo (fourteen times), and Tervagant (twelve times). Even the sophisticated Wolfram referred to the language of non-Christians as "hea-then": Cundrie "spoke all languages well, Latin, French, and heathen," *Parzival,* p. 169; line 312:20; see also *Parzival,* p. 224; line 416:25; *Wolfram von Eschenbach. Willehalm,* trans. Marion E. Gibbs and Sidney M. Johnson (New York: Penguin, 1984); *Wolfram von Eschenbach. Willehalm,* ed. Albert Leitzman (ATB 15, 16, Tübingen: Max Niemeyer, 1963), p. 54; lines 83:18-23; p. 103; line 192:23.

16 Rosalind Hill, ed., *The Deeds of the Franks and the Other Pilgrims to Jerusalem* (London: Thomas Nelson & Sons, Ltd., 1962), 9, 21:52.

17 Fulcher of Chartres, *A History of the Expedition to Jerusalem 1095-1127,* trans. Frances Rita Ryan (Knoxville: University of Tennessee Press, 1969), 1, 28.2, p. 122. Cf. Stein, pp. 43-44. See also Matthew Bennett, "First Crusaders' Images of Muslims: The Influence of Vernacular Poetry?" *Forum for Modern Language Studies* 22/2 (April 1986): 101-22.

18 *Kaiserchronik,* ed. Hans Ferdinand Massmann (Quedlinburg & Leipzig: Gottfried Basse, 1949), line 23.

19 Cf. S. Aurelii Augustini, *De civitate dei contra paganos* (Saint Aurelius Augustine, *The City of God Against the Pagans*), 1.19; 5.12.

20 Heraclius, the epitome of Christian humbleness, is contrasted with the Persian King Codras, who represents pagan arrogance (*superbia*): "vil gerne wolt er got sîn" (he very much wanted to be God), *Kaiserchronik,* line 11147. Christian knights not only win reward in heaven but also worldly honor (*êre*); for the first time we confront the idea that being for God does not necessarily mean that one is against the world, lines 14366-67, Wentzlaff-Eggebert, p. 68. Later the possibility of winning the love of a lady becomes important also; see note 37.

21 Preceding the account of the First Crusade there is a passage which, according to Naumann, expresses a positive attitude towards non-Christians, *Kaiser-chronik,* lines 16612-17: Duchess Agnes of Bavaria is inspired by God to make a pilgrimage to the Holy Sepulchre. Before she reaches her goal, she is cap-tured by the Muslims and eventually marries one of them. Naumann viewed this as a foreshadowing of the love matches between Christians and Saracens so common in courtly epics, p. 89. Stein felt that the author's unwillingness to say anything more about

the incident was an indirect expression of his disapproval of this type of alliance, p. 32. According to Kaplowitt, the passage merely mentions the birth of a son about whom the author will have more to say at the appropriate time and thus contains no explicitly or implicitly expressed attitude toward non-Christians, p. 24.

22 Cf. Stein, pp. 30-31.

23 Cf. Stein, p. 35.

24 Eberhard Nellmann, "Pfaffe Konrad," in *Die deutsche Literatur des Mittelalters. Verfasserlexikon*, 2nd ed. (Berlin/New York: Walter de Gruyter, 1986), 5:115-31. Kaplowitt, p. 34. Wentzlaff-Eggebert, pp. 77-79, points out in the German *Rolandslied* that although Karl fights against the Persian King Paligan, he does not fight for France but rather for the heavenly kingdom; he and his knights are less interested in conquering the enemy kingdom and more concerned with converting nonbelievers to the service of God.

25 *Rolandslied*, lines 7697ff. Naumann, p. 86, characterizes the attitude of the *Rolandslied*, as follows: "Die Heiden sind unkeusch, beten ihre unreinen Abgötter an, sind die Kinder des Teufels, sind nebelfinstere Nacht, stiften Raub und Brand, zerstören die Kirchen, opfern die Christen ihren Abgöttern, sind übermutig, töricht, unselig, vermessen, eine *verfluochete meintâtige thiet, verworht, vertân*, mordgierig, grimmig, prahlerisch; ihre Fürsten sind grausame Wüteriche, Höllenwirte, Valande, Abgründe des Teufels."

26 *Rolandslied*, line 4595.

27 *Rolandslied*, line 4600.

28 The author of the *Gesta Francorum* declared that if they had been willing to be Christians, "you could not find stronger or braver or more skillful soldiers," Hill, 3, 9, p. 21. This sentiment is expressed time and again in medieval literature; e.g., *Parzival*: "If they were baptized men as mine are, and of the same color of skin, there would never be a man crowned but that he would get his fill of fighting from them," p. 28; lines 49:13-17. Denecke, pp. 68-73, considers it important to distinguish whether the "heathens" are treated like any other enemy or whether they are treated as non-Christians.

29 *Rolandslied*, lines 4604-06.

30 *Rolandslied*, line 8006.

31 *Rolandslied*, lines 3725ff.

32 It has been suggested that Gahmuret was modeled after Richard I of England, cf. Steven Runciman, *A History of the Crusades* (Cambridge: Cambridge University Press, 1955), vol. 3, *The Kingdom of Acre and the Later Crusades*, pp. 59-60, who offered to hold two Palestinian cities as fiefs under the suzerainty of Saladin and proposed a marriage alliance between his sister, Queen Joanna of Sicily, and Saladin's brother Saphadin; neither suggestion came to fruition. Friedrich Panzer, "Gahmuret. Quellenstudien

zu Wolframs Parzival," *Sitzungsberichte der Heidelberger Akademie der Wissenschaften*, Phil.-hist. Klasse (1940), pp. 62-68.

33 *Parzival*, p. 53; lines 94:11-15.

34 When King Richard first proposed marriage between his sister and Saphadin, there was no suggestion that Saphadin would have to convert to Christianity; it was only when his sister refused to consider marrying a Muslim that Richard asked Saphadin if he would consider embracing Christianity (Runciman, p. 59). In *Parzival* we find the same tendency to ignore at first the distinction between Christian and non-Christian, but ultimately the necessity of conversion becomes evident. The mutual respect between Gahmuret and the Baruch (Caliph of Baghdad) generally parallels reports from the Third Crusade, such as the joint hunting expedition of Reynald of Sidon and Saphadin (Runciman, p. 60), the great banquet given by Saphadin for Richard (Runciman, p. 59), and Saladin's gift of fruit and snow to Richard when he was ill (Runciman, p. 72).

35 *Parzival*, p. 395; lines 758:17-20.

36 *Parzival*, p. 420; lines 805:28-806:3.

37 *Parzival*, p. 425; lines 816:25-30.

38 *Parzival*, p. 425; lines 817:1-3.

39 Kaplowitt, p. 125.

40 *Willehalm*, pp. 24-25; lines 17:3-22.

41 *Willehalm*, p. 218; lines 450:15-20.

42 See, for example, descriptions of "heathens" in *Willehalm*: Noupatris, lines 22:14-29; the Persian king Arofel, line 78:19; Tesereiz, lines 87:16-19; 204:1-30; 205:1-206:2; 419:12-24; King Tybalt of Arabia, Gyburg's first husband, lines 310:16; 342:13-19; 354:24-355:3; King Matribleiz of Scandinavia, lines 461:30-462:9.

43 Kaplowitt, p. 136.

44 *Graf Rudolf*, ed. Peter F. Ganz (Berlin: Erich Schmidt Verlag, 1964).

45 Heinrich von Sybel, "Über die geschichtliche Grundlage des grafen Rudolf," *ZfdA* 2 (1842):235-48, suggested that the character of Rudolf was loosely modeled after Count Hugh of Le Puiset, who deserted to the Muslims between 1131 and 1141. According to John L. La Monte, "The Lords of Le Puiset on the Crusades," *Speculum* 17 (1942): 100-18, this would have to be Hugh II of Jaffa, pp. 104-6.

46 Denecke, pp. 58-59, considers this portrayal to be the purest expression of what German knights knew about heathendom between the Second and Third Crusades.

47 Maurice O'C. Walshe, *Medieval German Literature. A Survey* (Cambridge, Mass.: Harvard University Press, 1962), p. 134.

48 Kaplowitt, p. 97.

The Pilgrim as Tourist:
Travels to the Holy Land as Reflected in the Published Accounts of German Pilgrims Between 1450 and 1550

Gerhard Weiss

There are three acts in a man's life which no one ought either to advise another to do or not to do. The first is to contract matrimony, the second is to go to the wars, the third is to visit the Holy Sepulchre. . . . These three acts are good in themselves, but they may easily turn out ill; and when this is so, he who gave the advice comes to be blamed as if he were the cause of its turning out ill.

(Count Eberhard the Bearded of Württemberg, to Brother Felix Fabri, 1480.)[1]

One of the most fascinating aspects of the early German book market is the abundance of travel accounts published in the major printing centers, in Frankfurt, Nuremberg, and Mainz. In this period between 1450 and 1550 other nations sailed the oceans on journeys of exploration or in search of new trading routes, while the Germans excelled in the preparation of maps, the printing of nautical guidebooks, and the publication of travel accounts, which ranged from pure fiction to hard fact. Many of these works were written in German, or they were translated into German, to make them accessible to the growing middle class that made up an increasing portion of the book-buying public[2] (Fig. 1).

Among the travel literature published at that time, descriptions of journeys to the Holy Land assumed a particularly prominent place. The books vary greatly in quality, ranging from monotonous recitations of places visited or helpful hints for any potential traveler wanting to embark on such a journey on his own (a kind of early Baedeker), to keen observations presented with considerable literary skill. Although even the best accounts sometimes mixed fact with fancy, they nevertheless enable the modern reader to get a glimpse of what it must have been like to travel in those days. The great detail and care with which a number of travel accounts had been prepared also reflect another purpose of the pilgrim reports: They served as a surrogate or "spiritual" pilgrimage for those who could not go themselves. Brother Felix Fabri, for example, wrote his *Evagatorium in terrae sanctae* (1494) at the request of Swabian nuns who wanted to share in the spiritual benefits of his journey, so that in their own convents they might become "with a little training virtuous pilgrims of the Holy Land."[3] In the sixteenth century, accounts of journeys to the Holy Land had become so popular that the Frankfurt publisher Sigmund Feyrabend found it commercially advantageous to compile an anthology of the "best of travels," which he called *Reyszbuch dess Heyligen Lands. . . . (Book of Travels to the Holy Land).* It contained the writings of seventeen Germans who between 1095 and 1573 had journeyed to Jerusalem. An appended eighteenth account, by "Joh. De Monte Villa," is the Holy Land portion of Sir John Mandeville's popular *Travels.* Feyrabend published the entire book in German, thereby making accessible to the general public even those reports that previously had been available only in Latin. The *Reyszbuch dess Heyligen Lands. . . .* was first published in 1584. Subsequent editions appeared in Frankfurt, Nuremberg, and Cologne. All told, Feyrabend's anthology went through eleven printings, with the last edition recorded in Cologne in 1704, evidence of its popularity among the wealthy burghers of the time.

The most famous book, however, was Bernard von

Breydenbach's *Peregrinatio in Terram Sanctam*, which initially had been printed in Latin by Gutenberg's associate Peter Schöffer in Mainz (February, 1486). It saw twelve editions between 1486 and 1522 and almost immediately was translated into German, Dutch, French, and Spanish. The book's main attraction, however, was not so much its text, but rather its abundance of illustrations and pictorial maps—superb woodcuts that for the first time combined a visual impression with a verbal account. Breydenbach had hired the Utrecht artist Erhard Reuwich to accompany him on the journey as a "visual recorder"—a clear indication that the travelers had become interested in more than just a prayer at a holy place (Fig. 2). Reuwich's woodcuts were such a success that they were immediately copied and "borrowed" by others. The two existing manuscripts of Conrad Grünemburg's *Pilgerfahrt ins Heilige Land* (1486), for example, contain pen-and-ink drawings almost identical to Reuwich's works[4] (Figs. 3, 4, 5, 6).

Copying from other sources was common practice in those days. Authors often lifted whole portions from other books and at times even reported on sights that they themselves could not possibly have visited. Sometimes an aristocratic pilgrim hired an educated monk to do the actual writing, or at least to supply the scholarly and theological trimmings. Ghostwriters certainly were not unknown.[5] Rarely was a writer as honest as the monk Felix Fabri, who faithfully divulged his own borrowings and even pointed to some of Breydenbach's sources: "Whosoever will see the most beauteous and most ancient description of the Holy Land, let him read the book of Brother Burcard. . . . From this book . . . Bernard von Braitenbach . . . has copied the description of the Holy Land. . . ."[6]

Indeed, plagiarism was not considered a crime in the Middle Ages. Therefore, it comes as no surprise that the pilgrims' books published to the end of the sixteenth century often are very close to one another and at times almost identical. They have enough

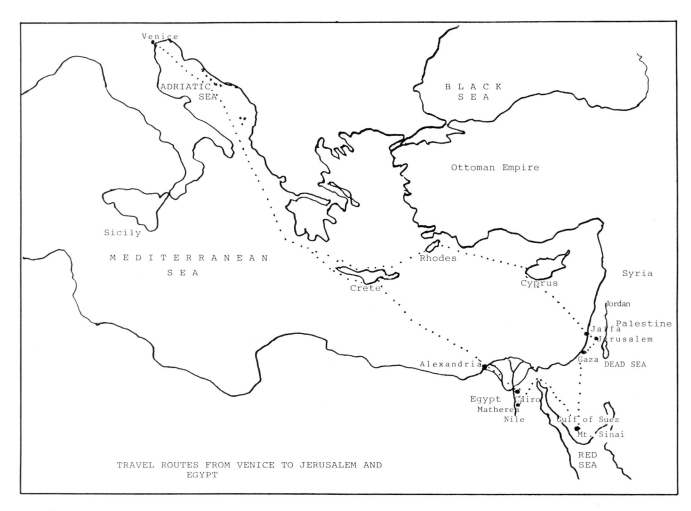

TRAVEL ROUTES FROM VENICE TO JERUSALEM AND EGYPT

Efscheff	schuster	baß	thór	esuet	swartz
Hyiath	schnyder	trijck	weg	mattem	meister
Tobach	koch	abijt	knecht	kekem	priester
Amara	wyß	ebrr	sun	ocht	swester
Szama	hymel	nesme	stern	mattir	regen
Layl	nacht	baß	port	maristan	siechhuß
Tauß	rock	choff	hoß	bardt	kaldt
Ezekeß	berg	kestarr	vffgang	carre	nessel
Faras	pferd	cathy	sunder	endom	yr
ij oder eij	ja	gadda	morgen	kr	syrr
Vd	holtz	dahan	mulier	ceryen	maydt
kadelocht	glockner	ebß	vatter	kenthr	tochter
Mekeß	frundt	schiemß	sunn	gear	wolcken
Daw	liecht	dalme	vinsternuß	madbach	kuchen
Coket	cappe	camiß	kembde	serbul	schuch
Harr	hitze	wodirr	tatt	segara	baum
Schocke	dorn	krami	dieß	kij	myrr
Hadack	der	la	neyn	buckara	morgen
Methay	myrr	hasar	steyn	keßyan	kecker
Ostkopffß	Bischoff	rasol	man	omm	mütter
Achß	Brüder	nazerani	crist	kamar	mon
Hauwa	wyndt	naßar	tag	soßß	lufft
Mensel	kamer	stabrim	hütt	zennar	gurtell
Goffara	mantkel	ard	erde	achßyn	acker
Hasis	kruth	ßymel	kemeltßyr	sarrir	schalck
Lack	dyrr	ena	ich	ylkom	keudt
Swoy	schlecht	hadid	yßen	lumen	fuer
Mokeijt	eyns	etneyn	zwey	relate	dry
Arba	vier	campß	funff	sißy	seßs
Sada	süßen	thmani	acht	tyßza	nun
Eyschara	zeßen	woßeyttasch	eylff	temetasch	zwolff

Telatasch	dryzeßen	arbatasch	viezeßen
Campßtasch	funffzeßen	sythtasch	sechzeßen
Sabatasch	süßenzeßen	thmantasch	achzeßen
Tyßtasch	nunzeßen	Acharyn	zwenzyg
woßeyttascharin	eyns vñ zweßig	etnentascharin	zwey vñ zwenzig
Telateraschein	dry vñ zweßig	arbatascharin	vier vñ zwenzig
Campßtascharin	funff vñ zweßig	syttascharin	seßß vñ zwenzig
Sabatascharin	süßen vñ zweßig	tementascharin	acht vñ zweßig
Teßzatascharin	nun vnd zwenzig	Talatyn	dryssig

Fig. 1. Arabic-German word list (from Breydenbach, *Die Reise ins Heilige Land*).

in common to allow us to draw some valid conclusions about the general nature of the travel experiences facing the German pilgrims between 1450 and 1550[7] (Fig. 7).

A perusal of the accounts reveals that in spite of the avowed holy purpose of the journey, many pilgrims were very much like tourists today and were facing some similar problems. Like tourists, they often found it difficult to comprehend the alien world that confronted them, and they often tried to relate it to the familiar environment back home. They compared the Nile at Alexandria to the Rhine near Cologne,[8] and Jerusalem to Basle ["as the city of Basle is hilly, even so is this city; for in Basle St. Leonard's Hill answers to Mount Sion, St. Peter's Hill to Mount Calvary, and St. Martin's Hill to Mount Moriah—albeit, in shape and configuration there is much difference between the one and the other"[9]]. They also felt comforted and reassured when they found the familiar names and coats-of-arms of their countrymen scratched into sacred walls, and they enjoyed meeting fellow-Germans, even if they were Mamluks of German origin, or German Jews who had emigrated to Palestine.

What, then, was the journey of our pilgrims really like, and who was able to embark on such a trip at a time when travel was still quite limited? Travel to the Holy Land was very expensive. It became customary, therefore, that pilgrims of lesser means attached themselves to the affluent as chaplains, guides, cooks, barbers, bodyguards, servants, interpreters, and so on.[10]

A number of travel books contain detailed accounts of what a journey cost. Georg Wilhelm the Brave of Thuringia ranked among the most extravagant. He traveled in style and managed to spend a record 20,000 gold marks.[11] Most did it for appreciably less. Even the cost of the ship passage varied greatly and was subject to keen negotiations between the ship owners and their clients.

Venice was the customary port of embarkation, and it was here that most of the travel business was transacted (Fig. 8). The Republic controlled the sea routes of the eastern Mediterranean and virtually held the monopoly on passenger transportation. Venice had developed pilgrim travel to a fine art, allowing prospects to purchase a number of package tours. Even the schedule of departure was fixed in general terms. Originally, two travel periods were set for pilgrim ships, in spring and summer, taking advantage of favorable winds and weather. Later, commercial travel was limited to spring departures only. However, rich and influential pilgrims always could

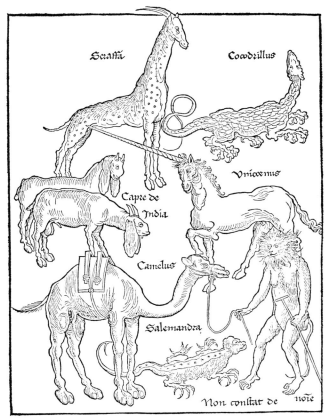

Fig. 2. Erhard Reuwich: animals, including a unicorn, which he claimed to have seen during his travels through the Holy Land (from Breydenbach, *Peregrinatio . . .*).

charter galleys for departure at any time.[12]

On their arrival in the city, the Germans usually found shelter in one of the many German inns, or, if they were clerics, in one of the local monasteries.[13] They sold or boarded their horses and stored their armor for safekeeping until their return. They also had to change their money to drafts on various international banks. Any cash they might carry on board they usually hid among the pork, to keep it out of the hands of inquisitive Muslims inspecting the ship in Jaffa.[14]

A trip to St. Mark's Square brought the pilgrims in contact with the shipping agents, whose banners advertised the names of the major owners. The Republic had regulated the passenger trade quite well. To assure compliance with the regulations, inspectors would at times travel with the pilgrims and report on infractions. Every traveler had to negotiate a detailed contract, containing special clauses about provisions (including the assurance of receiving one glass of Malvasia wine before each

Fig. 3. Erhard Reuwich: woodcuts (from Breydenbach, *Peregrinatio . . .*).

Fig. 4. Ritter Grünemburg: pen-and-ink copies of Reuwich's woodcuts, 1487 (from Lehmann-Haupt, "Die Holzschnitte der Breydenbachschen Pilgerfahrt als Vorbilder gezeichneter Handschriftenillustrationen," *Gutenberg-Jahrbuch*, 1929, pp. 156-160).

meal); payments (one half of the fare was due at the beginning of the journey, the other half on arrival in Jaffa); the assurance of immediate departure from Venice; and a guarantee of a direct journey without delays en route. Included were the promise of a guided tour to Jerusalem and the River Jordan; the assurance of a refund of eight to ten ducats for those pilgrims intending to go on their own to Sinai; and, finally, the provision that each passenger would have enough room on the vessel for his own kitchen and for ten to twelve chickens. This contract was

signed by all parties and notarized by Venetian officials. It carried the power of a legal document—and often was honored in the breach.[15]

In spite of all the promises, long delays were common before the ships set sail (Fig. 3). The wealthy travelers used the time to enjoy the abundant social life of Venice. The poor, meanwhile, inspected the local churches. But finally the day of sailing did arrive, and the last provisions were stored on board.[16] Felix Fabri gives us a detailed account of life at sea, and describes the Venetian galleys in such a way that even the nuns in Swabia could gain an impression of what these ships might look like: "Venetian galleys are like one to another as swallows' nests. They are built of the stoutest timbers. . . . The first and foremost part . . . which is called the prow, is sharp where it meets the sea, and has a strong beak, made somewhat like a dragon's head, with open mouth, all of which is made of iron, wherewith to strike any ship which it may meet. . . ."[17] (Fig. 10). We learn about the meals at sea, the heat and stench below deck, the "unquiet sleep" experienced by the passengers, and we receive all kinds of good advice of what to avoid while on board.[18] There were other warnings, too, for those pilgrims wanting to go ashore in strange harbors. This should be done only in broad daylight. Under no circumstances should one frequent any inns, or visit private homes, because "no one receives German pilgrims into his house save the keepers of houses of ill-fame, who for the most part are Germans who dwell there with courtezans."[19]

The sea voyage took between six and eight weeks. Once the pilgrims caught sight of the Holy Land, many of the troubles of a tedious journey were forgotten quickly in the loud "Te deum" celebrated on deck (Fig. 11). Yet the difficulties were by no means over. Once ashore, the pilgrims were locked up in a large cave that served as customs and immigration station. Here they were closely examined and taxed. Princes and nobles quickly changed to simple pilgrim brothers, trying to continue their journey incognito, not out of piety but rather to avoid the particularly high taxes reserved for them. The name of each traveler was recorded, and so was his father's name. Felix Fabri reports: "I was obliged to repeat my name to them several times, and even then they could neither pronounce it or write it without putting some outlandish diphthong before it, and gurgling its syllables in their throat so as not to say 'Felix,' but some word which I cannot pronounce in the place thereof."[20] In this cave, the pilgrims often had to wait several days, and sometimes over a week, until the local authorities and the Christian Guardian (the abbot of the Franciscan monastery) had arrived from Jerusalem to guide them to the holyplaces. The Guardian greeted the pilgrims with a long list of directions and rules. He informed them that he was empowered to issue the necessary ecclesiastic dispensations for those who had failed to receive papal permission to embark on their pilgrimage from the authorities back home, and who thus had been officially excommunicated. He further told them that they never should go out alone, that they should avoid stepping on Muslim graves, that they should not knock off any parts of the Holy Sepulchre or any other shrines for souvenirs, that they should not engrave their names, mottos, or emblems in the church walls, that they should not push or shove while visiting holy places, that they should not have traffic with local women, that they should avoid lewd behavior in church and, finally, that they should remember the monks at Mount Sion with their gifts and not hold the convent responsible if their journey did not work out the way they had expected. The Guardian's proclamation was usually presented in Latin and simultaneously translated into the languages spoken by the pilgrims. His admonitions were based on centuries of experience, both in dealing with pilgrims and with the Muslim authorities.[21]

Having been properly instructed, the pilgrims moved on to Jerusalem, where they visited the Holy Sepulcher and other sacred places. They bitterly complained about the hefty admission charges often extracted by Muslim door keepers. The Holy Sepulcher, for example, offered free admission only twice a year. Pilgrims who could not afford the five to nine ducats normally required, were ruthlessly

Fig. 6. Ritter Grünemburg: pen-and-ink copies of Reuwich's woodcuts (from Lehmann-Haupt).

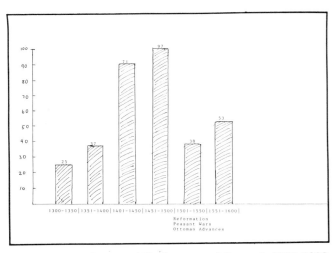

Fig. 7. Major German Pilgrimages of Record, 1300-1600 (based on Röhricht, *Deutsche Pilgerreisen nach dem Heiligen Land,* Neue Ausgabe, [1900]).

Fig. 5. Erhard Reuwich: woodcuts (from Breydenbach, *Peregrinatio . . .*).

turned away.[22] The reports give us a detailed image of the church of the Holy Sepulcher, the worship services conducted by the pilgrims, the special knighting ceremonies performed, and the strict division of the church into denominational segments. The most precise physical description can be found in the writings of the Nuremberg monk Johannes Tucher (1479), of whom Felix Fabri says that he had "examined the Lord's sepulchre with the most minute care, and took its measurements with his hands, feet, and outstretched arms."[23] Tucher's description and Reuwich's illustrations served as model for the many replicas of Christ's tomb constructed in Germany on the pilgrims' return (Fig. 12).

Most pilgrims paid little or no attention to the Muslim world surrounding them. They had a strong Christian myopia and were primarily interested in the spiritual benefits of their journey. A few openly defied the "pagan devils" and showed their contempt by sneering at the mosques or committing other acts of insult. Fabri tells us: "A fair mosque adjoined our inn, and we could see into it through the openings in the roof; indeed, by night one of the pilgrims defiled it through one of these openings, whereby he brought us into extreme peril, but we had departed before anyone came into the church."[24] Again and again we find in Fabri's book admonitions that Christians should show respect to the churches of other religions. Although he is by no means an apostle of tolerance, he nevertheless believes that what is sacred to some should not be ridiculed by others: "Simple men think that they are doing God service when they play some insolent trick in Saracen mosques, or in Jewish synagogues. But this is no service of God, for our holy Mother Church tolerates the synagogues of the Jews and does not destroy them as it might; wherefore the sons of the Church ought not to defile that which their mother endures. The same argument applies to the mosques. . . ."[25]

Breydenbach and Fabri offer fairly detailed descriptions of urban Jerusalem. They comment

Fig. 8. Erhard Reuwich, Venice (from Breydenbach, *Peregrinatio . . .*).

on the deteriorating buildings, and they are fascinated by the many ethnic groups that inhabit the town: Arabs, Syrians, Jews (Breydenbach tells us that during his visit there lived 400 Jews in Jerusalem), Coptic Christians (Breydenbach calls them "Abbasini oder Indiani"), Greek and Roman Christians. Reuwich's illustrations show these groups in their peculiar costumes, engaged in their typical occupations. It is interesting to note that Reuwich's depiction of the Jews reflects the medieval stereotype of the Jew as moneylender (Fig. 13). Indeed, his picture is an illustration that could fit many other works of the time that have nothing to do with Jerusalem or the Holy Land.

Felix Fabri made it a habit to wander the streets of Jerusalem. His curiosity led him to peek into houses and to observe the life of the "natives." He even visited one of the schools in which "the heathen children are instructed in the law of Mahomet." He found the boys sitting "in rows upon the ground,

and all of them were repeating the same words in unison in a shrill voice, bowing their heads and their backs, even as the Jews are wont to do when saying their prayers."[26] He records both the words they were chanting and the musical notes of their chant (Fig. 14).

On the average, pilgrims stayed in Jerusalem for about two weeks before beginning their return journey to Jaffa. They usually made a side trip to Bethlehem and they always bathed in the River Jordan. They also collected relics and souvenirs. Like modern tourists, they often were cheated by the local merchants, who had developed a lively industry producing nails of the cross and similar items, for which the travelers paid dearly. A great favorite was bottled Jordan water—although superstitious sailors often dumped this and other relics overboard, because it was a common belief among navigators that the magic power of these artifacts could wreck the ship. Other favorite souvenirs

Fig. 9. Erhard Reuwich, shipyards at the outskirts of Venice (from Breydenbach, *Peregrinatio . . .*).

were thorns from the vicinity of Jerusalem, fragments from various holy places (although this was strictly forbidden), copies of Christ's footprints, pebbles from Mount Zion, mothermilk from Bethlehem, nails from various churches in Jerusalem, and Palestine-made shirts, shoes, and jewelry.[27]

The return journey to Jaffa was as tedious as any previous trip. The pilgrims were by now exhausted. They were often sick, suffering from the heat and from various diseases. They also had to be constantly on the alert for marauding Arabs, who found them an easy target for robberies and worse. The Nuremberg merchant Sebaldus Rieter tells us that on his journey in 1464 the "pagans" had seized four "poor fellows" of his group, with the intention of abducting them into their own pagan land. Rieter's group in turn threatened to kidnap the four "pagans," whom they had engaged to row them back to their galley, leading finally to an exchange of hostages and a great shoot-out, as the ship left the harbor: ". . . and we defended ourselves against the heathens and fired many a shot into them with our guns, while at the same time they fired on us with a big gun from the tower of Jaffa."[28]

The more adventurous pilgrims added a trip to Egypt to their journey, to visit the sacred places there and to see some of the extraordinary sights. Such a journey required a special contract with the "Saracen Lords of Jerusalem," to assure an "escort and safe-conduct through the wilderness."[29] One also had to procure the necessary provisions for a lengthy and "toilsome" journey through desert and mountains. The route led via Bethlehem, Ramla, and Hebron to Gaza, where the travelers enjoyed the bathhouses, worrying only that sharing the bath with a Muslim or a Jew might be a sinful act.[30] The convoluted theological arguments put forward by Felix Fabri are comparable to similar Dominican sophisms ridiculed in the famous *Epistolae Obscurorum Virorum*, published some twenty years later.

From Gaza, the pilgrims proceeded to Mount Sinai and St. Catherine's monastery, which offered

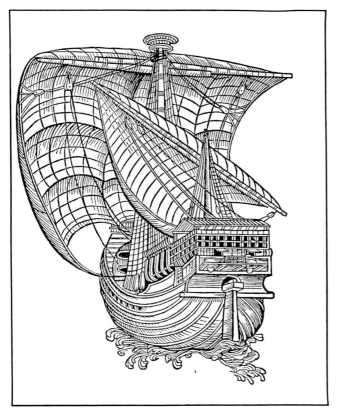

Fig. 10. Erhard Reuwich, typical pilgrims' ship (from Breydenbach's, *Peregrinatio . . .*).

Fig. 11. Erhard Reuwich, map of Palestine, landing at Jaffa, road to Jerusalem (from Breydenbach, *Peregrinatio . . .*).

127

them an opportunity for rest and contemplation. As the travelers approached Egypt, they came to Matherea, known for its magnificent balsam gardens and worshipped by the Christians as the place where the Virgin and Joseph had rested with the Christ Child on their flight to Egypt. Most accounts report in considerable detail how this garden was laid out, and how it was guarded by some fierce-looking gatekeepers. Before entering, one had to pay admission and promise not to break any twigs. Out of sight of the watchmen, the travelers never failed to test the juices contained in the plants, of which they had heard that they had miraculous healing powers. The fragrance of the balm was so penetrating that a drop placed on one side of the hand could be smelled on the other.[31] While observations of this kind satisfied the pilgrims' fascination with curiosities, some had interests that went beyond the collection of oddities. Felix Fabri, for example, on approaching Egypt, contemplated the possibilities of a kind of "Suez Canal," connecting the Red Sea with the Nile, so that ships from England and other European ports could move more efficiently through Alexandria, the Nile, and the Red Sea to India. Fabri remembered that this idea had been considered in the past, but that it was not carried out because "wise philosophers" anticipated that such a water link might harm all of Egypt, since the Nile would be polluted with the salt of both the Red Sea and the Mediterranean, killing fish and wildlife, and harming agriculture dependent on Nile

Fig. 13. Erhard Reuwich, money-lending Jews in Jerusalem in his images of ethnic groups in the Holy City (from Breydenbach, *Peregrinatio . . .*).

Ha y la Halyl la lach   Ha y la Ha lyl la lach   Ha y la Ha lyl la lach

Fig. 14. Words and musical notes of chants repeated by Muslim boys (Felix Fabri, *Fratris Felicis Fabri Evagatorium*, 1:322).

water for irrigation.[32] Felix Fabri's thoughts reflect an early awareness of the conflicts between the needs of commerce and the environment.

Once the pilgrims arrived in Cairo (or Babylon, as many of them called it), they found themselves in a big city with many sights to be seen. They usually were not interested in the remnants from antiquity, or even the pyramids. Those are mentioned merely in passing. What really struck their fancy, however, was a phenomenon that they described with awe worthy of one of the seven wonders of the world: the large chicken incubators that anyone visiting Cairo simply had to see (Fig. 15). It is obvious that the Europeans had never encountered anything like them, and they were deeply impressed. In a travel report written as early as 1350 we read: "In Cairo there are low buildings like ovens; in them are furnaces, wherein eggs are laid upon dung, and by this heat chickens are hatched. . . . The master then takes them to an old woman, who nurses and cherishes the chicken in her bosom. . . . There are numberless old women in those parts who have no means of

Fig. 12. Erhard Reuwich, the Holy Sepulchre (from Breydenbach, *Peregrinatio . . .*).

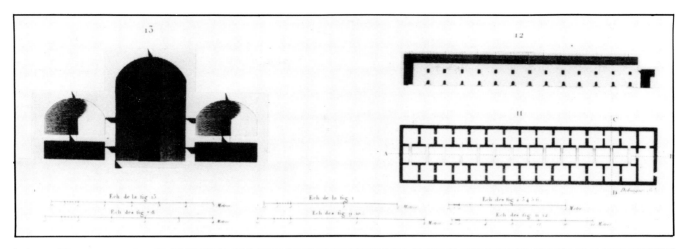

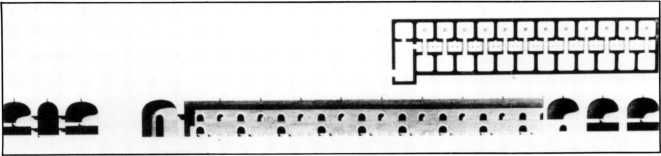

Fig. 15. Cross-sections of Cairo incubators, 1828, similar to those described by medieval pilgrims (from Commission des sciences et arts d'Egypte, *Description de l'Egypte . . .*).

livelihood save by nursing and taking care of chickens. . . ."[33] Similar accounts can be found in practically all travel books describing a visit to Cairo. They even entered the world of German fiction writing. In Grimmelshausen's novel *Simplicissimus* (1669), the hero visits the great city of Alkayr and has only one major impression: "What seemed strangest to me was that the inhabitants again and again were hatching many hundreds of chickens in specially prepared ovens, the eggs of which had not been touched by the hens since they had laid them, and the whole hatching business was attended to by old women."[34]

The pilgrims also were impressed by the general hustle and bustle in the streets of Cairo, and they were amazed by the many food vendors. They were convinced that the natives did very little cooking at home, because warm meals were so readily available everywhere. Breydenbach writes with awe that he had heard that 12,000 cooks were employed in Cairo, catering to the public.[35] His native city of Mainz had nothing comparable to offer!

From Cairo, one traveled by boat to Alexandria, the political center of the Mamluk empire, and one of the great trading hubs of the Mediterranean world.

From here one hoped to return to Venice. On the Nile, the pilgrims marveled at the crocodiles, which reminded them of the legendary dragons back home (Fig. 16). Arnold von Harff tells us that merchants often sold dried crocodile skins, claiming that they

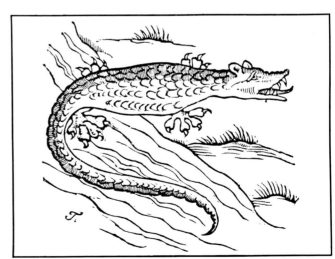

Fig. 16. Crocodile on shores of Nile (from Arnold von Harff, *Pilgerfahrt*, p. 82).

were taken from "dragons" (lyntworme), "which is a lie."[36]

In Alexandria, the travelers had to endure very strict customs controls and police investigations before they could take shelter at one of the trading enclaves belonging to Christian merchants. They found Alexandria both glorious and frightening. By the end of the fifteenth century, much of the city was "dilapidated," except for the newer parts and the most impressive castle of the Sultan, which was facing the sea. It was a magnificent structure that was rumored to have been built by a German Mamluk from Oppenheim. Frightening was the open slave market, in which Christian children were sold. Although some of the pilgrims expressed their abhorrence, many visited the slave market as a local curiosity, an important tourist sight.[37] On the whole, Felix Fabri surmised, Alexandria was very much like Cologne. It was a city with high steeples and elegant walls surrounding it.

From Alexandria, the travelers returned to Venice—often encountering rough seas, dangerous pirates, and many additional hardships. But when the ship approached St. Mark's and the bells of the Venetian churches tolled their welcome, all toil was forgotten. The returning pilgrims enjoyed the admiration with which they were greeted in their home communities, and they displayed their souvenirs and their holy relics, which gave credence to their journey. They were the heroes—they had seen the world, and they found a grateful audience eager to hear their stories. What they reported broadened the horizons of the many who would never have a chance to make such a trip. It encouraged the few to embark on journeys of their own. As pilgrims to the Holy Land, they had performed a religious task. As travelers and tourists, they helped to draw away the curtains of cultural isolation that had hung over medieval Europe for so long.

Notes

1 Aubrey Stewart, trans., *The Wanderings of Felix Fabri*, Palestine Pilgrims' Text Society (London, 1896), 7:3-4.

2 One of the best examples of such travel accounts is *The Travels of Sir John Mandeville*. Of its German translation there exist fifty-eight known manuscript editions and thirteen editions printed before 1600 (see Josephine Waters Bennet, *The Rediscovery of Sir John Mandeville* [New York, 1954]). The German editions are known especially for their imaginative and excellent illustrations. Many of the popular chapbooks published before 1600 also contain elaborate travel reports. The story of *Dr. Faustus* (printed in Frankfurt in 1587) is one example.

3 Reinhold Röhricht and Heinrich Meisner, *Deutsche Pilgerreisen nach dem Heiligen Lande* (Berlin, 1880), p. 282.

4 Hellmut Lehmann-Haupt, "Die Holzschnitte der Breydenbachschen Pilgerfahrt als Vorbilder gezeichneter Handschriftenillustrationen," *Gutenberg-Jahrbuch* (1929), pp. 152-63.

5 Bernard von Breydenbach himself engaged the Dominican monk and Master of Theology Martin Roth to deal with the theological portions of his book and to assist with the historical-anthropological parts. Roth in turn sought advice from Paul Walther of Guglingen, who at that time was writing his own account of the journey to the Holy Land. In its final version, Breydenbach's book is very much indebted to Paul Walther. What Breydenbach did was common practice. E. Gordon Duff informs us that the account of Sir Richard Guildforde's pilgrimage "is a word for word translation of Breydenbach, and many of the more personal observations are lifted bodily from the same source." *Information for Pilgrims unto the Holy Land 1524* (London, 1893), p. xi.

6 *Fabri*, Palestine Pilgrims' Text Society, 7:206.

7 We shall base our report primarily on the following works: Frater Felix Fabri, *Evagatorium in terrae sanctae* (1494) and its German versions; Bernard von Breydenbach's *Reyse ins Heylige Land* (1486); Ritter Arnold von Harff's *Pilgerfahrt von Cöln durch Italien, Syrien, Aegypten, Arabien, Aethiopien, Nubien, Palästina, die Türkei, Frankreich und Spanien* (1499); the *Itinerarium* of Frater Paul Walther of Guglingen, a Heidelberg monk (approximately 1482); Count Albert von Löwenstein's journey of 1561, as recorded in Feyrabend's *Reyszbuch* (1584); the *Reisebuch der Familie Rieter*, a collection of travel reports from the fourteenth through the sixteenth centuries. These are the most reliable, detailed, and thorough accounts available to us.

8 Arnold von Harff, *Pilgerfahrt* (Cöln, 1860), p. 80.

9 *Fabri*, Palestine Pilgrims' Text Society, 9:225.

10 Fabri, in *Reyszbuch*, p. 122, gives a complete list of the members of his party, recording their social standing, their occupations, and their backgrounds.

11 Röhricht and Meisner, p. 7.

12 Margaret W. Labarge, *Medieval Travellers* (New York, 1983), p. 72.

13 Röhricht and Meisner, p. 11.

14 Röhricht and Meisner, p. 7.

15 Röhricht and Meisner, pp. 13-14. See also the accounts of Albert von Löwenstein, in *Reyszbuch*, pp. 191-92; *Fabri, Palestine Pilgrims' Text Society*, 7:87ff.; Röhricht [Neue Ausgabe, 1900], p. 154.

16 Felix Fabri writes in *Reyszbuch*, p. 124: "Als wir nun auff die Galee verdinget waren/da haben die Herren on alles spahren lassen reichlich bestellen/für sich und uns alle auff das Schiff/guten Wein, weiss und rot/Piscoten weiss mit Zucker/Truhen/Laden oder Kisten/Matratzen und Bettlein mit aller zugehörung/ Grauwe Pilgerröcke/rot und gele Stieffeln/viel Schächtlein oder Lädlein mit mancherley Confect und Specerey/Und irem Koch haben sie gekaufft/ Kessel/Pfannen/Hafen/Schüsseln und Teller/und was man erdencken mochte/das not auff das Meer war/das liessen die Herren für sich und uns alle bestellen."

17 *Fabri, Palestine Pilgrims' Text Society*, 7:127.

18 Ibid., 7:154, 158ff.

19 *Fabri, Palestine Pilgrims' Text Society*, 7:163. The journey usually proceeded along the northern coastline of the Mediterranean, past Rhodes and Cyprus, ending in the port of Jaffa.

20 Ibid., 7:223.

21 Fabri, in *Reyszbuch*, p. 130. In the German version, Fabri cites only ten rules. In the Latin text, he quotes twenty-seven (*Fratris Felicis Fabri Evagatorium*, Bibliothek des Literarischen Vereins in Stuttgart, vol. 2, pp. 212-17).

22 Röhricht and Meisner, p. 30.

23 *Fabri, Palestine Pilgrims' Text Society*, 7:404.

24 Ibid., 10:428.

25 Ibid., 9:255.

26 Ibid., 8:396. The words the boys chanted were "Hayla Halylalach" (see Fig. 14).

27 Röhricht and Meisner, pp. 35-36.

28 *Das Reisebuch der Familie Rieter*, p. 15.

29 *Fabri, Palestine Pilgrims' Text Society*, 10:395.

30 Ibid., 10:441.

31 *Das Reisebuch der Familie Rieter* (Bibliotek des litterarischen Vereins in Stuttgart, Band 168, Tübingen, 1889), p. 113; Breydenbach, in *Reyszbuch*, p. 106; Ludolph von Suchem, *Palestine Pilgrims' Text Society*, 12:68.

32 Felix Fabri, in *Reyszbuch*, p. 169.

33 Ludolph von Suchem, *Palestine Pilgrims' Text Society*, 12:67; Fabri, in *Reyszbuch*, p. 174; Breydenbach, in *Reyszbuch*, p. 109.

34 Hans Jacob Christoph von Grimmelshausen, *Der abenteuerliche Simplicius Simplicissimus* (Berlin, 1961), p. 483. I am also very much indebted to Professor Oliver Nicholson of the University of Minnesota, who has referred me to a study by E. W. Lane, *Manners and Customs of the Modern Egyptians* (London, 1836). In the 1895 edition of this book, we read "The Egyptians have long been famous for the art of hatching fowls' eggs by artificial means. This practice, though obscurely described by ancient authors, appears to have been common in Egypt in very remote times." Lane describes the incubators and the process of hatching in detail and offers statistical data on their efficiency (pp. 312-13).

35 Breydenbach, in *Reyszbuch*, p. 109.

36 Arnold von Harff, *Pilgerfahrt*, p. 82.

37 Fabri, in *Reyszbuch*, p. 109.

Contributors

Catherine B. Asher, Minneapolis, Minnesota

Jonathan M. Bloom, Harvard University

Clara Estow, University of Massachusetts - Boston

Oleg Grabar, Harvard University

*Ivan Havener, O.S.B., Saint John's University

W. Eugene Kleinbauer, Indiana University

L. S. B. MacCoull, Society for Coptic Archaeology

Mark D. Meyerson, University of Toronto

Marvin H. Mills, Columbia University

Sybil H. Mintz, Wayne State University

Oliver Nicholson, University of Minnesota

Thomas Noonan, University of Minnesota

Moshe Sokolow, Yeshiva University

Stephanie Cain Van D'Elden, University of Minnesota

Ann T. Walton, St. Paul, Minnesota

Gerhard Weiss, University of Minnesota

*Deceased, April 24, 1988.

Selected Publications of Carl D. Sheppard

Books:

Looking at Modern Painting, 1st Edition, Ford Foundation, 1957; 2nd Edition, Norton, New York, 1961, co-author.

Creator of the Santa Fe Style, Isaac Hamilton Rapp, Architect, University of New Mexico Press, 1988.

Articles:

"Monreale and Chartres," *Gazette des Beaux-Arts*, ser. 6, 35 (1949).

"Iconography of the Cloister of Monreale," *The Art Bulletin* 31 (1949).

"A Chronology of Romanesque Sculpture in Campania," *The Art Bulletin* 32 (1950).

"Two Romanesque Capitals," *The Art Quarterly* 13 (1950).

"Stylistic Analysis of the Cloister of Monreale," *The Art Bulletin* 34 (1952).

"The East Portal of the Baptistery and the West Portal of the Cathedral of Pisa: A Question of Date," *Gazette des Beaux Arts*, ser. 6, 52 (1958).

"Romanesque Sculpture in Tuscany: A Problem in Methodology," *Gazette des Beaux Arts*, ser. 6, 54 (1959).

Introduction to the catalogue in *Old Favorites Revisited: A Loan Exhibition of Paintings* (Los Angeles, CA: Municipal Art Gallery) 1959.

"An Earlier Dating for the Transept of Saint-Sernin, Toulouse," *Speculum* 35 (1960).

"Romanesque and Pre-Romanesque Sculpture in Stone," *Art Quarterly* 23 (1960).

"Subtleties of Lombard Marble Sculpture of the Seventh and Eighth Centuries," *Gazette des Beaux Arts* 63 (1964).

"Carbon-14 Dating and Santa Sophia, Istanbul," *Dumbarton Oaks Papers*, 1965.

"Byzantine Carved Marble Slabs," *Art Bulletin* 51 (1969).

"The Bronze Doors of Augsburg Cathedral," *Essays in Honor of Harold Wethey*, University of Kansas, 1974.

"Classicism in Romanesque Sculpture in Tuscany," *Gesta* 15 (1976).

"A Note on the Date of Taq-i-Bustan and Its Relevance to Early Christian Art in the Near East," *Gesta* 20 (1981).

"Pre-Romanesque Sculpture: Evidence for the Cultural Evolution of the People of the Dalmatian Coast," *Gesta* 23 (1984).

"The Frankish Cathedral of Andravida, Elis, Greece," *Journal of the Society of Architectural Historians* 44 (1985).

"Minnesota Adobe," *La Crónica de Nuevo México*, March, 1985.

"Excavations at the Cathedral of Haghia Sophia, Andravida, Greece," *Gesta* 25 (1986).

"Romanesque Art," in *Dictionary of the Middle Ages*, vol. 10, Joseph R. Strayer, ed., Scribner's, New York, 1988.

Review articles:

Review of Carl A. Willemsen, *Kaiser Friedrichs II. Triumphtor zu Capua: Ein Denkmal Hohenstaufischer Kunst in Süditalien* for *Speculum* 32 (1957).

Review of J. Deér, *The Dynastic Porphyry Tombs of the Norman Period in Sicily* for *The Art Bulletin* 42 (1960).

Review of John Fitchen, *The Construction of Gothic Cathedrals: A Study of Medieval Vault Erection* for *Speculum* 36 (1961).

Review of Roberto Salvini, *The Cloister of Monreale and Romanesque Sculpture in Sicily* for *Speculum* 40 (1965).

Review of Virgil Vataşianu, *Architectura şi sculptura romanica in Panonia medievala* for *Speculum* 43 (1968).

Review of C. Verzár, *Die romanischen Skulpturen der Abtei Sagra di San Michele* for *Art Bulletin* 53 (1971).

Review of Hugo Buchtal, *Historia Troiana, Studies in the History of Medieval Secular Illustrations* for *Speculum* 47 (1971).

Other titles from the Center for Medieval Studies at the University of Minnesota:

The Medieval Castle
   ($16.95 plus $1.50 for shipping.)
ORDER FROM:
   Center for Medieval Studies
   304 Walter Library
   117 Pleasant St. S.E.
   Minneapolis, MN 55455

The Medieval Monastery
   ($16.95 plus $1.50 for shipping.)
ORDER FROM:
   North Star Press of St. Cloud, Inc.
   P.O. Box 451
   St. Cloud, MN 56302-0451
(Minnesota residents please add 6% sales tax.)